The uses of drama

by the same author

IMPROVISATION
(with Ernest Richards)

The Uses of Drama

SOURCES GIVING A BACKGROUND TO ACTING AS A SOCIAL AND EDUCATIONAL FORCE

edited by JOHN HODGSON

EYRE METHUEN LTD
LONDON

First published 1972
by Eyre Methuen Ltd
11 New Fetter Lane, London EC4P 4EE
This collection copyright © 1972 by John Hodgson
Printed in Great Britain
by Cox & Wyman Ltd
Fakenham, Norfolk

SBN 416 19730 2 Hardback
SBN 416 19740 X Paperback

Contents

Acknowledgements

It was reading Eric Bentley's collection of extracts in *The Theory of the Modern Stage* that set me wondering which documents would give the background to the social and educational side of acting. I then began to draw together some pieces I had been using in my teaching at Bretton Hall and the Old Vic Theatre School in Bristol and talked over the whole concept with Ernest Richards. Since then I have recast both the shape and the selections but I am nevertheless grateful to Ernest Richards for the stimulus of those early discussions.

For permission to quote from the works listed below my thanks are due to the following: to the Clarendon Press for the lecture by Jean-Louis Barrault, first published in the original French under the title *Le Phénomène Théâtral* (Zaharoff Lecture at Oxford, 1961); to the Clarendon Press for *The Medieval Stage* by E. K. Chambers; to A. D. Peters and Company for *Play in Childhood* by Margaret Lowenfeld; to Penguin Books Ltd for *Classical Literary Criticism* ('The Poetics of Aristotle'); to Macdonald and Evans Ltd for *The Mastery of Movement* by Rudolf Laban; to Calder and Boyars Ltd for *Silence* by John Cage; to James Nisbet and Company Ltd for *Voice and Speech* by Gwynneth L. Thurburn; to Geoffrey Bles Ltd for *An Actor Prepares* by Constantin Stanislavski; to Methuen and Co Ltd for *Brecht on Theatre* by Bertolt Brecht; to Penguin Books Ltd for *Dreams and Nightmares* by J. A. Hadfield; to Beacon House Inc. for *Psychodrama Vol. I* by J. L. Moreno; to Curtis Brown Ltd for *The Play Way* by Caldwell Cook; to Mrs Dorothy Heathcote for her essay 'Drama as Challenge'; to Routledge and Kegan Paul Ltd and the University of Toronto Press for *Drama in a World of Science* by Glynne Wickham; to Mr Charles Marowitz for his essay 'Whatever Happened to Happenings?'; to Calder and Boyars Ltd for the introductory material to *US* by Michael Kustow, Albert Hunt and Geoffrey Reeves.

J. H.

USES OF DRAMA
Motivation and Materials

DRAMA in education and the community.

Personal potential and skills: Imagination, Speech, Observation, Movement, Feeling.

Human relationships: Conflicts, Personal and social problems & conditions, Attitudes, Fears, Prejudices.

Literature past and present: Myth, Legend, Plays, Newspapers, Biographies, Novel, Poetry, New writing.

Other aspects of society: Art, Music, Film, T.V., Radio, Science, Civics, Religion, History, Geography.

Investigation
Preparation
Stimulation
Development
Co-ordination
Experience
Sublimation
Therapy
Expression
Communication
Recapitulation
Celebration
Relaxation

SECTION ONE
The State of Affairs

1 **Drama as a Social and Educational Force—An Introduction**/*John Hodgson*

It may seem strange that drama should be considered to be of any *use* at all – other than as relaxation and entertainment. But it is being used, and abused, in many other and varied ways. To inquire into these is not to deny its function as a means of enjoyment. Greater understanding of its nature and potential as a means of human inquiry and expression should, however, facilitate the appreciation of its importance and help to enrich the quality of entertainment we look for.

In his preface to the printed edition of *US*, Peter Brook says 'there are times when I am nauseated by the theatre, when its artificiality appals me, although at the same moment I recognize that its formality is its strength!' In a way, any health there is in the theatre will only be maintained by such ambivalent approaches as this. Scepticism about the arts of the drama is important if drama is to remain alive. The questioning and re-examination of aims and purposes can only lead to a stronger and more virile approach in the long run. So, on this score there is no cause for alarm! What *is* worrying is the confusion and lack of clarity about the questions (or the sheer inability to be aware of any). It seems it is only too easy to become pre-occupied with issues which cloud, fuzz, or totally obscure the important lines of investigation. We seem to be lacking any fundamental basis for a philosophy of the drama.

Recent years have seen some fresh thinking about approaches to certain aspects of drama in education; and there has been some building of more varied and flexible theatres. Yet some people still find it difficult to see the common ground between such manifestations as national theatre companies, local repertory theatres, drama in the classroom, school plays, set dramatic texts, children's dramatic play, actors' training and amateur theatre – and role playing amongst adults. There are still those who decline to use the word 'drama', because they feel it too associated with work in schools and summer courses, and others who disdain the word 'theatre', because they feel it reeks of artificiality and raised stages.

Some are worried about the study of plays becoming too academic or analytic and too divorced from the players, while others complain about people spending too much time acting the dramas, instead of devoting adequate energy to studying the texts. In some quarters improvisation is the only acceptable form of acting, while others give no truck to it, because they need all the time to get on with the play. Acting for some is a shared activity – for others 'performance' is a denigrated word.

Fortunately expansion goes ahead. Each year more public money is poured into some theatre companies. New theatres are planned and built; older theatres are improved and modernized. Several provincial theatres are extending their sphere of influence, and emphasising their awareness of their place in the community. Some are arranging experimental and studio theatre activities designed to appeal to a range of audiences. There are exhibitions and displays, lunch hour and late night presentations; there are readings of verse and recitals of folk song, concerts and revues. There are clubs catering for all ages of patrons, clubs for young people and children, and more and more theatres are establishing teams of actor/teachers in a department of theatre in education.

Arts centres and labs with a strong theatre core are flourishing in many more areas. There are small professional touring companies visiting theatres, schools and colleges; and universities are at last discovering that a resident theatre company on the campus can stimulate the work in many departments and bring in the townsfolk for a community activity.

Yet so many of the influential money-wielders, as well as the general public, are confused. And the confusion is over many of the basic issues.

Just what is the force on which we are now spending so much money? Why do people devote themselves to it? As actors? As audiences? How could it be used? How should it be used? Is it anything more than a pastime? Does it matter? On what standards can you judge it? By what standards can you appreciate it?

Many know drama and acting as an enjoyable activity, but have no clear idea of how to improve the enjoyment of it or how to extend its range. There are arguments about programmes at local and national theatres, suitability of particular plays, whether drama has any place in the curriculum and whether money ought to be spent on new buildings. It is obvious that for some people it is a very absorbing game, but there are not many who understand why or realize which aspects of it are of more lasting value.

One has only to read the first Department of Education and Science report 'Drama: a survey' to have all this confirmed. Confusion abounds. 'The value of improvisation', states the report, 'should not divert attention from the extreme importance of studying plays for their own sake . . . Dramatic literature is an art form in its own right.' Cannot improvisation have any relationship with the discovery of the text? Isn't a dramatic text meant to be acted? How do you study plays 'for their own sake'? Nor is this confusion confined to education. We even find theatre men of considerable standing planting red herrings about acting. Sir Bernard Miles is quoted by the *Sheffield Star* as saying, 'Acting is a frontal activity because the actor's means of expression, his eyes and his mouth, are in the front of his face.' What about his voice and his body? What about relationships with fellow actors? Do these count for nothing?

It is not difficult to see why issues easily become confused. Drama, whether it takes place in a London theatre, a schoolroom, or a village hall, tends to draw attention to itself. It is an outgoing activity and its very nature is to be seen. There is a tendency for us to observe it most when it is most spectacular and then to take the part for the whole. If some plays which are set around the kitchen sink come to our notice, the tendency is that we accept them as typical of the whole of modern drama. If some actress takes off all her clothes in one play, we seem very ready to believe that this is the trend of the latest writing.

Because so few people have a wide experience or understanding of drama, these more sensational moments can lead to misunderstanding. It is surprising to find how much the conception of theatre of that large percentage of the population who are the non-theatre-going public, stems from the Victorian and earlier theatre rather than the theatre of the here and now. And even amongst those who consider themselves theatregoers there is a large proportion whose only experience is of actors raised on a stage and seen through a proscenium arch in a picture-frame setting. Because for so long theatre has been a profitable concern, many find it difficult to appreciate why it still should not be made to pay its way. Why is it charged to the rates like the library? Why do we spend Arts Council subsidies on it? What is it doing in education? What has it got to do with everyday life? Is it a highly specialized art form? Has it anything to do with English or literature or examinations? Can it make a contribution to town or country life? We've got the telly – what do we need with a theatre? If we are responsible for the provision of a theatre company in our town, do they have any responsibility to us?

If only we could give ourselves the space to think and re-examine the issues, instead of rushing to take up attitudes. If only we would allow ourselves to view the issues in a wider context (often an historical context), and realize that although most of the problems have never been solved for good and all, many of them have been faced before and some have already been clarified.

What I have tried to do is to collect together some important documents dealing with many aspects of dramatic expression and communication, and to suggest ways in which I think they can throw light on aspects of the problems which are facing us in the theatre and educational drama today. In selecting the contributions, I have tried to take as broad a view as possible, because I think it is in seeing the range and associated uses of drama that we can best employ it at the present time. It seems to me that we have yet to see our way clearly beyond many of the attitudes which were set up by puritan and industrial attitudes to leisure and theatre, and to look at both once again in a broader social context. The order of the pieces is important, though by no means self-determining. In the process of planning, I have organized these in several different arrangements: I have tried a chronological (by date of writing) order, an historical (by topics) order, and several orders of logic. The arrangement that I have finally settled for has a logic, which will, I hope, be evident as the book is read, but a few words of overall explanation will perhaps make the position still clearer.

Some kind of introductory essay seemed vital: I have had by me for some time Jean-Louis Barrault's lecture on the 'Phenomenon of the Theatre' and have found it a valuable reference on many occasions.

Jean-Louis Barrault is such an eminent theatre man, discussing his profession in both social and human terms, aware of its shortcomings as well as its virtues, that his lecture seemed to make a well-nigh ideal beginning, firmly establishing many of the broad issues which are to follow.

Next I felt that there was a need to examine the basic nature of drama. Although it often seems to us that we stand on the threshold of drama, especially in appreciating its educational implications, we are inclined to overlook the fact that man has always employed drama from the earliest times and still does employ it quite openly in his early years. So, the two articles which follow Barrault consider some of the dramatic expressions which we find: first of all, in primitive societies, and then in the play of the child. Both these inquiries are about representation and a kind of drama away from the script. It seemed, therefore, appropriate to follow these with an early examination of the kind of drama which became literary – Aristotle's consideration of some of the fundamental aspects of drama.

The second section is a group of articles discussing the fundamentals of drama. Interestingly enough, the matters considered here are closely related to those main elements of drama which Aristotle had considered in his *Poetics*. First we look at movement expression, then voice and sound, followed by Stanislavski's consideration of emotional training and the kind of reality he was aiming for in his actors' training. Brecht's examination of the purpose and content of theatre stands as an interesting contrast.

Two articles which inquire into possible sub-conscious values and uses of drama then follow – drama in dreams and then as a therapy. Both chapters suggest the need and value of drama in the increasing of expression and inquiry in adult life, and both prepare some ground for the next part of the book.

After this is a section of chapters concerned with varying approaches to drama in education. The first writer is concerned with the discovery and development of literature, the second is eager for its link with life, and the third helps in realizing its importance as a branch of investigation. Each lays a different point of emphasis – all share a common awareness of broad educational values. It becomes evident that from one standpoint or another the writers consider drama to be primarily for the benefit of those taking part. They see at least part of its contribution to be the way in which it helps the individual in his social adjustment.

From the individual in the centre of society, we can turn to the last group of contributions, which consider problems of keeping drama (whether in or out of the theatre) vital, both as a force contributing to man's spiritual wellbeing, and as a means of helping society in understanding or facing some of its problems and burning issues.

Alas, many important writers and practitioners are omitted. Here are only some of the things which have been thought and said. This book does not set out the final answers neatly; all it attempts to do is to organize some of the more relevant comments. We still have to do our own individual thinking, but these chapters should stimulate our own investigations. They let us see that many of the paths have been trod before. They let us see that there are some directions in which we no longer need to flounder, there are some mistakes we do not need to make again and some confusions we do not have to perpetuate any more.

2 **Best and Worst of Professions**/*Jean-Louis Barrault, translated by Manolo Santos and John Hodgson*

In 1961 the University of Oxford invited Jean-Louis Barrault to deliver the Zaharoff Lecture, and he chose to talk about 'The Phenomenon of Theatre' from the standpoint of a practitioner. In this talk, which he gave in French from the stage of the Oxford Playhouse to a packed audience of Oxford graduates and undergraduates, he clearly and effectively summarizes the place of the actor and his work and his contribution to society. He is not blind to the shortcomings of some of the work which passes for theatre and is well aware of some of the poverty of a number of actors, but the fact that a force may be abused does not diminish its importance or value.

Jean-Louis Barrault here introduces many aspects of our investigation and raises and faces some of the fundamental issues which are taken up by other writers.

Barrault speaks from a lifetime of work in and thought about the theatre. He was born in 1910 and, although he began studying as a painter, he was soon involved in the art of the actor, studying mime with Etienne Ducreux, and working with Antonin Artaud. In 1940 he was working both as actor and director for the Comédie Française and, after a break, returned in 1959 as artistic director to the Comédie Française which was re-named the Théâtre de France.

During the student riots in 1968, the theatre building was taken over by Paris students. Barrault made a desperate appeal from the stage to the young people involved, but it appears that he attempted to pacify both Government and students, without satisfying either. Some months later, he was dismissed from his post.

Jean-Louis Barrault has written on the theatre in *Reflections on the Theatre* and *The Theatre of Jean-Louis Barrault*. For him 'drama is as old as man: it is as closely linked to him as his double, for the theatrical game is inherent in the existence of any living being'.

After thirty years of experience, the theatre appears to me to be at one and the same time the greatest of trades and the most absurd profession. It frequently happens that I am affected by that healthy malady, doubt. Many a time I've said to myself: 'Heavens! I practise a profession which is absolutely stupid, false, deceptive. I have completely missed the course which I would like to have followed. Theatre is not at all a justifiable human activity. On a social, on an individual, and on an aesthetic plane, it has to be rejected.' That was in periods of despair, but I believe that a period of despair is a healthy trial. There is always a need to go through great despair, but if, beyond that despair the desire remains, the faith becomes impregnable, indestructible and imperishable. André Gide had a very palatable definition of sin, which went: 'Sin is the thing we cannot help doing.' So if beyond the great despair the theatre remains, like sin, the thing we cannot help doing – theatre is our vocation. But vocation matters little. What we want to know is this: Is theatre a valuable phenomenon, individually as well as socially and aesthetically.

Let's start with a process of destruction of the theatre and see if, after this, the desire remains – in short, if the phenomenon of theatre survives.

Destruction of theatre

Judged by a harsh critic, the theatre is social delusion, individual incapacity, and doubtful aesthetics.

Social delusion: Under the pretext that people need to be distracted – that is, that governments are interested in distracting people's minds and lulling their critical sense – the dramatic art can be used by the theatre, the cinema and television in a degrading manner, appealing to sexual excitement, money-making and cheap laughter.

The manner in which the cinema or certain productions in the theatre exploit vulgar eroticism, both morbid and senile, the manner in which the Press overestimates this eroticism and profits from the private lives of certain stars in order to sell newspapers, cannot but give a feeling of shame to those who sincerely perform their trade. To this one must add the mirage of fame and of lightning success, with the result that kings, queens, governments of great countries will more readily receive a star than a sage. The dramatic art which ought to serve the people and which should, at least, entertain through educating, becomes, then, a depraving drug, and consequently criminal.

Individual incapacity : Many amongst the younger generation who think they are devoting themselves to the theatre are, in fact, running away from life, they obey an important reflex; they do not go into theatre because of their richness, but as a result of their poverty. They are not looking for theatre, they are running away from the true problems of living. Once a young man came to me saying that he wanted to go into the theatre. To my question: 'Why?' he replied, 'Because I hate work!' I questioned him further, forcing him to consider his own limitations. I said, 'What does your father do?'

'He is a lawyer.'

'Is he happy about you?'

'No! He has thrown me out!'

I said, 'Well, you must work so that one day you can prove to your father that he is a fool.' He said to me, 'But he knows that!' There was absolutely nothing to be done – he did not want to work.

Another young man came. He was thin, curly and seemed to breathe the wrong way round – his chest caved in! I was very proud but a little astonished at having attracted him. I asked him why he wanted to go into the theatre and he said, 'Because my health does not allow me to do anything else.'

All these boys and girls who rush into drama courses are unfortunates who take the coward's way out, turning their backs on life, believing they will find in illusion and dream some excuse for their incapacity and laziness.

Doubtful aesthetic : Theatre has often been considered a minor art. To allow it the freedom of the city it would be necessary to consider it as a branch of literature.

In fact, what is a trade? It is an activity which renders service to the corporate life. And an art? An activity which is not a trade but one which, by reflection, renders service to the corporate life, being a sort of token of life and of reaction against death. Art is a revenge taken against death. Take a canvas, a paint brush and some paint; rub the brush over the canvas and suddenly, out of these inert but faithful materials you have a beginning of life, a being, a revelation which is a profound victory over death. Take a box which has the shape of a woman's trunk and in whose belly is the soul. From the top of the neck to the base of the trunk stretch, like nerves, some catgut strings. With a sort of stick of horsehair, begin tickling, stroking this woman's bust, making it creak, and it will release an echo of life which is none other than music. Take a stone, which is inert, take a chisel, which is steel, hit the steel on the stone and suddenly (thanks to *Maillol*, the sculptor) living flesh appears. Scratch your pen over paper and poetry begins to sing. So, through the conflict of two inert materials, whether we rub, stroke, strike or tickle, art re-creates life and man takes his revenge on death.

But these arts are pure and true only because the inert materials are constant. Now, theatre has no recourse to these inert materials. It uses the human being who moves in space. The actor is dependent on the vicissitudes of his health. His voice, his breathing, his precision depend on his balance and metabolism. His nerves, submerged by his sensitivity, may give way. His emotion may escape his control. Then, he will no longer be able to bring to the true creator, the author, that obedience, that faithfulness which is indispensable to all true art. This is what has made all those who have conscientiously considered the dramatic art say that the art of theatre is an impure art. As a reaction, people like Gordon Craig or Baty were tempted by the marionette or the ueber marionette, which were themselves precise and faithful objects. If we once entrusted the actor with the responsibility of expressing dramatic art it would not be anything but a second-hand art, impure and minor.

If the art of the drama leaned on a worthy text, it would become an estimable branch of literature. The theatre, an off-shoot of writing, would then most definitely be a minor art, but capable of meriting the freedom of the city alongside literature. This is what has made many say, 'Above all, theatre is a text!'

Combining the Arts : Theatre is also practised according to Baudelaire's definition, 'a convergence of arts'. To put it another way, a crossroads where all arts meet. It very frequently becomes, we must admit, a complicity of arts. Whether the art of the drama is subservient to the man of letters or is delivered bound hand and foot, to the producer, it no longer sits at the head of the table at the banquet of the muses. Alongside the other arts it is considered aesthetically impure and minor.

Now that we have in this painful manner demonstrated the social delusion, the individual incapacity and the doubtful aesthetic of this incongruous profession, we realize that we have taken a false route. We must, then, forget the theatre temporarily and turn to life.

Look at life : For me life is like the pursuit of the tight-rope walker, who tries, more or less skilfully, to maintain his balance on a rope which has been stretched. But by whom and to where we do not know! We cannot see the point of departure, nor very clearly the destination. We know that sooner or later, as the tight-rope walker feels his way, trying to keep his delicate balance on his rope, there will be a given moment when he will fall headlong into the pitch darkness. So far this is all we know for sure. Obviously it is not terribly encouraging. However, when we start living and reflecting on life, we can observe three rather interesting points: the first is that we are not born once only. True, when we leave our mother's womb, the little being we are is *one*. While we are being breast-fed, while we cry, while we have a vegetable existence, we are *one*. Then we grow and, one fine day, we become aware that we are *seen*, we become aware of others. At that precise moment when we are aware of the fact that we are seen by others, a second birth, a second organic revolution takes place, a second umbilical cord is broken and from *one* we become *two*. We even project a second being which will be the person we wish to appear. From the moment we are not simply ourselves but another, our person is born, we are two.

The others weigh in on us. The community involves us, oppresses us, feeds us in case of need. The exchanges between the individual and the community begin. And we begin to live on two planes: that which we believe we are and that which we want to seem. In fact, it is on *three* planes that we live, because we are mistaken about what we believe we are. This third plane is what we are not, and in effect it is that of which we are ignorant.

From the moment the human being becomes aware of others, he lives hidden behind his person in the same way that the warrior takes refuge behind his shield. From then on, the human being will not only have to fight the others, but will also have to avoid being dominated by his own person. How many people, in the street, have been eaten by their own person! I am talking about adults. When we are young, the essential Me, the being of the first birth is still full of sap; it has nothing to fear from its double – the invertebrate person. But, with the years, the sap recedes and the person develops and one day the second has devoured the first. It is no longer human beings that go about in the street, but the teacher, the policeman, the actor, the general, the director, the subaltern, the businessman, the civil servant – individuals void of their substance, who are no more than what they wish to appear. Here we gamble the higher stake of our existence. Our life will succeed if we resist the person we wish to appear. We must safeguard in ourselves that gleam in our eyes we had as a child, a baby, when we were *one* – one complete world in ourselves.

Since I am addressing young people, I take the liberty of drawing their attention to this problem. It is in the course of your youth that perhaps you die while becoming a person or, alternatively, you remain living while safeguarding that self which was you since birth, that first little being you were and must preserve. That being in you was the child. It is important to safeguard childhood. Youth is a malady in the course of which you either remain living, if you protect your childhood, or you die, if, your childhood stifled, you become adult.

Knowing we are dual, that each of us, in himself, lives with at least two persons, and moves on at least three planes:

What we are

What we believe we are

What we want to appear to others

is a revelation which, amongst the majority of us, gives the desire to become acquainted with the behaviour of the others. Knowing that each of us does not present himself exactly as he is, gives us the desire to shoulder the personality of the others so that we can learn to recognize what they are. This duality determines the desire to change our skin. So there exists in us a desire for metamorphosis of personality.

Training for life : Let's go on to the second point. The second thing that strikes me in our existence is that everything is done out of interest and out of the instinct for preservation. The struggle for life is such that we have no time to do things for nothing, except in periods of decadence. Our existence is guided by usefulness. Human behaviour like the behaviour of all living beings on earth is guided by usefulness. What forms does this behaviour take? Sleeping, eating, working – in order to get something to eat, procreating – in order to survive one's existence (always that resistance against death), and, surprisingly, besides eating, sleeping, working and procreating, *playing*. Every living creature in nature plays. So since I have just said that the behaviour of every living creature is guided by usefulness and the instinct for preservation, we must conclude that playing is useful.

When you see a dog playing with a ball, you cannot say, 'It is like Dafcadio – André Gide's hero – a being acting without purpose.' It cannot help but do something useful. Play may be the outlet for an over-flow, a means of avoiding physical congestion, or just as well a discharge released to prevent the batteries becoming over-charged, a liberation of excess energy. But the phenomenon is much more profound. Watch a dog playing with a ball. The dog cowers before the ball. He behaves in such a way that the ball becomes the enemy. He circles it and uses all his cunning. Suddenly, when looking elsewhere as though unconcerned, pff! He springs on the ball. He traps it. There it is. By tactics, he has taken his enemy. He holds it between his teeth, munches it and mimes injuring his enemy. Then, when the enemy is supposedly dead, he throws it into the air. It falls again. He circles it as if in a scalp dance, then recaptures it, throwing it again, and so on. He plays and suddenly, finally, what does he do? He makes a hole, puts the ball in it and buries it for the next time. He has experienced danger, courage, victory and after victory, reinforcement. He has done no more than that which armies do in times of peace. He has trained himself. He has carried out manoeuvres. Over a certain period of time he has inoculated himself with the danger of existence and the threat of death in a controlled manner as if with a vaccine. Then, as though this danger and this menace of death were pale shadows, he has been able to take his time to analyse his actions well. By then he has organized his fighting so well that he is ready to combat more skilfully at a time when, instead of a ball, he will have another dog – that is to say, a real enemy. This play, therefore, enables us to understand that it is a training for living, a sort of temporary inoculation of evil and danger, a disruption of the balance, like a vaccine which allows us to live, in a substitute way, all the danger-ous circumstances of life, so that we can conduct ourselves better when the dangerous circumstances of life are real. Play is then a training for life, and not an activity without purpose. Observation of life has there-fore given me the notion of person and the explanation of play as a utilitarian activity – a training for life.

Ways of meeting life : Now a third point, which is the synthesis of the other two. We may play to train ourselves for life. We may become aware of the others, of our personal life in the midst of a greater number. We may become aware of this major problem posed by life – the problem of the individual in conflict with the community, the pressure of the community on the individual, the pressure of the Universe on both community and individual. We may have both direct and indirect ways of facing this pressure and this state of existence; yet before long, in spite of the person behind which we take shelter and in spite of the exercises to which we may devote ourselves, the only result is that we feel alone.

When we become conscious of this existence, of this grotesque walk of life on the wire which leads us to death, we are filled with anxiety. In spite of the person, which is the result of a defensive reaction, and in spite of play, which is the result of a training reaction, the individual in society feels *alone* and *anxious*.

There are two solutions to this anxiety. First we are endowed with a vitality quite extraordinary, an excess of strength. In this case, rather than turn his back on death, from fear, man braces himself and charges straight ahead. He cries out with Aeschylus, 'God, release me from my unproductive anxiety.' He bulldozes straight ahead. He defies death beyond his instinct for preservation. He goes further. At this moment, the phenomenon of tragedy emerges. Tragedy begins where the instinct for preservation ends. Surplus energy has turned its nose up at the instinct for preservation. This is why no matter how gloomy the circumstances, a sort of joy, a sort of living tension is always released from tragedy. On the other hand, apart from this direct response, there is an indirect way of reacting to our anxiety. It is by doing a somersault at the precise moment when the preservation of our being is threatened. Here the instinct for preservation is strongest and man reacts by evasion. Then the phenomenon of comedy emerges. So comedy is born out of evasion. The instinct for preservation leads man to joke, to minimize the danger. And man cries out with Menander, 'My joy prevents me from knowing who I am.' These are the two emotional reactions with which man responds to anxiety.

The indestructibility of theatre

Tragedy, rising from an excess of energy, in spite of the tears, releases a certain pleasure. Comedy, on the other hand, rising from an emotional evasion, in spite of the laughter, releases a certain melancholy. For this reason the works of Molière are sadder than the tragedies of Racine. But both these opposing forms of the theatrical phenomenon – tragedy and comedy, specializing in turn in Laughter or Terror and Pity – rise from the same source: our anxiety and solitude. It is this feeling of solitude which we meet with in life which has given us a desire to gather in one agreed meeting place. It is this feeling of solitude which has evoked the theatrical representation.

Actors and audience: A theatrical representation is a meeting of two human groups. First, the audience. Second, the players. The audience is the quintessence of the whole community, or alternatively, the quintessence of the others. The spectator is part of the others, he belongs to the world. The audience is a sort of magnet that brings together humanity in all its numbers and in all its varieties, and it is really only the audience when all the human varieties are closely gathered and people brush shoulders. It is noteworthy that in theatres where there are two arm-rests between the seats the atmosphere is much colder. Where there is only one, the house is much warmer. There is a need for promiscuity. The audience is a sort of synthesis of the whole community of the world, of the promiscuity of all the others pressing one against the other; a sort of human stirring, shoulder to shoulder, like one vast magnetic pile which releases, in a chemical precipitate, a monstrous god, a sole personality which fills all the space of the house, with a huge head and huge arms. The audience is a kind of enormous baby. The phenomenon is logical: taken as a whole, all the adults lose their personality, they no longer have to present themselves because it is going to present itself for them. And through it they re-find themselves. Then their childhood re-appears. The audience has all the qualities and vitality of the child. It finds a unity which is the unity of the collective being, of the childhood of humanity.

On the other hand, on the stage, there is another human group – the players. This company has been formed in the opposite way. It was formed on the principle of quality, of individuality. It is the quintessence of humanity in all its quality. It is human prototypes that have been chosen and selected. There is the lover, there is the captain, there is the lady, there are all the servants: the first servant, the second servant, the mischief maker, the man who gets all the blows, and so on. They are human prototypes who are going to unfold their selfishness for the consideration of the others and represent all the excesses which the others have. The performance is the establishing of contact, an exchange between the individual and the collective. So it is a true artistic representation, the re-creation of that major problem we had already seen when we observed life – Self and the others. On the stage there will be all the 'self' and, in the house will be all the 'others'.

What have they come for, those people who make up the audience? They've come, first of all, to forget self, to forget their personality, to forget their daily life. They've come also to witness the concerns of others. They themselves have their little individual concerns and they want to see others having much greater ones. This is going to purge them of their own anxieties. It is a quest for purification. There is a putting to death in a theatre performance. Then, after it has forgotten itself, after it has seen all the others well troubled, well entangled, after it has taken part in their concerns, their conflicts, their tears, their wounds, their excesses, their passions, the audience comes looking for a place of dream, an ideal place. They come to dream; they come looking for the sublime, that is to say, for a purified life and, through the flight of fancy, they want to reach the plane that one always expects from life, that plane where justice is dispensed. They want to witness a readjustment of the balance of life.

They desire that all conflicts be revealed on the stage – conflicts in which everyone selfishly pleads for himself, in which everyone appears to be what he is not, believes himself to be what he is not, is what he does not know he is and pleads his own rights against the rights of the others, but in fact pleads for his passion of which he is the first victim – they desire, after witnessing all this struggle for existence, they desire to witness justice, that is to say a final judgement, because it is only justice which is going to settle the accounts of all the individuals on the stage. In the last analysis it is justice that will decree the death of those who indulged in excess, and victory for those who have worked for the preservation of life – but only when everybody is dead.

In fact, they want to witness the perfect balance of that tight-rope walker along the wire, that wire of life, because they suffer greatly every time they see him stumble and fall.

At the end of a performance, if it has been a good one, the audience will leave purged of their personal anxieties, and reassured, revitalized, tranquillized by what seemed a dispensing of justice. It is for this reason that I consider that, socially, the theatre is first and foremost an art of justice. Given that, the theatre no longer appears as social delusion, but on the contrary as an activity useful to the public, since it purifies and revitalizes human beings, since it reassures them against anxiety and against solitude.

Let's go on now to the actor on the stage. For him to be able to represent in a selected and crystallized form a human prototype, he will have had to draw upon a great deal of love. It is only through the greatest love that one can fit perfectly inside another's skin. You well know that lovers come to have the same colour eyes, the same way of looking, the same tone of voice, the same handwriting. Sincere lovers come to be infected by simulation – the phenomenon of mimetism. They have the same gestures. It is through the greatest love of life, and particularly of man, that the actor, called on by his profession, will come to resemble the man he wants to interpret, the man he wants to become. Here we are far from impotence, far from evasion of life. The theatrical vocation is the vocation of giving of self.

By force of love, and love not only of men but of life, one lends to life a human soul. The phenomenon of lending a soul to everything that surrounds us is called animism. The oak then becomes the king of the forest, as the lion is the king of animals. The wind is a mischievous lad, fire a wicked person. Liberty is a woman – no doubt because of her frailty!

It is through these two phenomena which result from the greatest love – the mimetism and the animism – that we come to be able to fit perfectly inside the skin of others and to change personality. It seems to me it is in this way that the theatrical phenomenon takes place as far as the actor goes. Here we are opposed to exhibitionism and narcissism. I have in this breakdown of the theatre overtaken the first two objections – social delusion and individual impotence – and have replaced them by public usefulness and the very greatest love of man.

The art of the present moment

It remains for me to prove to you that the theatre – a social necessity and the giving of self – is, on the aesthetic plane, an independent art. For it to be a true art we need to be able to separate it from the other arts. Now if we compare the theatre with the other arts, there is apparently not much room for the theatre. The other arts satisfy all our senses: painting, in a straightforward manner, satisfies the sense of vision; music, the sense of hearing; poetry satisfies our understanding; and so on till we reach the culinary art, which satisfies the papillae of our tongue. I can't very well see where the theatre can take its place. All our specific senses are reached by the other arts. But they are reached one after the other. When we look at a picture, theoretically we become deaf, we only have eyes. When we listen to music we often close our eyes, we only have ears.

At this moment I would like you to be well aware of the present instant. I have been talking to you in abstract terms. But at this moment, now, this very second, the present appears to us in a concrete manner. We can grasp it, touch it. During the fleeting flash of the present, we are reached not only in our eyes and in our ears, but all over the surface of our skin. Sounds, shapes, colours, waves of every kind strike us from all sides. From everywhere the world contacts us and all our radar receivers are open. At each instant of the present our being is like a besieged town on the alert. At each instant of the present, the future is changed to the past. That which awaited life shines like lightning and at once becomes the past. The abstract concept of what is to come, in contact with concrete reality, is transformed into abstract recollection of the past. So it is uniquely at the lightning moment of the present that life exists, that reality is here, concrete, and it is precisely that moment which we have come to grasp.

Is it not surprising to come to realize that what men speak of most – the future and the past – is what does not exist, and that which exists – the present – is actually ungraspable? We need to find an amusement, a recreation, which will consist of enticing this present, of unfolding it like a skin over something, to see what there is inside and to define and enumerate all that co-exists. We need to find an art, an amusement, capable of recreating life accurately observed from the standpoint of the present, and not from the standpoint of colour and shape like painting, or from sound like music, but from the standpoint of silence and the co-existence of sensations.

Let's analyse this present, this time present which we have brought to life perhaps for a fifth of a second. We hardly realized that it was no longer present. It was movement, change. The present is a continuous metamorphosis which takes place on a moving belt. It is the walk of life. But there was something else. While we kept silent, there was contact and exchange between us, our lungs exchanged their life. At any rate, we lived in a certain rhythm, the rhythm of a lecture, but which could covertly be the rhythm of a lecture at Oxford, the rhythm of a lecture in

Great Britain, on Earth, in Space. This minor rhythm, admittedly of no great interest, which exists in this lecture, is covertly in harmony with the universal rhythm, with gravitation. It is not a useless and isolated thing. The present can, therefore, be analysed by movement, exchange and rhythm. In order to re-create the present in its co-existence, there is, then, the need to find an instrument which contains these three characteristics – movement, exchange and rhythm – in their natural state. I only know of one – man. Man who is made up of a vertebral column, the centre of motion, from which all movement flows. Man, who is composed of breath, respiration, centre of exchanges. And man, who holds within himself a sort of wizard, the heart, which beats in accordance with life. That heart which beats regularly its two strokes, short and long, systole – diastole, systole – diastole, that heart which beats the iamb. The beat of the heart is iambic, the fundamental rhythm of poetry. Man is the only instrument who can reproduce the present observed at the moment of the co-existence of all sensations.

If I take a man and set him in space, at strife in a cube of air, and if movements and exchanges, all at a certain rhythm, are established between the man and the air, I will be able to re-create in space the present moment of life which no other art can reproduce. In this way I will have an amusement absolutely independent of other arts – the theatrical phenomenon or the art of the present.

Movement and rhythm

Now let us analyse this instrument which is man. From his vertebral column flows movement. Movement is divided into attitudes, into actions in the strict sense of the word, and into signs. The attitude is the subject, the action is the verb and the sign is the complement. Movement is therefore a language. In the enthusiasm of rhythm, movement becomes dance. From his chest man emits a sound which by the changing shape of his mouth will form the vowel; which by bringing the lips together will create the consonant; which by the unifying of breath and movement will bring to life the syllable, then the word, after this the subject, the verb and the complement. The word is another language which, in the enthusiasm of rhythm, becomes song. But there is no solution of continuity between his movement, which is a muscular contraction supported by breathing, and the word, which is a result of breathing supported by a muscular contraction. Their constitution is the same. There is no difference between movement and the word. The word is an intelligible mouthing which vibrates in space. So the man who moves in space, as he makes exchange with the exterior world, will reach not only our eyes and our ears, but will affect the whole of our skin also. He will reach us not only by vision and hearing but above all, by the sense of touch as well.

I believe that we live in an age where we can pay attention to the importance of the sense of touch. Already during the Renaissance, and before, in the time of the alchemists, we represented man surrounded by his halo of light. We knew well that man was a transmitting station, which sent out waves. We knew well that he reached others beyond the confines of his own skin, that he had the power of radiation. In our age, we have the scientific confirmation of that. We are stations transmitting waves and our most important and powerful sense, the most efficient is without doubt the sense of touch. We can even say that touch is the mysterious sense, the sense divine.

When just now I kept silent, a sort of physical phenomenon occurred between us. We touched each other at a distance. We lived the mystery of presence. When we say of an actor that he has greater or lesser presence, it is to his magnetic power that we refer. When the wizard in the forest goes to meet the explorer 50 kilometres from his hut, although nobody has foreseen it, the fact is that his senses were alerted by the explorer's presence. He has been knocked at, touched, reached. It would not surprise me if sight were a ramification of the sense of touch, and hearing the same. We are touched through the eyes, we are touched through the ear. On the religious plane, to be touched by grace is not a poetic image. It is reality! We are touched. It was not for nothing that men invented the 'hand of God'. Saints are touched. Molière says that in theatre the first rule is to please. He is right. Why to please? It is to open first of all. To open for love, good! But Racine adds, in his preface to Berenice, 'We must please and touch.' Undoubtedly he says it in the eighteenth-century sense of touching sensibility. In our modern world, we can well extend the definition of the verb 'to touch' to include the physiological sense – we must please and touch. This is what makes the magic virtue of Claudel's word. Claudel is sometimes intellectually incomprehensible, but his spoken word is as definite as dough, as physiology, so the audience is physically affected by the word of Claudel. By dint of being drummed at by his word, the audience comes to be in a certain physical state outside all cerebral understanding.

Thanks to the sense of touch, the dramatic art is fundamentally a carnal, a sensual amusement. The theatrical performance is a collective mingling, an act of true love, a sensual communion of two human groups. One opens itself, the other touches and penetrates. The two become one. They devour each other. It is for this that the theatre essentially represents the act. Now the act can only be understood at the present moment, because, what is an act? An act is made up of three elements: the neuter, the masculine, the feminine. The preparation, the act proper and the consequence. The preparation is slow – it is the future, it is the neuter of future. Then comes the act and suddenly there is the flashing gush of lightning at the present moment and following after, the long consequence which is called the past. The three moments of the act are: the slow rise of desire, the lightning of fruition, and the gestation which is slow as well.

The art of theatre, addressing itself essentially to the sense of touch, is then above all the art of sensation. It is opposed to all intellectual preoccupation. We are therefore a long way from literature and writing. There is nothing in common between literature and theatre except poetry, the verbal poetry of the theatre, much more ancient than the poetry which is handed down through writing. We rediscover in the dramatic poem, the poet of antiquity who sang and danced before the others his own creation at the present moment. It is only later because of the decline of song and the decline of dance that the poet wrote and had others speak his text. We turned to literature because total poetry, that is theatrical poetry, was exhausted. Then, syntax prevailed over prosody. But if in literature it is syntax that counts, in theatre it is without doubt prosody, because prosody is respiration, respiration is exchange and exchange is the present life.

I believe then that I am showing from the point of view of the present that theatre is very much an independent art, independent of literature and of all other arts. It will always be objected that it is impure, because the human being is a weak and uncertain instrument. I have made that point already at the outset. It is for that reason that we have grafted on to the dramatic art another art which is that of the actor. The art of the actor consists of making an undisciplined human being become a disciplined instrument. It is a very complicated and absurd art which is only possible owing to the duality of every individual, the duality of his deeper being and his personality. An art which is disrupting since it must, on the one hand develop to the pitch of hysteria within himself the actor's capacity for sensibility, and must, on the other, develop by means of will, a constant control of himself. The art of the actor consists in achieving that absolute contradiction – the control of spontaneity. If the theatrical phenomenon is the art of the present, the art of the actor is that of the will.

Now we have overcome the test of doubt, we have denounced the theatre for what it has of falsehood and shame. We have taken refuge in life and observed it in its more striking aspects: the duality of being, the useful significance of amusement, solitude and anguish. The theatrical phenomenon now appears to us afresh as a desire, rising out of man's need to congregate, to reassure, to purify, to revitalize himself. Since in this way, we have rediscovered our faith, now more indestructible than ever, theatre will be for us the finest of trades, embracing art and religion – the thing which, like sin, we cannot help doing.

There is a story of a bishop who dined with a psychoanalyst. The psychoanalyst said, 'Nowadays, my Lord, it is not to the confessional that one comes to purify oneself, it is to my consulting-room which is more comfortable – one does not scrape one's knees, one lies comfortably on a couch. It is pleasanter.' The bishop replied, 'Yes, dear doctor, you are right. The only difference between us is that you do not forgive.'

We people of the theatre do not have the right of forgiveness; we do not, like doctors, have the power of healing. But we do frequently have the feeling of comforting, of reassuring our fellow creatures. And that, I believe, is what makes the nobility of our trade.

This lecture was first published in French by Oxford University Press in 1961, and has not been previously printed in English because Oxford say they must assume that all their readers would be capable of reading it in the French! The version here is slightly abridged, though all Barrault's main points are included.

Barrault's is a somewhat romantic view in that he talks in terms of the magic of the theatre. He believes the effect on the audience is one of tranquillizing and reassuring in the presentation of an ultimate justice. He does not discuss political or other committed approaches to theatre. He is still thinking in terms of traditional theatre practice of the actor as an interpreter and does not seem to be considering him as a possible creator. The rhythm and approach are certainly those of an Oxford lecture, in that there is a safe academic comfort about procedure. There is an awful irony in that he seems to have such a regard for the young people to whom he is speaking and yet it was the equivalent young people in France who contributed towards his losing his key post in the French theatre.

Nevertheless, the following points seem important and are likely to come up again:

1. acting *can* be a form of running away from life
2. theatre appeals to the quick money-making instinct
3. drama can help in preparing for life – some plays are ways of meeting aspects of life (theatre ought to entertain through educating)
4. audiences experience a solidarity in the theatre – they lose identity to find it
5. actors can present prototypes – they take on identity
6. drama is the art of the 'now' – 'a co-existence of sensations'
7. good acting demands a generosity of spirit
8. acting draws on mimetism and animism
9. the art of the actor involves turning the undisciplined human being into a disciplined instrument
10. theatre is escape – but escape to understanding and awareness

SECTION TWO
Some Basic Attitudes

3 Human Needs and the Drama
E. K. Chambers

If drama has a natural place in the lives of men, it is sensible to look next at two areas of investigation where this could be exemplified.

First, we can examine some of the dramatic activities of early man and then look at aspects of dramatic play in early childhood.

Sir Edmund Chambers was by occupation a civil servant in the field of education, and, in the second half of the nineteenth century began research into dramatic history. His work is exact and scholarly, splendidly documented and carefully annotated. In attempting to understand medieval drama as a means of understanding Elizabethan drama, he found himself delving into early ritual and festivals – drama without a theatre. Much of his information is drawn from, or related to, that other associated study, Sir James Frazer's *The Golden Bough* (the first volume of which was published in 1890).

The eighteenth- and nineteenth-century practice of the theatrical art has tended to obscure thinking with regard to the fundamental meaning and purpose of acting and impersonation, rhythm and ritual. The growing importance in those centuries of the proscenium arch, dividing actor and audience, helped to create a separate world of escapism and associated the word 'theatrical' with the illusionary and phoney.

By considering the earliest manifestations, it is possible to see more clearly how drama is linked with the central desire of man to find form, pattern and purpose in his very existence. It is from such investigations as these that Freud formulated his own interpretation, and developed our understanding of taboo.

The central fact of the agricultural festivals is the presence in the village of the fertilization spirit in the visible and tangible form of flowers and green foliage or of the fruits of the earth. Thus, when the peasants do their 'observance to a morn of May', great boughs of hawthorn are cut before daybreak in the woods, and carried, with other seasonable leafage and blossom, into the village street. Lads plant branches before the doors of their mistresses. The folk deck themselves, their houses, and the church in green. Some of them are clad almost entirely in wreaths and tutties, and become walking bushes, 'Jacks i' the green'. The revel centres in dance and song around a young tree set up in some open space of the village, or a more permanent Maypole adorned for the occasion with fresh garlands. A large garland, often with an anthropomorphic representation of the fertilization spirit in the form of a doll, parades the streets, and is accompanied by a 'king' or 'queen', or a 'king' and 'queen' together. Such a garland finds its place at all the seasonal feasts; but whereas in spring and summer it is naturally made of the new vegetation, at harvest it as naturally takes the form of a sheaf, often the last sheaf cut, of the corn. Then it is known as the 'harvest-May' or the 'neck', or if it is anthropomorphic in character, as the 'kern-baby'. Summer and harvest garlands alike are not destroyed when the festival is over, but remain hung up on the Maypole or the church or the barn-door until the season for their annual renewing comes round. And sometimes the grain of the 'harvest-May' is mingled in the spring with the seed-corn.

The rationale of such customs is fairly simple. They depend upon a notion of sympathetic magic carried on into the animistic stage of belief. Their object is to secure less the beneficent influence of the fertilization spirit by bringing the persons or places to be benefited into direct contact with the physical embodiment of that spirit. In the burgeoning quick set up on the village green is the divine presence. The worshipper clad in leaves and flowers has made himself a garment of the god, and is therefore in a very special sense under his protection. Thus efficacy in folk-belief of physical contact may be illustrated by another set of practices in which recourse is had to the fertilization spirit for the cure of disease. A child suffering from croup, convulsions, rickets, or other ailment, is passed through a hole in a split tree, or beneath a bramble rooted at both ends, or a strip of turf partly raised from the ground. It is the actual touch of earth or stem that works the healing.

The magical notions which, in part at least, explain the garland customs of the agricultural festival, are still more strongly at work in some of its subsidiary rites. These declare themselves, when understood, to be of an essentially practical character, charms designed to influence the weather, and to secure the proper alternation of moisture and warmth which is needed alike for the growth and ripening of the crops and for the welfare of the cattle. They are probably even older than the garland customs, for they do not imply the animistic conception of a fertilization spirit immanent in leaf and blossom; and they depend not only upon the 'sympathetic' principle of influence by direct contact already illustrated, but also upon that other principle of similarity distinguished by Dr Frazer as the basis of what he calls 'mimetic' magic. To the primitive mind, the obvious way of obtaining a result in nature is to make an imitation of it on a small scale. To achieve rain, water must be splashed about, or some other characteristic of a storm or shower must be reproduced. To achieve sunshine, a fire must be lit, or some other representation of the appearance and motion of the sun must be devised. Both rain-charms and sun-charms are very clearly recognizable in the village ritual.

With the growth of animistic or spiritual religion, the mental tendencies, out of which magical practices or charms arise, gradually cease to be operative in the consciousness of the worshippers. The charms themselves, however, are preserved by the conservative instinct of cult. In part they survive as mere bits of traditional ritual, for which no particular reason is given or demanded; in part also they become material for other instinct, itself no less inveterate in the human mind, by which the relics of the past are constantly in process of being re-explained and brought into new relations with the present. The sprinkling with holy water, for instance, which was originally of the nature of a rain-charm, comes to be regarded as a rite symbolical of spiritual purification and regeneration. An even more striking example of such transformation of intention is to be found in the practice, hardly yet referred to in this account of the agricultural festivals, of sacrifice. In the ordinary acceptation of the term, sacrifice implies not merely an animistic, but an anthropomorphic conception of the object of cult. The offering or oblation with which man approaches his god is an extension of the gift with which, as suppliant, he approaches his fellow men. But the oblational aspect of sacrifice is not the only one. In his remarkable book upon *The Religion of the Semites*, Professor Robertson Smith has formulated another, which may be distinguished as 'sacramental'. In this the sacrifice is regarded as the renewal of a special tie between the god and his worshippers, analogous to the blood-bond which exists amongst those worshippers themselves. The victim is not an offering made to the god; on the contrary, the god himself is, or is present in, the victim. It is his blood which is shed, and by means of the sacrificial banquet and its subsidiary rites, his personality becomes, as it were, incorporated in those of his clansmen. It is not necessary to determine here the general priority of the two types or conceptions of sacrifice described. But, while it is probable that the Kelts and Teutons of the time of the conversion consciously looked upon sacrifice as an oblation, there is also reason to believe that, at an earlier period, the notion of a sacrament had been the predominant one. For the sacrificial ritual of these peoples, and especially that used in the agricultural cult, so far as it can be traced, is only explicable as an elaborate process of just that physical incorporation of the deity in the worshippers and their belongings, which it was the precise object of the sacramental sacrifice to bring about. It will be clear that sacrifice, so regarded, enters precisely into that category of ideas which has been defined as magical. It is but one more example of that belief in the efficacy of direct contact which lies at the root of sympathetic magic. As in the case of the garland customs, this belief, originally pre-animistic, has endured into an animistic stage of thought. Through the garland and the posies the worshipper sought contact with the fertilization spirit in its phytomorphic form; through sacrifice he approaches it in its theriomorphic form also. The earliest sacrificial animals, then, were themselves regarded as divine, and were naturally enough the food animals of the folk. The use made by the Kelto-Teutonic peoples of oxen, sheep, goats, swine, deer, geese, and fowls requires no explanation. A common victim was also the horse, which the Germans seem, up to a late date, to have kept in droves and used for food. The strong opposition of the Church to the sacrificial use of horse-flesh may possibly account for the prejudice against it as a food-stuff in modern Europe. A similar prejudice, however, in the case of the hare, an animal of great importance in folk belief, already existed in the time of Caesar. It is a little more puzzling to find distinct traces of sacrificial customs in connection with animals, such as the dog, cat, wolf, fox, squirrel, owl, wren, and so forth, which are not now food animals. But they may once have been such, or the explanation may lie in an extension of the sacrificial practice after the first rationale of it was lost.

At every agricultural festival, then, animal sacrifice may be assumed as an element. The analogy of the relation between the fertilization spirit and his worshippers to the human blood bond makes it probable that originally the rite was always a bloody one. Some of the blood was poured on the sacred tree. Some was sprinkled upon the worshippers, or smeared over their faces, or solemnly drunk by them. Hides, horns, and entrails were also hung upon the tree, or worn as festival trappings. The flesh was, of course, solemnly eaten in the sacrificial meal. The crops, as well as their cultivators, must benefit by the rites; and therefore the fields, and doubtless also the cattle, had their sprinkling of blood, while heads or pieces of flesh were buried in the furrows, or at the threshold of the byre. The wearing of the skins of the victims is precisely parallel to the wearing of the green vegetation, the sprinkling with blood to the sprinkling with lustral water, the burial in the fields of flesh and skulls to the burial of brands from the festival fire. In each case the belief in the necessity of direct physical contact to convey the beneficent influence is at the bottom of the practice. It need hardly be said that of such physical contact the most complete example is in the sacramental banquet itself. It is entirely consistent with the view here taken of the primitive nature of sacrifice, that the fertilization spirit was sacrificed at the village festivals in its vegetable as well as in its animal form. There were bread offerings as well as meat offerings. Sacramental cakes were prepared with curious rituals which attest their primitive character. Like the *tcharnican* or Beltane cakes, they were kneaded and moulded by hand and not upon a board; like the loaf in the Anglo-Saxon charm, they were compounded of all sorts of grain in order that they might be represent-ative of every crop in the field. At the harvest they would naturally be made, wholly or in part, of the last sheaf cut. The use of them corres-ponded closely to that made of the flesh of the sacrificial victim. Some were laid on a branch of the sacred tree; others flung into the sacred well or the festival fire; others again buried in the furrows, or crumbled up and mingled with the seed-corn. And like the flesh they were sol-emnly eaten by the worshippers themselves at the sacrificial banquet.

With the sacrificial cake went the sacrificial draught, also made out of the fruits of the earth, in the southern lands wine, but in the vineless north ale, or cider, or that mead which Pytheas described the Britons as brewing out of honey and wheat. Of this, too, the trees and crops received their share, while it filled the cup for those toasts or *minnes* to the dead and to Odin and Freyja their rulers, which were afterwards transferred by Christian Germany to St John and St Gertrude.

The animal and the cereal sacrifices seem plausible enough, but they do not exhaust the problem. One has to face the fact that human sacrifice, as Victor Hehn puts it, 'peers uncannily forth from the dark past of every Aryan race'. So far as the Kelts and Teutons go, there is plenty of evidence to show, that up to the very moment of their contact with Roman civilization, in some branches even up to the very moment of their conversion to Christianity, it was not yet obsolete. An explanation of it is therefore required, which shall fall in with the general theory of agricultural sacrifice. The subject is very difficult, but, on the whole, it seems probable that originally the slaying of a human being at an annually recurring festival was not of the nature of sacrifice at all. It is doubtful whether it was ever sacrifice in the sacramental sense, and although in time it came to be regarded as an oblation, this was not until the first meaning, both of the sacrifice and of the human death, had been lost. The essential facts bearing on the question have been gathered together by Dr Frazer in *The Golden Bough*. He brings out the point that the victim in a human sacrifice was not originally merely a man, but a very important man, none other than the king, the priest-king of the tribe. In many communities, Aryan-speaking and other, it has been the principal function of such a priest-king to die, annually or at longer intervals, for the people. His place is taken, as a rule, by the tribesman who has slain him. Dr Frazer's own explanation of this custom is, that the head of the tribe was looked upon as possessed of great magical powers, as a big medicine man, and was in fact identified with the god himself. And his periodical death, says Dr Frazer, was necessary, in order to renew the vitality of the god, who might decay and cease to exist, were he not from time to time reincarnated by being slain and passing into the body of his slayer and successor. This is a highly ingenious and fascinating theory, but unfortunately there are several difficulties in the way of accepting it. In the first place it is inconsistent with the explanation of the sacramental killing of the god arrived at by Professor Robertson Smith. According to this, the sacrifice of the god is for the sake of his worshippers, that the blood-bond with them may be renewed; and we have seen that this view fits in admirably with the minor sacrificial rites, such as the eating and burying of the flesh, as the wearing of the horns and hides. Dr Frazer, however, obliges us to hold that the god is also sacrificed for his own sake, and leaves us in the position of propounding two quite distinct and independent reasons for the same fact. Secondly, there is no evidence, at least amongst Aryan-speaking peoples, for that breaking down of the very real and obvious distinction between the god and his chief worshipper or priest, which Dr Frazer's theory implies. And thirdly, if the human victim were slain as being the god, surely this slaughter should have replaced the slaughter of the animal victim previously slain for the same reason, which it did not, and should have been followed by a sacramental meal of a cannibal type, of which also, in western Europe, there is but the slightest trace.

Probably, therefore, the alternative explanation of Dr Frazer's own facts given by Dr Jevons is preferable. According to this the death of the human victim arises out of the circumstances of the animal sacrifice. The slaying of the divine animal is an act approached by the tribe with mingled feelings. It is necessary, in order to renew the all-essential blood-bond between the god and his worshippers. And at the same time it is an act of sacrilege; it is killing the god. There is some hesitation amongst the assembled worshippers. Who will dare the deed and face its consequences? 'The clansman', says Dr Jevons, 'whose religious conviction of the clan's need of communion with the god was deepest, would eventually and after long waiting be the one to strike, and take upon himself the issue, for the sake of his fellow men.' This issue would be twofold. The slayer would be exalted in the eyes of his fellows. He would naturally be the first to drink the shed blood of the god. A double portion of the divine spirit would enter into him. He would become, for a while, the leader, the priest-king, of the community. At the same time he would incur blood-guiltiness. And in a year's time, when his sanctity was exhausted, the penalty would have to be paid. His death would accompany the renewal of the bond by a fresh sacrifice, implying in its turn the self-devotion of a fresh annual king.

These theories belong to a region of somewhat shadowy conjecture. If Dr Jevons is right, it would seem to follow that, as has already been suggested, the human death at an annual festival was not initially sacrifice. It accompanied but did not replace the sacramental slaughter of a divine animal. But when the animal sacrifice had itself changed its character, and was looked upon, no longer as an act of communion with the god, but as an offering or bribe made to him, then a new conception of the human death also was required. When the animal ceased to be recognized as the god, the need of a punishment for slaying it disappeared. But the human death could not be left meaningless, and its meaning was assimilated to that of the animal sacrifice itself. It also became an oblation, the greatest that could be offered by the tribe to its protector and its judge. And no doubt this was the conscious view taken of the matter by Kelts and Teutons at the time when they appear in history. The human sacrifice was on the same footing as the animal sacrifice, but it was a more binding, a more potent, a more solemn appeal.

In whatever way human sacrifice originated, it was obviously destined, with the advance of civilization, to undergo modification. Not only would the growing moral sense of mankind learn to hold it a dark and terrible thing, but also to go on killing the leading man of the tribe, the king-priest, would have its obvious practical inconveniences. At first, indeed, these would not be great. The king-priest would be little more than a rain-maker, a *rex sacrorum*, and one man might perform the ceremonial observances as well as another. But as time went on, and the tribe settled down to a comparatively civilized life, the serious functions of its leader would increase. He would become the arbiter of justice, the adviser in debate; above all, when war grew into importance, the captain in battle. And to spare and replace, year by year, the wisest councillor and the bravest warrior would grow into an intolerable burden. Under some such circumstances, one can hardly doubt, a process of substitution set in. Somebody had to die for the king. At first, perhaps, the substitute was an inferior member of the king's own house, or even an ordinary tribesman, chosen by lot. But the process, once begun, was sure to continue, and presently it was sufficient if a life of little value, that of a prisoner, a slave, a criminal, a stranger within the gates, was sacrificed. The common belief in madness or imbecility as a sign of divine possession may perhaps have contributed to make the village fool or natural seem a particularly suitable victim. But to the very end of Teutonic and Keltic heathenism, the sense that the substitute was, after all, only a substitute can be traced. In times of great stress or danger, indeed, the king might still be called upon to suffer in person. And always a certain pretence that the victim was the king was kept up. Even though a slave or criminal, he was for a few days preceding the sacrifice treated royally.

He was a temporary king, was richly dressed and feasted, had a crown set on his head, and was permitted to hold revel with his fellows. The farce was played out in the sight of men and gods. Ultimately, of course, the natural growth of the sanctity of human life in a progressive people, or in an unprogressive people the pressure of outside ideals, forbids the sacrifice of a man at all. Perhaps the temporary king is still chosen, and even some symbolic mimicked slaying of him takes place; but actually he does not die. An animal takes his place upon the altar; or more strictly speaking, an animal remains the last victim, as it had been the first, and in myth is regarded as a substitute for the human victim which for a time had shared its fate. Of such a myth the legends of Abraham and Isaac and of Iphigeneia at Aulis are the classical examples.

There is another group of myths for which, although they lack this element of a substituted victim, mythologists find an origin in a reformation of religious sentiment leading to the abolition of human sacrifice. The classical legend of Perseus and Andromeda, the hagiological legend of St George and the Dragon, the Teutonic legend of Beowulf and Grendel, are only types of innumerable tales in which the hero puts an end to the periodical death of a victim by slaying the monster who has enforced and profited by it. What is such a story but the imaginative statement of the fact that such sacrifices at one time were, and are not? It is, however, noticeable, that in the majority of these stories although not in all, the dragon or monster slain has his dwelling in water, and this leads to the consideration of yet another sophistication of the primitive notion of sacrifice. According to this notion sacrifice was necessarily bloody; in the shedding of blood and in the sacrament of blood partaken of by the worshippers, lay the whole gist of the rite: a bloodless sacrifice would have no *raison d'être*. On the other hand, the myths just referred to seem to imply a bloodless sacrifice by drowning, and this notion is confirmed by an occasional bit of ritual, and by the common superstition which represents the spirits of certain lakes and rivers as claiming a periodical victim in the shape of a drowned person. Similarly there are traces of sacrifices, which must have been equally bloodless, by fire. At the Beltane festival, for instance, one member of the party is chosen by lot to be the 'victim', is made to jump over the flames and is spoken of in jest as 'dead'. Various Roman writers, who apparently draw from the second-century B.C. Greek explorer Posidonius, ascribe to the Druids of Gaul a custom of burning human and other victims at quinquennial feasts in colossal images of hollow wickerwork; and squirrels, cats, snakes and other creatures are frequently burnt in modern festival fires. The constant practice, indeed, of burning bones in such fires has given them the specific name of bonfires, and it may be taken for granted that the bones are only representatives of more complete victims. I would suggest that such sacrifices by water and fire are really developments of the water and fire-charms described earlier; and that just as the original notion of sacrifice has been extended to give a new significance to the death of a human being at a religious festival, when the real reason for that death had been forgotten, so it has been still further extended to cover the primitive water and fire-charms when they too had become meaningless. I mean that at a festival the victims, like the image and the worshippers, were doubtless habitually flung into water or passed through fire as part of the charm; and that, at a time when sacrifice had grown into mere oblation and the shedding of blood was, therefore, no longer essential, these rites were adapted and given new life as alternative methods of effecting the sacrifice.

This is an abridged version of Chapter 6, Village Festivals, in Sir E. K. Chambers' monumental study of the Medieval Stage, which was first published in 1903. This two-volume work was itself the result of preliminary investigations for 'a little book of Shakespeare'.

While Chambers' investigations are often rather drily presented, this account still seems readable and apposite. The more important points which emerge seem to be:

1. a strong dramatic ritual element in early festivals
2. that both animism and mimetism are present
3. clear association of the magical qualities of imitation and physical contact
4. that costume is a considerable aid in assisting identification
5. the value of myth and legend in human understanding
6. that this dramatic expression is a tangible and active approach to matters which are often intangible
7. that there are certain themes emerging which are universal in nature – fundamental questions about life itself are being investigated
8. the development of imaginative substitution in development of the rituals.

It is interesting to compare Chambers' discussion of Frazer's and Jevon's narratives with Freud's account of the growth of social restrictions and the Uranus' myth. Put as simply as possible, Freud's account goes something like this:

Man originally lived in a tribe or group of families, ruled over by a male leader. This ruler dominated all, until members of the group got together, rose against him, killed and ate him. Then the men, soon after the killing, felt a sense of regret and the need to make up for their wrong doing (possibly this could be explained by suggesting that, without this expression of sorrow, the killing might continue and who could say who the next victim might be).

Then follows the idea that the spirit or life-force of the dead leader has gone into some animal or plant. This animal or plant then becomes sacred or, as they say, the 'totem' and must on no account be killed or destroyed. Until there comes a time when they feel the need to re-enact the deed of killing.

When we act something out, we always seem to have a healthier control of it than if we try to pretend that it doesn't exist. So, a ceremony or ritual begins to be established, and at a set time the killing is acted out but the sacred animal or plant is substituted for the man. It is at this point when people seem to have, through this ceremony, regained some control of the situation, that certain rules or laws or 'taboos' are formed. The most obvious one is that no man should kill any other human. So death becomes concerned with the forbidden and from here we can see how the next important set of taboos is connected with the making of life. Two things are important: to avoid strife over the women, and to avoid weakening the tribe by in-breeding. Other early taboos were concerned with the maintenance of health: the avoidance of certain meats which seemed to cause disease, the importance of hand washing in the handling of food, and so on.

From this kind of ceremony and ritual it can be seen how ideas of power – of unseen forces and so of superstition and the concern with gods (who seem to have powers over men) – could grow. In man's primitive rituals, drama is seen as one of the ways in which man comes to terms with aspects of the unknown.

4 Drama and Childhood Play
Margaret Lowenfeld

There have been several important studies of the play of children and perhaps the best known of these, at least by name, is that undertaken by

Jean Piaget, in *Play, Dreams and Imitation in Childhood* (published in 1962). Piaget's observations are detailed records of the progress of his own three children. Only later did he extend his study to the examination of children in a school community. This somewhat narrow range, and his incredibly detailed and scholarly recordings, make his account less readable than that of Margaret Lowenfeld, whose observations are drawn from work with children from a wider range of backgrounds and abilities.

Piaget's terminology tends to make his work particularly specialist. He refers constantly to terms like 'assimilation', 'accommodation' and 'schema'. The child absorbs new experiences, he 'assimilates' these to his 'schema', which is his own sequence of actions. This process he refers to as 'accommodation', or as he puts it: 'imitation is a continuation of accommodation, play is a continuation of assimilation, and intelligence a harmonious combination of the two'.

As Piaget established earlier in *Language and Thought of the Child* (published in 1926), he tends to relate his observations to the *intellectual* development of the child. Margaret Lowenfeld's classification of children's play according to physical action, realization of experience, demonstration of fantasy, realization of environment and use of comedy, is a study more relevant and illuminating in considering drama as a social and educational force. 'Play', she points out, 'is an exceedingly complex phenomenon. It is an activity which combines, into a single whole, very diverse strands of thought and experience. Many of these persist in adult life. . . . It is the author's contention that the mechanisms of play do not entirely disappear with the ending of childhood.'

The standpoint from which we approach the study will tend to influence the way we attempt to classify or group the different purposes we discern. As Margaret Lowenfeld emphasizes, classification is only a means by which we attempt further understanding. The play of children in any particular hour may well range through many different kinds and at times may be employed on several levels. For the most part, it is a subconscious manifestation, an outward expression of the conflicts and perplexities which face individuals as they grapple with old and new experiences. By studying the absorbed play of children, we can appreciate further the functions and purposes of drama, free from conventions and pseudo-sophisticated associations.

There is hardly any feature of human life to which so little serious consideration has been given as that of children's play. The present study is offered because of the writer's belief that there is a connection between the play of children and the life of adult man, and that in this little-regarded aspect of the life of the juvenile fraction of humanity can be found clues to some of the most perplexing puzzles that face adult man in his relationships to his fellows.

Our increased control over nature seems to be exactly balanced by an increasing bewilderment about ourselves. Unconquered, however, in the fact of this paradox, the human mind refuses to admit defeat, and from the darkest aspects of its peril begins to forge new weapons of attack.

The field is so vast, and our knowledge of it so infinitesimal, that an attack at practically any point may yield the most valuable results. Modern work in dynamic psychology has given indications that, in the study of children, clues can be found to laws of general significance that may not be attainable in any other way; and it is such a belief that lies behind this study of childhood play.

To a primitive society young people are important in three ways – they are a relaxation from toil, an earnest of future strength to the tribe, and as they grow to marriageable age they become the focus of the economic cares and ambitions of the family. In very primitive societies, where a child must rely upon itself for protection from danger, adults devote a great deal of time to play with their young.

So much ambiguity has arisen from time to time over the use of the word 'play', as also over the exact interpretation of the word 'child', that before any useful examination can be made either of play itself, or of matters concerning a child or children, some agreement must be arrived at as to the sense in which either word is used.

As regards the word 'child', it has during the history of the English language borne very many meanings, and here will be taken as embracing the years between eighteen months (early toddler) and early adolescence – that is to say, the period covered by the nursery school and ordinary school years of the elementary school child.

An equivalent term to the English word 'play' is to be found in all European languages. In each language the meaning of the word 'play', like that of the word 'child', has shown great flexibility. In the Oxford English Dictionary among the very large number of meanings given, the following groups may be distinguished: Play as free activity or movement in general; play as the carrying out of something which is not to be taken seriously, but is done merely in sport or frolic; to engage in a game, to play it; to perform dramatically, and, with the derived sense, to represent in mimic action, to play out; to play on musical instruments. In the study of children's play, each and every form of meaning will be found to be implied.

Children have played since the dawn of civilization, and descriptions of their games are to be found throughout the literature of mankind. Every civilization has handed on to its children, from one generation to another, traditional types of games. Moreover, in reference to children, it is in this sense that to the present day the word 'play' is most generally used.

Since all the activities of children, other than lessons, eating, and sleeping, seem to the watching adult to have no serious purpose, a description of them as play appears apt and fitting, and to draw a line rigidly, for example, between the play of an individual playing alone, and games which are played in groups, seems the act of a purist.

It was Froebel who, in the early part of last century, first pointed out that the games that children play in groups to set rules are only part, and a very small part, of the total play life of children and that play in itself in children is not relaxation, but the most significant aspect of childhood.

'Play', said Froebel, 'then, is the highest expression of human development in childhood, for it alone is the free expression of what is in the child's soul. It is the purest and most spiritual product of the child, and at the same time it is a type and copy of human life at all stages and in all relations. . . . For to one who has insight into human nature, the trend of the whole future life of the child is revealed in his freely chosen play.' It was Froebel's genius to have discovered play as the appropriate vehicle and helpmate of education. Primarily an educationalist, with his whole mind and heart centred in education, he was at the same time an amazingly intuitive, acute, and sympathetic observer of children. Throughout his writings illuminated remarks are scattered, almost as if by chance, on the varieties and significance of play, but at no point does he attempt a systematic classification of children's play as play.

Towards the end of the nineteenth century, Spencer put forward the theory that children's play arises out of the discharge of an excess of energy in the brain centres in childhood, and that the child plays because he has a superabundant supply of energy.

In 1886, Grasberger remarked that hitherto no satisfactory classification of play had been made, and in 1896 Professor Karl Groos published the first scientific study of the Play of Animals, which was followed a few years later by his book on the Play of Man. At about the same time, working in America, Stanley Hall and his colleagues had begun to put out a series of papers that were systematic and painstaking studies of various aspects of child life, and which were afterwards collected into *Aspects of Child Life and Education* and *Youth: Its Education, Regimen, and Hygiene*. In England, Sully, then Professor of Psychology at University College, London, published in 1896 his *Studies of Childhood*.

Groos, working from a theory which links the play of childhood with the play of animals, grouped play into seven major and sixty minor varieties. He regarded play as the expression of instinct, and particularly of that form of instinct which impels animals to train themselves in infancy for the roles they are to play in maturity.

Stanley Hall, on the other hand, writing between 1896 and 1904, takes the view that in play the child epitomizes and recapitulates the progress of the race. 'True play', he writes, 'never practises what is phyletically new; . . . I regard play as the motor habits and spirit of the past of the race, persisting in the present, as rudimentary organs'; and again: 'Thus the boy is father of the man in a new sense, in that his qualities are indefinitely older, and existed, well compacted, untold ages before the more distinctly human attributes were developed.' Hall, at the same time, places overwhelming emphasis upon muscular development: 'Muscles', he writes, 'are in a most intimate and peculiar sense the organs of the will. They have built all the roads, cities, and machines in the world, written all the books, spoken all the words, and, in fact, done everything that man has accomplished with matter. Character might be in a sense defined as a plexus of motor habits.'

Sully, as a psychologist, viewed play objectively and with less moral bias than Froebel, or Stanley Hall, but unlike Groos and Hall, he did not attach a specialized function to play. Indeed, he cast doubts on the assumption that the adult, with his superior understanding, would easily comprehend this activity of his intellectual inferiors. In his Studies of Childhood, he says, talking of children at play: 'We talk . . . glibly about their play, their make-believe, their illusions; but how much do we really know of their state of mind when they act out a little scene of domestic life or of the battlefield?'

To Sully, children's play was essentially the expression of childish imagination and ideas. There was imitative play on the one hand, which copies those adult activities constantly seen, and there was play that expressed ideas conjured up by a vivid imagination fed by stories from books and by things seen and not completely understood. Later, for example, in the chapter from which the above quotation is taken, he says of play: 'The source of play is the impulse to realize a bright idea: whence as we shall see by and by, its close kinship to art as a whole.'

Sully conceives play as essentially the spontaneous activity of the child. He lays particular stress upon the difficulty of observing children's play, and he gives more than one striking example of children distressed at adult interruption of their play – interruption either by physical interference or by failure to enter into the play then in progress. For example, in Chapter II, he relates the following story told him by a mother:

> 'a little girl of four was playing shops with her younger sister. The elder one was shopman at the time I came into her room and kissed her. She broke out into piteous sobs – I could not understand why. At last she sobbed out: "Mother, you never kiss the man in the shop." I had with my kiss quite spoilt her illusion.'

He nowhere essays a survey of the whole field of play.

If we would, therefore, attempt the task of passing the field of children's play in review, it is to Stanley Hall and to Groos that we must turn for classification of the forms of play and for theories of the meaning of play. There are, however, considerable difficulties in the way of acceptance of the views put forward by either.

To consider first the standpoint of Karl Groos: the first difficulty that appears is that Groos nowhere separates the play of children from the play of adult men and women. He classifies as play many activities which, when practised by adults, are indeed play, but when performed by children, if ever this occurs, they have a different significance. Groos further makes no distinction between activities which are undertaken by a child in its normal process of gaining control of the muscles of its body and play. For example, he writes:

> 'Almost as soon as the child has learned to preserve his equilibrium in ordinary walking, he proceeds to complicate the problem by trying to walk on curbstones, in a rut, on a beam, on a balustrade or narrow wall.'

While Groos classes this as play, because in an adult it would be play, to a child it is not play, but serious effort at motor control. That is to say, activities of this kind are the parallel in childhood of the gradual undertaking of more and more difficult tasks that an adult sets himself in the enterprise of learning a difficult exercise, and are not in any sense play at all.

As a result, Groos fails to distinguish between movements made by the child in the effort to gain control over his body, which are to the child purely purposive in function, and movements and activities made by the child for the sake only of the pleasure they bring. The classification of group play into fighting plays, love plays, etc. makes Groos's work inapplicable to the activities of the ordinary child at play in a civilized country, as will be found by anyone who attempts to put these classifications into practice. Finally, many important aspects of children's play are omitted altogether: for example, all infantile play, and all such play as is described [later in this book].

Stanley Hall, on the other hand, takes play almost exclusively as motor play – indeed states that 'play is motor poetry'. At one point in *Youth: Its Education, Regimen and Hygiene,* he writes: 'The field of play is as wide as life and its varieties far outnumber those of industries and occupations in the census.' This promises well, but he goes on to say:

'Play and games differ in seasons, sex, and age. McGhee has shown, on the basis of some 8,000 children, that running plays are pretty constant for boys from six to seventeen but that girls are always far behind boys, and run steadily less from eight to eighteen. In games of choice boys showed a slight rise at sixteen and seventeen, and girls a rapid increase at eleven and a still more rapid one after sixteen. In games of imitation girls excel and show a marked, as boys do a slight, pubescent fall. In those games involving rivalry boys at first greatly excel girls, but are overtaken by the latter in the eighteenth year, both showing marked increment. Girls have the largest number of plays and specialize in a few less than boys, and most of these plays are of the unorganized kinds.'

This shows he has again only 'games' in mind; a viewpoint which is shared by Helen Marshall, one of the most recent writers on Children's Plays, Games and Amusements.

Finally, in this century, Professor Freud put forward a different view. In *Beyond the Pleasure Principle* he analyses the play of a single child of eighteen months, and writes as follows:

'We see that children repeat in their play everything that has made a great impression on them in actual life, that they thereby abreact the

c

strength of the impression and so to speak make themselves masters of the situation. But on the other hand it is clear enough that all their play is influenced by the dominant wish of their time of life: viz. to be grown-up and to be able to do what grown-up people do. It is also observable that the unpleasing character of the experience does not always prevent its being utilized as a game . . . In the play of children we seem to arrive at the conclusion that the child repeats even the unpleasant experiences because through his own activity he gains a far more thorough mastery of the strong impression than was possible by mere passive experience. Every fresh repetition seems to strengthen this mastery for which the child strives.'

He also relates play to an impulse to repetition:

'In the light of such observations as these, drawn from the behaviour during transference and from the fate of human beings, we may venture to make the assumption that there really exists in psychic life a repetition-compulsion, which goes beyond the pleasure-principle. We shall now also feel disposed to relate to this compelling force the dreams of shock-patients and the play-impulse in children.'

This conception of play has been developed by the psychoanalytic school into a theory by which play is regarded exclusively as the representation in symbolic form of wishes, ideas and thoughts related to the theory of infantile sexuality. This view of play, primarily put forward by Melanie Klein, has been further developed by M. N. Searl and Dr. M. Schmideberg. For further exposition of this conception, reference can be made to papers by these authors, published in the *International Journal of Psycho-Analysis*.

In the view of the writer, play in children is the expression of the child's relation to the whole of life, and no theory of play is possible which is not also a theory which will cover the whole of a child's relation to life. Play, in the sense, therefore, in which it will be used here, is taken as applying to all activities in children that are spontaneous and self-generated; that are ends in themselves; and that are unrelated to 'lessons' or to the normal physiological needs of a child's own day.

It is essential, if the nature of play is to be grasped, that its various manifestations be divided into categories. If the categories are appropriate, the entry of each item into its place will tell us a great deal about it.

Now, play has an outer and inner aspect: an outer aspect, which is the form which appears to the playfellow or adult observer, and an inner or psychological aspect, which is the meaning that the type of play has to the child. Classifications of play made by various observers differ according as emphasis is laid upon the outer form or the inner content. No ultimate classification will be possible which does not take into account both aspects. The grouping here suggested shows a combination of both points of view, but with the emphasis upon the psychological content.

The standpoint from which the classification has been made is the function each form of play serves to the child who plays it. It is suggested, therefore, that there is play that expresses the bodily impulses of the child; that apperceives his environment; that prepares the child for life; that enables him to mix harmoniously with his fellows. Within each of these groupings an attempt has been made to show the existence of a number of interrelated varieties of play within the group.

Play as bodily activity is the earliest form of all children's play. During the time that speech is being acquired, play as the realization of experience gained in previous years is the next necessity of childhood. Play as the demonstration of phantasy follows hard upon the footsteps of play as interior realization, and interweaves all the way with it; experience feeds phantasy and phantasy interprets experience.

The child of five and six, who is learning to wield the tool of speech, and has made terms with his earlier experience, turns naturally outwards towards his environment. Play as the realization of environment is his means of expressing his new orientation.

In and out of play as a realization of environment goes play as a preparation for life. As early as children think of 'life' at all, they may 'play-train' themselves to fit into it. This form of play comes to its climax in middle school years, and with adolescence fades into reality.

Every adult has at some time to come to terms with the reality that surrounds him. No individual can comprehend even a tenth part of the phenomena he daily meets, and without the help of literature and the drama even that tenth would be beyond his power. The ordinary man in these days relies for his picture of the meaning of the events he sees around him, as A. P. Herbert has so delightfully illustrated in the *Water Gipsies*, on the novelist, the dramatist, and the scenario writer, for the functions which, in earlier days, were performed by scriptural writings, ballads, and heroic stories. This necessity of the human mind to dramatize these elements of its environment that it perceives, in order to be able emotionally to assimilate them, is a characteristic that runs throughout the whole fabric of human life. Realism, romance, and satire all find their beginning in the play of children and in the child's play-relation to its environment. Examples of each rudimentary form of art will be found in the play of the children we are reviewing.

No child combines naturally with its fellows before the age of four or five years; after that, delight in social play appears and grows until it reaches its maximum at about twelve to fourteen years. Group games, therefore, are considered at the end of this series, because, although many group games are played in far earlier years, yet it is the only form of children's play which is carried forward to form a major element in adult life.

Comedy and the mechanisms that determine the choice of play are common to all ages. Perhaps there is nothing in which the kinship of child and adult stands out more clearly, or in which the persistence of 'childish' traits in adults can be more vividly seen, than in buffoonery. All the world loves a clown, and in the great Christmas circuses the clown's fooling evokes as sure a response from adults as from the children they have accompanied. There are many causes and kinds of laughter. . . .

The basis of the order of classification of the main groups of play considered is, therefore, the basis of historical growth. After four, each child may play all these games at any age. It is the particular feature of neurotic children that they may adopt any form of play at any age, and in the examples cited it is not by any means always the younger child who plays the chronologically youngest type of play. Such anomalies are characteristic of the neurotic temperament throughout life.

A classification, if it is to be true and organically inter-related, as well as logical, must also be provisional. Every classification represents the point of view from which it has been made. In a new subject at any time there may emerge new elements which may make the older classification of the subject a grouping by qualities which have now become of subsidiary rather than primary importance. When this has occurred, the classification in question should be thrown overboard and a newer one made more closely in accordance with the qualities now proved to be essential.

A classification is a finger-post, not a railway system, and in a living subject the object of a classification is to stimulate thought and to enable assimilation of the present aspects of a situation.

The classification adopted in these chapters is, therefore, provisional, in that little is as yet known of the ultimate nature of play. It is experimental, in that it has arisen out of experimental work; and it is put forward with the hope that it can be used as a practical tool by which the varieties of meaning that underlie the behaviour we speak of as 'play' may be differentiated by those at work with children, and so enable a better understanding of the children we love and teach.

Play has been regarded here not as an accident, but as an essential function of childhood, and related in its essence to the basic qualities of mankind.

A child, as is an adult, is a creature of varied needs and activities. A child needs to learn, to eat, to excrete, and to sleep. We see here that it needs, as adults also do, to relax, to laugh, and to create; and that the problems of adaptation and understanding that oppress the adult so hardly, bear upon the child as well.

Play, when looked at from this angle, may be seen to serve four purposes:

(a) It serves as the child's means for making contact with his environment. Such play in childhood partakes of the nature of, and fulfils, much of the same social purpose as work in adult life.

(b) It makes the bridge between the child's consciousness and his emotional experience, and so fulfils the role that conversation, introspection, philosophy, and religion fill for the adult.

(c) It represents to the child the externalized expression of his emotional life, and therefore in this aspect serves for the child the function taken by art in adult life.

(d) It serves the child as relaxation and amusement, as enjoyment and as rest.

Play is to a child, therefore, work, thought, art, and relaxation, and cannot be pressed into any single formula. It expresses a child's relation to himself and his environment, and, without adequate opportunity for play, normal and satisfactory emotional development is not possible.

Moreover, if the author is correct in this view of play as an essential function of the passage from immaturity to emotional maturity, then any individual in whose early life these necessary opportunities for adequate play have been lacking will inevitably go on seeking them in the stuff of adult life.

Though he must do this, he will be unaware of what he is seeking. Emotional satisfactions, which the mind has missed at the period to which they properly belong, do not present themselves later in the same form. The forces of destruction, aggression, and hostile emotion, which form so powerful an element for good or evil in human character, can display themselves fully in the play of childhood, and become through this expression integrated into the controlled and conscious personality. Forces unrealized in childhood remain as an inner drive forever seeking outlet, and lead men to express them not any longer in play, since this is regarded as an activity of childhood, but in industrial competition, anarchy and war.

The less a man or a child is aware of the interior forces of his mind the more irresistibly is he driven to express them. We have seen how fantastic is the content of much of this interior life of the mind in children; in another volume the author hopes to show how real is the logic that underlies this phantasy. The nature of this logic, is, however, at utter variance with the logic of the conscious mind, and man's disharmony with himself is due to the fact that he is unaware of this situation; that, once childhood is over, he takes his games for reality, his fantastic conceptions of the world for political sanity, and his momentary myths for considered thought.

This is abridged from Margaret Lowenfeld's book *Play in Childhood*, which was originally published in 1935. The book is a record of a series of lectures and discussions with teachers and members of the Board of Education attending a course at the Institute of Education of London University in the spring of 1934. The aim was to establish generalizations which apply to the play of children as a whole, rather than those from any specialized cultural background. In these sessions she tested her own findings, based on the records of the Institute of Child Psychology, against the experience of the staffs of nursery schools. Included is part of her Introductory Chapter, part of Chapter 1 on Historical Theories of Play, and almost all of the Concluding Section.

Omitted from her argument, then, are the many illustrations she gives and some of the argument justifying her generalized statements. We have to remember that she is talking about play in general and only incidentally has in mind dramatic play. She therefore leaves out any consideration of role playing and other imaginary situations involving imitation.

For comments on play which has clear characterization and emotional situation, we have to look to Peter Slade, who has pioneered the observation and classification of children's dramatic play. He points out that there is no border-line between a young child's realistic and his imaginative play. The only division he will admit is that between 'projected' and 'personal' play. Projected play is that play in which the child projects himself *mentally* into characters or situations outside himself (like dolls, bricks, paper) and personal play is more obvious drama in which the child is very much *physically* involved (an interesting link with ideas in Chapters 11 and 12).

Margaret Lowenfeld does not explore the value of play activities for older children or adults – she tends to feel that with maturity the need for play diminishes. She seems to feel that games are for the neurotic person only and does not see them as links with freedom from inhibitions. One wonders why, since she clearly recognizes the value of play in childhood understanding, she cannot see the same principles applying in adulthood, for externalized expression of emotional life, for amusement and relaxation. Pity she ignored Aristotle!

What Margaret Lowenfeld has to say seems important because:

1. she puts emphasis upon play as a means of growth of understanding – not relaxation only
2. she sees the value of play in aiding investigation and as a means of expression
3. she gives a simple survey of previous study and thought about play
4. she notes that adjustment through play helps in emotional development – it involves the *whole* of the child's relation to life
5. she realizes that play can help in developing skills (compare the emphasis here on the freedom of play with Barrault's point about the disciplined spontaneity)
6. she senses this link with primitive man, in that play can be employed to help cope with situations beyond our conscious comprehension
7. she notices the value of comedy in assisting with the distancing of problems and the way in which it prevents individuals from being overcome by some aspects of living.

5 The Purpose and Nature of Drama
Aristotle

The playwright David Rudkin once described Aristotle as 'the Harold Hobson of his day', but he is more of an academic or drama historian than a weekly critic – something of a cross between Neville Coghill and John Russell Taylor.

Born in Macedonia in 384 B.C., at seventeen Aristotle went to Athens where he was a pupil of Plato. On Plato's death twenty years later, Aristotle left Athens and worked as tutor to the lad who later became Alexander the Great. When Alexander came to the throne in 335 B.C., Aristotle returned to Athens and taught at the Lyceum, where his reputation attracted a large number of scholars. He died in 322 B.C.

His writing in *The Poetics* is clearly intended to act as a counter-balance to the views of Plato and Socrates on the poet. Plato wished to banish the poet from his ideal state because he seemed to him to be dealing in imagination and fiction, which Plato maintained to be a world of lies. The aim of drama (a branch of poetry) was unworthy because it did not inculcate moral and social virtues.

Aristotle considers that he is 'going back to first principles'. He points out that the term *drama* is given to works because they represent men doing things. The word drama literally means 'a thing done'. Important in our investigation is his emphasis upon imitation in dramatic art. For Aristotle, imitation is no slavish copying: it is out of imitation that man gains insight and eventually recreates and expresses artistically. *The Poetics* also introduces the theory of catharsis: that tragedy should result in a 'purging' by pity and terror.

Interpretation of Aristotle's meaning will no doubt go on for a long time yet, but his examination of the drama, its nature, form and function, remains basic. It is perhaps as well to emphasize that his description of tragedy results entirely from a consideration of Sophocles (496–406 B.C.), whose work he judged the best to have achieved in tragedy. At times, when there has been a revival of interest in the classics, especially in the Renaissance in England in the 15th and 16th centuries, and the neo-classical era of the 17th and 18th centuries, some of Aristotle's views have been given exaggerated importance, as though they were inimit-able laws, instead of observations drawn from the best poets and play-wrights.

'Comedy', he generalizes, 'aims at representing man as worse than they are nowadays, tragedy as better'. His comments begin our consideration of the possible moral values of drama and remind us that vexed questions like 'Why does drama deal so much with the violent, horrifying and sorrowful aspects of life?' were being faced a good two thousand years ago.

Aristotle stresses that, by purging the emotions it excites, the drama makes a very positive contribution. Those who participate, either as actors or audience, can be strengthened by the experience. Dealing as it does, both with the universal and the particular, it can deepen and broaden our understanding of the truth even more so than actual events, which often lack form and a frame of reference. Aristotle indicates value judgements and makes a distinction between 'historic truth' and 'poetic truth' and indicates the way man uses his own resources to cope with the mysteries of life.

Instinctive imitation

The creation of poetry generally is due to two causes, both rooted in human nature. The instinct for imitation is inherent in man from his earliest days; he differs from other animals in that he is the most imitative of creatures, and he learns his earliest lessons by imitation. Also inborn in all of us is the instinct to enjoy works of imitation. What happens in actual experience is evidence of this; we enjoy looking at the most accurate representations of things which in themselves we find painful to see, such as the forms of the lowest animals and of corpses. The reason for this is that learning is a very great pleasure, not for philosophers only, but for other people as well, however limited their capacity for it may be. They enjoy seeing likenesses because in doing so they acquire information (they reason out what each represents, and discover, for instance, that 'this is a picture of so and so'); for if by any chance the thing depicted has not been seen before, it will not be the fact that it is an imitation of something that gives the pleasure, but the execution or the colouring or some other such cause.

The instinct for imitation, then, is natural to us, as is also a feeling for music and for rhythm – and metres are obviously detached sections of rhythms. Starting from these natural aptitudes, and by a series of for the most part gradual improvements on their first efforts, men eventually created poetry from their improvisations.

Both tragedy and comedy had their first beginnings in improvisation.

The one originated with those who led the dithyramb, the other with the leaders of the phallic songs which still survive today as traditional institutions in many of our cities. Little by little tragedy advanced, each new element being developed as it came into use, until after many changes it attained its natural form and came to a standstill. Aeschylus was the first to increase the number of actors from one to two, cut down the role of the chorus, and give the first place to the dialogue. Sophocles introduced three actors and painted scenery. As for the grandeur of tragedy, it was not until late that it acquired its characteristic stateliness, when, progressing beyond the methods of satyric drama, it discarded slight plots and comic diction, and its metre changed from the trochaic tetrameter to the iambic. At first the poets had used the tetrameter because they were writing satyr-poetry, which was more closely related to the dance; but once dialogue had been introduced, by its very nature it hit upon the right measure, for the iambic is of all measures the one best suited to speech. This is shown by the fact that we most usually drop into iambics in our conversation with one another, whereas we seldom talk in hexameters, and then only when we depart from the normal tone of conversation. Another change was the increased number of episodes, or acts. We must pass over such other matters as the various embellishments of tragedy and the circumstances in which they are said to have been introduced, for it would probably be a long business to go into them in any detail.

The rise of comedy

As I have remarked, comedy represents the worse types of men; worse, however, not in the sense that it embraces any and every kind of badness, but in the sense that the ridiculous is a species of ugliness or badness. For the ridiculous consists in some form of error or ugliness that is not painful or injurious; the comic mask, for example, is distorted and ugly, but causes no pain.

Now we know something of the successive stages by which tragedy developed, and of those who were responsible for them; the early history of comedy, however, is obscure, because it was not taken seriously. It was a long time before the archon granted a chorus to comedies; until then the performers were volunteers. Comedy had already acquired certain clear-cut forms before there is any mention of those who are named as its poets. Nor is it known who introduced masks, or prologues, or a plurality of actors, and other things of that kind. Properly worked out plots originated in Sicily with Epicharmus and Phormis; of Athenian poets Crates was the first to discard the lampoon pattern and to adopt stories and plots of a more general nature.

Epic poetry agrees with tragedy to the extent that it is a representation, in dignified verse, of serious actions. They differ, however, in that epic keeps to a single metre and is in narrative form. Another point of difference is their length: tragedy tries as far as possible to keep within a single revolution of the sun, or only slightly to exceed it, whereas the epic observes no limits in its time of action – although at first the practice in this respect was the same in tragedies as in epics.

Of the constituent parts, some are common to both kinds, and some are peculiar to tragedy. Thus anyone who can discriminate between what is good and what is bad in tragedy can do the same with epic; for all the elements of epic are found in tragedy, though not everything that belongs to tragedy is to be found in epic.

The nature of tragedy

I shall speak later about the form of imitation that uses hexameters and about comedy, but for the moment I propose to discuss tragedy, first drawing together the definition of its essential character from what has already been said.

Tragedy, then, is a representation of an action that is worth serious attention, complete in itself, and of some amplitude; in language enriched by a variety of artistic devices appropriate to the several parts of the play; presented in the form of action, not narration; by means of pity and fear bringing about the purgation of such emotions. By language that is enriched I refer to language possessing rhythm, and music or song; and by artistic devices appropriate to the several parts I mean that some are produced by the medium of verse alone, and others again with the help of song.

Now since the representation is carried out by men performing the actions, it follows, in the first place, that spectacle is an essential part of tragedy, and secondly that there must be song and diction, these being the medium of representation. By diction I mean here the arrangement of the verses; song is a term whose sense is obvious to everyone.

In tragedy it is action that is imitated, and this action is brought about by agents who necessarily display certain distinctive qualities both of character and of thought, according to which we also define the nature of the actions. Thought and character are, then, the two natural causes of actions, and it is on them that all men depend for success or failure. The representation of the action is the plot of the tragedy; for the ordered arrangement of the incidents is what I mean by plot. Character, on the other hand, is that which enables us to define the nature of the participants, and thought comes out in what they say when they are proving a point or expressing an opinion.

Necessarily, then, every tragedy has six constituents, which will determine its quality. They are plot, character, diction, thought, spectacle, and song. Of these, two represent the media in which the action is represented, one involves the manner of representation, and three are connected with the objects of the representation; beyond them nothing further is required. These, it may be said, are the dramatic elements that have been used by practically all playwrights; for all plays alike possess spectacle, character, plot, diction, song, and thought.

Of these elements, the most important is the plot, the ordering of the incidents; for tragedy is a representation, not of men, but of action and life, of happiness and unhappiness – and happiness and unhappiness are bound up with action. The purpose of living is an end which is a kind of activity, not a quality; it is their characters, indeed, that make men what they are, but it is by reason of their actions that they are happy or the reverse. Tragedies are not performed, therefore, in order to represent character, although character is involved for the sake of action. Thus the incidents and the plot are the end aimed at in tragedy, and as always, the end is everything. Furthermore, there could not be a tragedy without action, but there could be without character; indeed the tragedies of most of our recent playwrights fail to present character, and the same might be said of many playwrights of other periods. Again, if someone writes a series of speeches expressive of character, and well composed as far as thought and diction are concerned, he will still not achieve the proper effect of tragedy; this will be done much better by a tragedy which is less successful in its use of these elements, but which has a plot giving an ordered combination of incidents. Another point to note is that the two most important means by which tragedy plays on our feelings, that is, 'reversals' and 'recognitions', are both constituents of the plot. A further proof is that beginners can achieve accuracy in diction and the portrayal of character before they can construct a plot out of the incidents, and this could be said of almost all the earliest dramatic poets.

The plot, then, is the first essential of tragedy, its life-blood, so to speak, and character takes the second place. It is much the same in painting; for if an artist were to daub his canvas with the most beautiful colours laid on at random, he would not give the same pleasure as he would by drawing a recognizable portrait in black and white. Tragedy is the representation of an action, and it is chiefly on account of the action that it is also a representation of persons.

The third property of tragedy is thought. This is the ability to say what is possible and appropriate in any given circumstances; it is what, in the speeches in the play, is related to the arts of politics and rhetoric. The older dramatic poets made their characters talk like statesmen, whereas those of today make them talk like rhetoricians. Character is that which reveals personal choice, the kinds of thing a man chooses or rejects when that is not obvious. Thus there is no revelation of character in speeches in which the speaker shows no preferences or aversions whatever; thought, on the other hand, is present in speeches where something is being shown to be true or untrue, or where some general opinion is being expressed.

Fourth comes the diction of the speeches. By diction I mean, as I have already explained, the expressive use of words, and this has the same force in verse and in prose.

Of the remaining elements, the music is the most important of the pleasurable additions to the play. Spectacle, or stage-effect, is an attraction, of course, but it has the least to do with the playwright's craft or with the art of poetry. For the power of tragedy is independent both of performance and of actors, and besides, the production of spectacular effects is more the province of the property-man than of the playwright.

The scope of the plot

Now that these definitions have been established, I must go on to discuss the arrangement of the incidents, for this is of the first importance in tragedy. I have already laid down that tragedy is the representation of an action that is complete and whole and of a certain amplitude – for a thing may be whole and yet lack amplitude. Now a whole is that which has a beginning, a middle, and an end. A beginning is that which does not necessarily come after something else, although something else exists or comes about after it. An end, on the contrary, is that which naturally follows something else either as a necessary or as a usual consequence, and is not itself followed by anything. A middle is that which follows something else, and is itself followed by something. Thus well-constructed plots must neither begin nor end in a haphazard way, but must conform to the pattern I have been describing.

Poetic truth and historical truth

It will be clear from what I have said that it is not the poet's function to describe what has actually happened, but the kinds of thing that might happen, that is, that could happen because they are, in the circumstances, either probable or necessary. The difference between the historian and the poet is not that the one writes in prose and the other in verse; the work of Herodotus might be put into verse, and in this metrical form it would be no less a kind of history than it is without metre. The difference is that the one tells of what has happened, the other of the kinds of things that might happen. For this reason poetry is something more philosophical and more worthy of serious attention than history; for while poetry is concerned with universal truths, history treats of particular facts.

By universal truths are to be understood the kinds of thing a certain type of person will probably or necessarily say or do in a given situation; and this is the aim of poetry, although it gives individual names to its characters. The particular facts of the historian are what, say, Alcibiades did, or what happened to him. By now this distinction has become clear where comedy is concerned, for comic poets build up their plots out of probable occurrences, and then add any names that occur to them; they do not, like the iambic poets, write about actual people. In tragedy, on the other hand, the authors keep to the names of real people, the reason being that what is possible is credible.

Whereas we cannot be certain of the possibility of something that has not happened, what has happened is obviously possible, for it would not have happened if this had not been so. Nevertheless, even in some tragedies only one or two of the names are well known, and the rest are fictitious; and indeed there are some in which nothing is familiar, Agathon's *Antheus*, for example, in which both the incidents and the names are fictitious, and the play is none the less well liked for that. It is not necessary, therefore, to keep entirely to the traditional stories which form the subjects of our tragedies. Indeed it would be absurd to do so, since even the familiar stories are familiar only to a few, and yet they please everybody.

What I have said makes it obvious that the poet must be a maker of plots rather than of verses, since he is a poet by virtue of his representation, and what he represents is actions. And even if he writes about things that have actually happened, that does not make him any the less a poet, for there is nothing to prevent some of the things that have happened from being in accordance with the laws of possibility and probability, and thus he will be a poet in writing about them.

Of simple plots and actions, those that are episodic are the worst. By an episodic plot I mean one in which the sequence of the episodes is neither probable nor necessary. Plays of this kind are written by bad poets because they cannot help it, and by good poets because of the actors; writing for the dramatic competitions, they often strain a plot beyond the bounds of possibility, and are thus obliged to dislocate the continuity of events.

However, tragedy is the representation not only of a complete action, but also of incidents that awaken fear and pity, and effects of this kind are heightened when things happen unexpectedly as well as logically, for then they will be more remarkable than if they seem merely mechanical or accidental. Indeed, even chance occurrences seem most remarkable when they have the appearance of having been brought about by design – when, for example, the statue of Mitys at Argos killed the man who had caused Mitys' death by falling down on him at a public entertainment. Things like this do not seem mere chance occurrences. Thus plots of this type are necessarily better than others.

Simple and complex plots

Some plots are simple, and some complex, for the obvious reason that the actions of which they are representations are of one or other of these kinds. By a simple action I refer to one which is single and continuous in the sense of my earlier definition, and in which the change of fortune comes about without a reversal or a discovery. A complex action is one in which the change is accompanied by a discovery or a reversal, or both. These should develop out of the very structure of the plot, so that they are the inevitable or probable consequence of what has gone before, for there is a big difference between what happens as a result of something else and what merely happens after it.

Reversal, discovery and calamity

As has already been noted, a reversal is a change from one state of affairs to its opposite, one which conforms, as I have said, to probability or necessity. In *Oedipus*, for example, the Messenger who came to cheer Oedipus and relieve him of his fear about his mother did the very opposite by revealing to him who he was. In the *Lynceus*, again, Lynceus is being led off to execution, followed by Danaus who is to kill him, when, as a result of events that occurred earlier, it comes about that he is saved and it is Danaus who is put to death.

As the word itself indicates, a discovery is a change from ignorance to knowledge, and it leads either to love or to hatred between persons destined for good or ill fortune. The most effective form of discovery is that which is accompanied by reversals, like the one in *Oedipus*. There are of course other forms of discovery, for what I have described may happen in relation to inanimate and trifling objects, and moreover it is possible to discover whether a person has done something or not. But the form of discovery most essentially related to the plot and action of the play is the one described above, for a discovery of this kind in combination with a reversal will carry with it either pity or fear, and it is such actions as these that, according to my definition, tragedy represents; and further, such a combination is likely to lead to a happy or an unhappy ending.

As it is persons who are involved in the discovery, it may be that only one person's identity is revealed to another, that of the second being already known. Sometimes, however, a natural recognition of two parties is necessary, as for example, when the identity of Iphigenia was made known to Orestes by the sending of the letter, and a second discovery was required to make him known to Iphigenia.

Two elements of the plot, then, reversal and discovery, turn upon such incidents as these. A third is suffering, or calamity. Of these three, reversal and discovery have already been defined. A calamity is an action of a destructive or painful nature, such as death openly represented, excessive suffering, wounding, and the like.

Tragic action

We saw that the structure of tragedy at its best should be complex, not simple, and that it should represent actions capable of awakening fear and pity – for this is a characteristic function of representations of this type. It follows in the first place that good men should not be shown passing from prosperity to misery, for this does not inspire fear or pity, it merely disgusts us. Nor should evil men be shown progressing from misery to prosperity. This is the most untragic of all plots, for it has none of the requisites of tragedy; it does not appeal to our humanity, nor awaken pity or fear in us. Nor again should an utterly worthless man be seen falling from prosperity into misery. Such a course might indeed play upon our humane feelings, but it would not arouse either pity or fear; for our pity is awakened by undeserved misfortune, and our fear by that of someone just like ourselves – pity for the undeserving sufferer and fear for the man like ourselves – so that the situation in question would have nothing in it either pitiful or fearful.

There remains a mean between these extremes. This is the sort of man who is not conspicuous for virtue and justice, and whose fall into misery is not due to vice and depravity, but rather to some error, a man who enjoys prosperity and a high reputation, like Oedipus and Thyestes and other famous members of families like theirs.

Inevitably, then, the well-conceived plot will have a single interest, and not, as some say, a double. The change in fortune will be, not from misery to prosperity, but the reverse, from prosperity to misery, and it will be due, not to depravity, but to some great error either in such a man as I have described or in one better than this, but not worse. This is borne out by existing practice. For at first the poets treated any stories that came to hand, but nowadays the best tragedies are written about a handful of families, those of Alcmaeon, for example, and Oedipus and Orestes and Meleager and Thyestes and Telephus, and others whom it has befallen to suffer or inflict terrible experiences.

The best tragedies in the technical sense are constructed in this way. Those critics are on the wrong tack, therefore, who criticize Euripides for following such a procedure in his tragedies, and complain that many of them end in misfortune; for, as I have said, this is the right ending. The strongest evidence of this is that on the stage and in the dramatic competitions plays of this kind, when properly worked out, are the most tragic of all, and Euripides, faulty as is his management of other points, is nevertheless regarded as the most tragic of our dramatic poets.

The next best type of structure, ranked first by some critics, is that which, like the *Odyssey*, has a double thread of plot, and ends in opposite ways for the good and the bad characters. It is considered the best only because of the feeble judgement of the audience, for the poets pander to the taste of the spectators.

But this is not the pleasure that is proper to tragedy. It belongs rather to comedy, where those who have been the bitterest of enemies in the original story, Orestes and Aegisthus, for example, go off at the end as friends, and nobody is killed by anybody.

Fear and pity

Fear and pity may be excited by means of spectacle; but they can also take their rise from the very structure of the action, which is the preferable method and the mark of a better dramatic poet. For the plot should be so ordered that even without seeing it performed anyone merely hearing what is afoot will shudder with fear and pity as a result of what is happening – as indeed would be the experience of anyone hearing the story of Oedipus. To produce this effect by means of stage-spectacle is less artistic, and requires the co-operation of the producer. Those who employ spectacle to produce an effect, not of fear, but of something merely monstrous, have nothing to do with tragedy, for not every kind of pleasure should be demanded of tragedy, but only that which is proper to it; and since the dramatic poet has by means of his representation to produce the tragic pleasure that is associated with pity and fear, it is obvious that this effect is bound up with the events of the plot.

Let us now consider what kinds of incident are to be regarded as fearful or pitiable. Deeds that fit this description must of course involve people who are either friends to one another, or enemies, or neither. Now if a man injures his enemy, there is nothing pitiable either in his act or in his intention, except in so far as suffering is inflicted; nor is there if they are indifferent to each other. But when the sufferings involve those who are near and dear to one another, when for example brother kills brother, son father, mother son, or son mother, or if such a deed is contemplated, or something else of the kind is actually done, then we have a situation of the kind to be aimed at. Thus it will not do to tamper with the traditional stories, the murder of Clytemnestra by Orestes, for instance, and that of Eriphyle by Alemaeon; on the other hand, the poet must use his imagination and handle the traditional material effectively.

I must explain more clearly what I mean by 'effectively'. The deed may be done by characters acting consciously and in full knowledge of the facts, as was the way of the early dramatic poets, when for instance Euripides made Medea kill her children. Or they may do it without realizing the horror of the deed until later, when they discover the truth; this is what Sophocles did with Oedipus. Here indeed the relevant incident occurs outside the action of the play; but it may be a part of the tragedy, as with Alemaeon in Astydamas' play, or Telegonus in *The Wounded Odysseus*. A third alternative is for someone who is about to do a terrible deed in ignorance of the relationship to discover the truth before he does it. These are the only possibilities, for the deed must either be done or not done, and by someone either with or without knowledge of the facts.

The least acceptable of these alternatives is when someone in possession of the facts is on the point of acting but fails to do so, for this merely shocks us, and, since no suffering is involved, it is not tragic. Hence nobody is allowed to behave like this, or only seldom, as when Haemon fails to kill Creon in the *Antigone*. Next in order of effectiveness is when the deed is actually done, and here it is better that the character should act in ignorance and only learn the truth afterwards, for there is nothing in this to outrage our feelings, and the revelation comes as a surprise. However, the best method is the last, when, for example, in the *Cresphontes* Merope intends to kill her son, but recognizes him and does not do so; or when the same thing happens with brother and sister in *Iphigenia in Tauris*; or when, in the *Helle*, the son recognizes his mother when he is just about to betray her.

This then is the reason why, as I said before, our tragedies keep to a few families. For in their search for dramatic material it was by chance rather than by technical knowledge that the poets discovered how to gain tragic effects in their plots. And they are still obliged to have recourse to those families in which sufferings of the kind I have described have been experienced.

I have said enough now about the arrangement of the incidents in a tragedy and the type of plot it ought to have.

The characters of tragedy

In characterization there are four things to aim at. First and foremost, the characters should be good. Now character will be displayed, as I have pointed out, if some preference is revealed in speech or action, and if it is a preference for what is good the character will be good. There can be goodness in every class of person; for instance, a woman or a slave may be good, though the one is possibly an inferior being and the other in general an insignificant one.

In the second place the portrayal should be appropriate. For example, a character may possess manly qualities, but it is not appropriate that a female character should be given manliness or cleverness.

Thirdly, the characters should be lifelike. This is not the same thing as making them good, or appropriate in the sense in which I have used the word.

And fourthly, they should be consistent. Even if the person who is being represented is inconsistent, and this trait is the basis of his character, he must nevertheless be portrayed as consistently inconsistent.

As an example of unnecessary badness of character, there is Menelaus in the *Orestes*. The character who behaves in an unsuitable and inappropriate way is exemplified in Odysseus' lament in the *Scylla*, and in Melanippe's speech. An inconsistent character is shown in *Iphigenia at Aulis*, for Iphigenia as a suppliant is quite unlike what she is later.

As in the arrangement of the incidents, so too in characterization one must always bear in mind what will be either necessary or probable; in other words, it should be necessary or probable that such and such a person should say or do such and such a thing, and similarly that this particular incident should follow on that.

Furthermore, it is obvious that the unravelling of the plot should arise from the circumstances of the plot itself, and not be brought about *ex machina*, as is done in the *Medea* and in the episode of the embarkation in the *Iliad*. The *deus ex machina* should be used only for matters outside the play proper, either for things that happened before it and that cannot be known by the human characters, or for things that are yet to come and that require to be foretold prophetically – for we allow to the gods the power to see all things. However, there should be nothing inexplicable about what happens, or if there must be, it should be kept outside the tragedy, as is done in Sophocles' *Oedipus*. [Aristotle is here referring to the fact that Oedipus remained for many years ignorant of the circumstances of Laius' death.]

Since tragedy is a representation of people who are better than the average, we must copy the good portrait-painters. These, while reproducing the distinctive appearance of their sitters and making likenesses, paint them better-looking than they are. In the same way the poet, in portraying men who are hot-tempered, or phlegmatic, or who have other defects of character, must bring out these qualities in them, and at the same time show them as decent people, as Agathon and Homer have portrayed Achilles.

These points must be carefully watched, as too must those means used to appeal to the eye, which are necessarily dependent on the poet's art; for here too it is often possible to make mistakes. However, enough has been said about these matters in my published works.

Taken from *The Poetics* of Aristotle, which though it cannot be dated accurately, seems to belong to the later part of his life when he was in Athens, after 335 B.C. It is difficult to know whether Aristotle's work is notes from a lecture which he gave, or was about to give, or notes taken by someone else from lectures which he gave. Understandably, then, the argument is sometimes elliptical.

Aristotle was a Greek Scientist and Philosopher. His theoretical observations are a formulation of his views from the standpoint of a literary critic, and form an interesting link with those of Jean-Louis Barrault, the Theatre Practitioner.

We still draw upon the terminology of Aristotle, especially his concepts of imitation, catharsis (or purging of emotions) and his definitions of tragedy and comedy, though today we challenge and contradict even his major assumptions.

Specially worth noting:

1. he emphasizes the innate quality of imitation and sees it as an important means of investigating problems
2. he mentions the joint values in drama of pleasure and learning
3. what does he intend by 'catharsis'? – in the 'Ethics' he bases his discussion on the desirable 'mean' and it seems likely that here the catharsis of pity and fear is their return to a desirable balance or controlled proportions
4. tragedy, far from encouraging the worst in us, helps us to purge it – it excites the emotions (which Plato and many others since say should be kept under control) but in doing so *releases* them and in this way they are more easily controllable
5. he sees the importance of a poetic truth, as well as an historic truth – the concern in drama is more with ultimate and universal truths than with facts (cf. Stanislavski)
6. drama, for him, should have a moral purpose in choice of subject matter, in characters and in the way the plot is resolved

SECTION THREE
Elements of Drama

6 **Movement, Dance and Dramatic Expression**
Rudolf Laban

If man is to be able to give expression to desires, fears, problems, of both his conscious and unconscious mind, he must not only be given the conditions in which to feel free and uninhibited, but he will need to have explored, developed and trained his expressive resources. The Greeks, of course, gave a good deal of attention to the training of body and voice for artistic play, but little systematic consideration was given to the art of movement until Rudolf Laban began his researches.

Laban was born in Bratislava, when that Czechoslovakian town was still part of the Austro-Hungarian Empire. As a young boy, he was given the job of custodian of the keys at the State Theatre, and, by 15, he had formed 'a dance-dramatic club'. At the age of 25 he had founded a school in Munich and developed theories of movement involving expressionist terms like 'effort-rhythm' and 'space harmony'. About the same time as Brecht was turning his back on Stanislavski and the Moscow Art Theatre, Laban was moving away from the romantic world of Diagilev's Russian Ballet and establishing a new approach to the Dance. Laban built up a reputation in Germany and became director of movement at the Berlin Opera, as well as other state theatres.

There was no place for Laban (any more than Brecht) in Germany when Hitler came to power. In 1936 Goebbels stopped a vast dance display Laban had directed, declaring that there was room for only one movement in Germany – the National Socialist Movement! For a time this terminated Laban's work, and it was not until Lisa Ullman came across him in Paris, almost penniless, and brought him to England, that his researches began again. At Dartington Hall, he was given opportunities for work once more. With F. C. Lawrence, an English businessman, he applied his understanding of movement to industry, commerce, and even to the techniques of parachute-jumping. His understanding was applied to education and strongly influenced many pioneers, especially in junior education (cf. 'Story of a School', see bibliography). In the late fifties, a permanent home was found for the Art of Movement Studio, at Addlestone in Surrey.

Like some of the other practitioners quoted in this volume, Laban is sometimes thought of as having a 'system' or method, but this is to do him a dis-service. Laban (like Stanislavski, Brecht and others) set out to understand further the art in which he had chosen to specialize. The codification should be seen as a further means of comprehension and expression, not as a limitation.

Man moves in order to satisfy a need. He aims by his movement at something of value to him. It is easy to perceive the aim of a person's movement if it is directed to some tangible object. Yet, there also exist intangible values that inspire movement.

Eve, our first mother, in plucking the apple from the tree of knowledge, made a movement dictated both by a tangible and an intangible aim. She desired to possess the apple in order to eat it, but not solely to satisfy her appetite for food. The Tempter told her that by eating the apple she would gain supreme knowledge: that knowledge was the ultimate value she desired.

Can an actress represent Eve plucking an apple from a tree in such a way that a spectator who knows nothing of the biblical story is made aware of both her aims, the tangible and the intangible? Perhaps not convincingly, but the artist playing the role of Eve can pluck the apple in more than one way, with movements of varying expression. She can pluck the apple greedily and rapidly or languidly and sensuously. She could, too, pluck it with a detached expression in the outstretched arm and grasping hand, and in her face and body. Many other forms of action are possible, and each of these would be characterized by a different kind of movement.

In defining the kind of movement as greedy, as sensuous, or detached, one does not define merely what one has actually seen. What the spectator has seen is only a peculiar, quick jerk or a slow gliding of the arm. The impression of greed or sensuousness is the spectator's personal interpretation of Eve's state of mind in a definite situation. If he should observe Eve grasping quickly into the air – that is to say, if he sees the same movement performed without the objective aim – he would probably not be induced to think either of the object or of the motive. He would perceive the quick, grasping movement without understanding its dramatic significance.

It may, of course, occur to the spectator to ask whether this movement, apparently without an objective aim, was made in order to reveal certain traits of Eve's then mood, or of her character. It is unlikely that one movement could convey to him more than a passing impression, since it could never give a definite picture of her character. On the other hand, several concurrent movements, as for example those including Eve's carriage and walking before the snatching gesture, would offer additional and clearer indications of her personality. But even then Eve's behaviour in the act of plucking the apple would be less characteristic of her personality than of her momentary eagerness in the particular situation. On other occasions she might develop quite different rhythms and shapes of movement which, comprising several actions, would show her general character in an altogether different light.

So movement evidently reveals many different things. It is the result of the striving after an object deemed valuable, or of a state of mind. In its shape and rhythm it shows a special attitude to meet the situation in which the action takes place. It can characterize the momentary mood, or the personality of the moving person. Movement can also be adapted to the surroundings of the mover. The *milieu* of a scene or action will heighten the movements of the actress. They will be different in the role of Eve in paradise, or of a society woman in an eighteenth-century salon, or of a girl in the bar of a public-house in the slums. All three women might be similar personalities exhibiting almost the same general movement-characteristics, but they would adapt their behaviour to the atmosphere of an epoch, or a locality.

A character, an atmosphere, a state of mind, or a situation cannot be effectively shown on the stage without movement, and its inherent expressiveness. Movements of the body, including the movements of the voice-producing organs, are indispensable to presentation on the stage.

There is yet another aspect of movement which is of paramount importance in acting. When two or more players are to meet on the stage, they have to make their entrance, approach one another (either touching, or keeping a due distance), and later they have to separate and make their exit.

The grouping of the actors on the stage occurs in movement, which is expressive in another sense than individual movement. The members of a group move in order to show their desire to get in touch with one another. The ostensible object of meeting might be to fight or to embrace, or to dance, or just to converse. But there exist intangible objectives, such as the attraction between sympathetic individuals or the repulsion felt by persons or groups antipathetic to each other.

Group movements can be brisk and pregnant with the threat of aggression, or soft and sinuous, like the movement of water in a placid lake. People can group themselves as hard, detached rocks on a mountain or as on a leisurely flowing stream in a plain. Clouds frequently form most interesting groupings which produce a strangely dramatic effect. Group movements on the stage resemble in a way the shifting clouds from which either thunder rolls, or sunshine breaks.

The individual actor will sometimes use his movements as if his limbs were the members of a group, and this is probably the solution of the riddle of the expressiveness of gesture. When Eve plucks the apple in a greedy or a languid manner, she will express her attitude by the movements of parts of her body. In greed the limbs, the whole body, shoots out suddenly, avidly, all together in one and the same direction towards the coveted object. The languid approach is characterized by a nonchalant, slow lifting of the arm, while the rest of the body is lazily curved away from the object. It is almost a dance-like movement, in which the outward action is subordinated to the inner feeling. No words are needed to convey this feeling to the spectator.

Eve reaching for the apple is not yet a dramatic scene. Drama starts when she offers the apple to Adam. Drama always happens between two or more people, and here is where group movement comes to its own.

The soliloquy and solo dance are in reality a dialogue between the two poles of an individuality divided by doubting reflection or controversial mood. The duality of the poles becomes visible in movements which display the antagonistic inner efforts.

In scenes of love and combat, the duality of the inner emotions is embodied in two real persons. Eve offers Adam the forbidden fruit. Her gesture of offering and his of accepting is more than a utilitarian move in which the apple passes from one to the other. It is a gathering storm, presaging thunder-clouds heavy with the fate of the race.

The gestures will be less conspicuous and less expressive if the impending thunderstorm is condensed into a spoken dialogue. The story of the forbidden fruit represented in a dance-mime will be enlivened by more elaborate gestures than the same story accompanied by words.

Pure dancing has no describable story. It is frequently impossible to outline the content of a dance in words; although one can always describe the movement. The spectator could not understand what Eve means by the movement of grasping quickly into the air, nor could he even be sure whether her movements expressed greed or any other emotion, although he could describe her movement as a quick grasp. One could say that the play of rhythms and shapes tells in dance its own story, a frequent happening in a world of undefined values and longings.

Movement in pure dancing does not need to adapt itself to characters, actions, epochs, and situations, but it does in dance-mime, which is virtually acting without words, but usually supported by background music. The performance of social dances on the stage characteristic of a historical period, of the social status of the dancers, and of the occasion and locality of the dance, cannot be considered as pure dancing. In pure dancing the inner drive to move creates its own patterns of style, and of striving after intangible and mostly indescribable values.

The art of movement on the stage embraces the whole range of bodily expression from the actors' speaking and acting, through dance-mime, to pure dance and its musical accompaniment.

Spoken drama and musical dance are, however, late flowers of human civilization. Movement has always been used for two distinct aims; the attainment of tangible values in all kinds of work, and the approach to intangible values in prayer and worship. The same bodily movements have always been used both in work and worship, but the significance of the movements is different. In order to achieve the practical purpose of work, the stretching out of an arm and the gripping and handling of an object have to be made in an entirely irrational sequence, though each of the gestures used in worship might also be part of a working action. The stretching out of the arm in the air might express the longing for something which cannot be grasped. The swinging of the arms and the body, which might resemble the handling of an object, might signify an inner struggle, and become the expression of a prayer for liberation from inner turmoil.

The European has lost the habit and capacity to pray with movement. The vestiges of such praying are the genuflexions of the worshippers in our churches. The ritual movements of other races are much richer in range and expressiveness. Late civilizations have resorted to spoken prayer in which the movements of the voice-organs become more important than bodily movements. Speaking is then often heightened into singing.

It is, however, probable that liturgical praying and ritual dancing co-existed in very early times; and so it is also probable that the spoken drama and the musical dance have both developed from worship; from liturgy on the one hand and ritual on the other. The whole complexity of human expressiveness, as comprised in the art of movement, is represented in the following diagram.

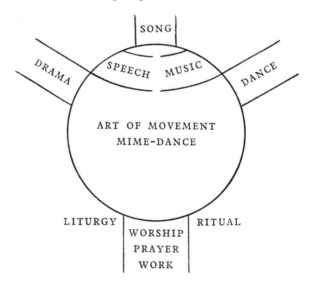

We never know whether man regards himself as taking part in a tragedy or a comedy with himself as the protagonist in the drama of existence and Nature forming the chorus. Yet it is an undeniable fact that man's extraordinary power of thought and action has placed him in a peculiar situation so far as his relationship to his surroundings is concerned.

Man tries to enact the conflicts arising from the solitary role of his race. Reflected in the mirror of tragi-comedy the public sees a character struggling and falling either to destruction or into ridicule. The tears for the first, as well as the laughter for the second, with which the public reacts to the representation of the character's inner and outer adventures appear to be equally comforting.

This is not a utilitarian explanation of, or an excuse for, acting. There is more beneath the co-operation of audience and actors than the fun of contemplating man's misery or folly, one eye laughing, and the other weeping. The theatre mirrors more than the everyday world of our sufferances and gaieties. The theatre gives an insight into the workshop in which man's power of reflection and action is generated. This insight offers more than an increased understanding of life; it offers the inspiring experience of a reality transcending that of our everyday fears and satisfactions.

Movements used in works of stagecraft are those of the body, the voice-producing organs, and, one may add, the motions performed by the instrumentalists of the orchestra. Human movement, with all its physical, emotional, and mental implications, is the common denominator of the dynamic art of the theatre. Ideas and sentiments are expressed by the flow of movement, and become visible in gestures, or audible in music and words. The art of the theatre is dynamic, because each phase of the performance fades away almost immediately after it has appeared. Nothing remains static, and the leisurely inspection of details is impossible. In music one sound succeeds another, and the first dies before the next is heard. The actors' lines and the dancers' movements are all in a continuous dynamical flux which is interrupted only by short pauses until it finally ceases at the end of the performance.

Theatrical acting, the artistic enhancement of human action, expresses the controversial dynamic of the thinking and feeling of the characters represented. In mime and ballet, the dynamic of thought and feeling is expressed in a visible form. It is, as it were, written into the air. What the music, the audible form of the ballet performance, adds to dancing is partly an underlining of the rhythmic components of the group movement, and partly a translation of its emotional content into sound-waves. In opera, speaking is replaced by singing, whereby the prominent role is given to music. The wide range of movement on the stage offers not only a common denominator for all stage work, but it also secures the basis for the common animation of all those participating in its creation.

The fluid transiency of works of dynamic art has to be contrasted with the solid durability of works of static and plastic art – architecture, sculpture, and painting – though one must remember that the last-mentioned contributes to the stage decor and costume. But the dynamics of action and dance are easily killed if the static components of the performance, costume, and decor are over-stressed. The highly pictorial theatre neglects the essential feature of stage-craft, which is movement.

Man expresses on the stage by carefully chosen efforts his inner attitude of mind, and he performs a kind of corporate ritual in the presentation of conflicts arising from the differences in his inner attitudes. In domesticating animals, man has learned how to deal with efforts, and how to change the basic effort-habits of living beings. In applying the principles of domestication to himself, he has broadened the scope of effort-training into the creation of works of dynamic art.

Man can domesticate his fellow-men – not just as slaves, but also as happy companions; and he has finally learnt to domesticate himself by training and developing his own personal effort-habits, both enlarging their range quantitatively and directing them more and more towards the specific humane forms of effort.

The way in which man has achieved this kind of effort-education is very remarkable. It has a parallel in the evolution of animal efforts.

Young animals learn to select and develop their efforts in play. Playing animals simulate all kinds of actions which resemble very strongly those real actions they will need to perform to provide for the necessities of their future life. Hunting, fighting, biting seem to be suggested, but they do not really hunt, fight, and bite – at least, not with the aim of procuring food. In young animals and children we call it play; in adult people we call it acting and dancing. During play, efforts are tried out, selected, and chosen as those best suited, say, for a successful hunt or fight. The young animal, and so also the child, experiments with all imaginable situations – offence, defence, ambush, ruse, flight, fear, and always courage is exhibited. Search for the best possible effort-combination for each occasion accompanies these experiments. The body-mind becomes trained to react promptly, and with improved effort-configurations, to all the demands of differing situations until the adoption of the best efforts becomes automatic.

The fighting and hunting methods of a cat are not fully developed in a kitten, but the impulse to them is already discernible in the kitten's first movements. The same is true of a puppy, a lamb, or any other young animal. Play is the great aid to growing effort-capacity, and effort-regulation.

Nothing could prevent our calling these play acrobatics dramatic acting if the words acting and drama were not reserved for man's conscious exhibition of life-situations on the stage. There exists also a difference, because stage performance demands a spectator whom the actor can address, while the playing puppy, kitten or child is unconcerned of a spectator. The play of young animals is thus nearer to dancing than to acting, since dancing does not always demand spectators. If children and adults dance – that is, perform certain sequences of effort-combinations for their own pleasure – no audience is necessary. In this sense dancing is a more genuine effort-exercise than acting. Dancing – or at least that which today we call dancing – is, however, different from play, but it is not in itself a stage art.

The resemblance to life's struggle is not so clearly evident in dancing. Dance is a stylized play which is not directly related to dramatic effort-behaviour. Some animals dance – that means they have learned to stylize their play in the same way that man has done. If we study the exhaustive descriptions of the movements of birds and apes as observed by scientists, we are amazed by the similarity of these movements to human dancing. While during play the efforts of these creatures are intermingled in an almost casual and irregular way, in human dances, they are neatly selected, worked out, and separated. Regular repetitions of efforts form rhythmical phrases, and are exactly repeated. What dancing animals intend would remain a riddle if we did not assume that the whole activity takes the form of a more or less conscious effort-selection and effort-training.

It is a well-known fact that the plays and dances of primitive tribes originate in a conscientious endeavour to make themselves aware of certain selected effort-combinations. Apart from the awareness, or rather combined with it is the fixation of the selected effort-combination in memory and movement-habit. It is a peculiar kind of building up of ideas about movement-qualities and their use.

It is perhaps not too bold to introduce here the idea of thinking in terms of movement as contrasted with thinking in words. Movement-thinking could be considered as a gathering of impressions of the happenings in one's own mind, for which nomenclature is lacking. This thinking does not, as thinking in words does, serve orientation in the external world, but rather it perfects man's orientation in the inner world of efforts, which surge within his mind and find an outlet in the decision to move and to act.

Man's desire to become orientated to the inner maze of the continuous flow of his intentions to move and to act results in definite effort-rhythms, as practised in dancing and mime. The repeated exercise of effort-configurations prevailing in the action-thinking of a community results in the creation of tribal or national dances. These express the efforts cultivated by social groups living in a definite milieu. The languid, dream-like dance of an Oriental, the proud, fierce dance of a Spaniard, the temperamental dance of the Southern Italian, the well-measured round dance of the Anglo-Saxon, are examples of the effort-manifestations of social units, selected and fostered during long periods of history until they have become expressive of their mentality.

Tribal or national dances remind the observer of the states of mind or traits of character cherished and desired within the particular community.

Formerly such dances were one of the main means of schooling the young to adapt themselves to the habits and customs of their forebears. They are in this way as much connected with education as with ancestor-worship and religion.

The primitive urge to play and dance has thus developed into an astonishing variety of movement-traditions in all fields of human activity. Dance has been used as a pleasurable aid to work, especially in rhythmical teamwork. Dance has become an adjunct to fighting, hunting, loving and much else. In dancing, or movement-thinking, man first became aware of a certain order in his higher aspirations towards spiritual life.

In religious dances man represented those superhuman powers which, as he conceived, directed the happenings of Nature, and determined his personal and the tribal, fate. In such personifications of efforts, primitive man learned the reconciling trend of events, and pictured the power behind it all, in his movement thinking, as a god of gliding gestures.

Gliding is an essentially sustained, light and straight action. In gliding movements man and his deity indulge in time and weight, but fight against space. Many dances of the aborigines of Africa, Asia, Polynesia and America show this feature of gliding in their dance-rituals and the pictures and statues of their gods are represented as figures making gliding gestures. The gods floating over the waters show in ritual, or pictorial representation, indulgence in all three motions. Floating is a sustained, light, and flexible movement. Soft floating characterizes states of mind of a similar content.

The malign gods of death and violence are figures indulging in thrusting, piercing, and compressing effort, which are either sustained, as in pressing, or quick, as in thrusting, or punching, but always strong, if not brutal. Punching, as well as pressing, are strong and direct movements, both striving against weight and space.

The glittering divinities of joy and surprise are characterized in racial dances by flickering, fluttering movements. The indulgence in weight – no struggle against it is shown in the lightness of a flick – is wedded to an indulgence in space, shown in the flexibility of the movement. In its quickness, the struggle against time gives the flicking-fluttering movement its brilliance.

Gods as conceived by primitive man were the initiators and instigators of efforts. They were more, they were the efforts themselves. There were dances and statues of wringing gods, indulging in space and time, but they were strong, sternly fighting against weight. There were slashing gods, fighting against time and weight in their quickness and strength, but indulging in their flexibility in space.

Meticulous dabbing dances characterize sprites and goblins, the movements of which fight against time and space quickly and directly, but there is no struggle against weight in their lightness.

The strange poetry of movement that has found expression in sacred dance enabled man to build up an order of efforts, which, in essence, is valuable and understandable to this day.

Man alone has become aware of the gods. That is to say, man is the only living being who is aware of and responsible for his efforts, and so he has thus become king of creatures and lord of the earth.

From effort-awareness in ritual and national dances arose the conventions of the various forms of economic and political order in human society. In the teaching of children and the initiation of adolescents, primitive man endeavoured to convey moral and ethical standards through the development of effort-thinking in dancing. The introduction to humane effort was in these ancient times the basis of all civilization.

But for a very long time, man has been unable to find the connection between his movement-thinking and his word-thinking. Verbal descriptions of movement-thinking found their expression only in poetical symbolism. Poetry, descriptive of the deeds of gods and ancestors, was substituted for the simple expression of effort-happenings in dance. This, the scientific age of industrial man, has yet to find ways and means to enable us to penetrate into the mental side of effort and action, so that the common threads of the two kinds of thinking can finally be re-integrated in a new form.

The old ways of effort-awareness and effort-training will certainly play a part in the investigation of the actor's movement. It is to be expected that mime, as expressive of effort, and a fundamental activity of man, will, after its long period of neglect, become once more an important factor of civilized progress, when its real sense and meaning have been re-acquired.

The value of characterization through dance-like mime movements lies in the avoidance of the simple imitation of external movement-peculiarities. Such imitation does not penetrate to the hidden recesses of man's inner effort. To effect contact with the audience, we need an authentic symbol of the inner vision, and this contact can be achieved only if we have learned to think in terms of movement, and to use this thinking for the purposes of the real mastery of movement on the stage is the central problem of the theatre.

This is from *The Mastery of Movement*, first published in 1950 by MacDonald and Evans as *The Mastery of Movement on the Stage*. It is related to his thinking expressed two years before in *Modern Educational Dance*.

Today there is still misunderstanding of Laban's aims. He was never out to form a particular movement theory or practice. The sections quoted do give some indication of the way in which he brings his thinking to analyse and synthesize movement, aiming to codify and understand it, rather than follow any narrow approach.

Laban indicates particularly:

1. the range of expression and communication possible through physical movement

2. the close link between dance and ritual and man's fundamental struggles

3. opportunities in movement for development of natural spontaneous expression

4. the transient and fluid element in movement and drama – which is its dynamic quality

5. learning from play resembling life situations – linked with Margaret Lowenfeld's ideas

6. observations of the movement of primitive man – tie in with the observations of Chambers

7. discussion of tragic and comic attitudes towards situations (worth comparing to those views of Barrault and Aristotle)

8. the idea of expression for its own sake without audience communication

9. that 'movement-thinking' is a means of inner orientation (how often national and period dances reflect feelings and attitudes).

7 Sound, Rhythm and Vocal Expression
John Cage

Unfortunately, there is no pioneer in sound to parallel the work which Laban undertook in movement, but the expressive qualities of the human voice is a field which requires just as much research. For, as Laban's studies took him into drama, dance, industry, vocational guidance and beyond, so the voice can find expression in sound rhythm and pattern, and in music, prose, poetry, drama, politics, work and day-to-day human relationships.

Movement and voice are the basic instruments which interact with mind and feeling in dramatic expression. Like the body, the voice (which Laban would claim as another branch of movement) can be employed in imitative, interpretive and expressive ways. In one aspect it is a musical instrument capable of incredible range and abstraction. In another aspect, it is an instrument of communication capable of conveying a range of meaning, interest, and association.

Amongst those who have written in a stimulating, if often irritating, way about the world of sound, is John Cage, the composer, who has experimented with all kinds of sound accompaniments for the dance, and has tried out lectures of silence, as well as those of apparent nonsense. The article included here serves as a brief indication of some of the opportunities of the expressive world of sound. Though Cage is concerned with non-human instruments, it is not difficult to see this approach relating to the voice and body. His comments form a useful link between movement and speech.

Percussion music is revolution. Sound and rhythm have too long been submissive to the restrictions of nineteenth century music. Today we are fighting for their emancipation. Tomorrow, with electronic music in our ears, we will hear freedom.

Instead of giving us new sounds, the nineteenth-century composers have given us endless arrangements of the old sounds. We have turned on radios and always known when we were tuned to a symphony. The sound has always been the same, and there has not been even a hint of curiosity as to the possibilities of rhythm. For interesting rhythms we have listened to jazz.

At the present stage of revolution, a healthy lawlessness is warranted. Experiment must necessarily be carried on by hitting anything – tin pans, rice bowls, iron pipes – anything we can lay our hands on. Not only hitting, but rubbing, smashing, making sound in every possible way. In short, we must explore the materials of music. What we can't do ourselves will be done by machines and electrical instruments which we will invent.

The conscientious objectors to modern music will, of course, attempt everything in the way of counter-revolution. Musicians will not admit that we are making music; they will say that we are interested in superficial effects, or, at most, are imitating Oriental or primitive music. New and original sounds will be labelled as 'noise'. But our common answer to every criticism must be to continue working and listening, making music with its materials, sound and rhythm, disregarding the cumbersome, topheavy structure of musical prohibitions.

These prohibitions removed, the choreographer will be quick to realize a great advantage to the modern dance: the simultaneous composition of both dance and music. The materials of dance, already including rhythm, require only the addition of sound to become a rich, complete vocabulary. The dancer should be better equipped than the musician to use this vocabulary, for more of the materials are already at his command. Some dancers have made steps in this direction by making simple percussion accompaniments. Their use of percussion, unfortunately, has not been constructive. They have followed the rhythm of their own dance movement, accentuated it and punctuated it with percussion, but they have not given the sound its own and special part in the whole composition. They have made the music identical with the dance but not co-operative with it. Whatever method is used in composing the materials of the dance can be extended to the organization of the musical materials. The form of the music-dance composition should be a necessary working together of all materials used. The music will then be more than an accompaniment; it will be an integral part of the dance.

This is from a collection of Cage's writing and lectures, appropriately called *Silence*, published by The Wesleyan University Press, in 1961. (Paperback edition by M.I.T. in 1966.)

This article, entitled 'Goal – New Music, New Dance', is one of four 'Statements on the Dance', and was part of a series 'Percussion Music, and its relation to Modern Dance' that appeared in the *Dance Observer* in 1939.

Cage has worked for many years, with Merce Cunningham's Dance Company, on new music.

His ideas are revolutionary only in that they are so basic and stimulating. From this kind of awareness of sound we are likely to train a sharper approach to listening, which is surely the best basis of any kind of speech work, and, if we follow Aristotle's belief in imitation, visual observation and training will be necessary for mime and movement; aural observation will be necessary for voice and speech work.

8 Speech, Voice and Sound
Gwynneth L. Thurburn

Nearly all the writing about voice and speech approaches the art from a very technical point of view – some kind of vocal equivalent of physical gymnastics in developing the tonal quality and pronunciation.

Training for professional actors always includes a great deal of this kind of approach. It may well have been important in the days of large theatres, before microphones, but these days one wonders whether preference should not be given to other aspects – flexibility, range, flow, development of clarity – alongside the full exploration of language, vocabulary and imagery. There seems to be a need for a more imaginative approach to training the voice – one which will illuminate the relationship between voice and character, voice and environment, voice and occupation, voice and emotion.

The voice is to some extent a more physical means of communication than even the body: the air vibrations set up through speech are conveyed physically to the ear of the listener whereas the eye interprets at a distance. Vocal movement is also more complex than bodily movement in that, through speech, we have developed a vast range of fairly precise symbols, each capable of being interpreted in different moods, attitudes and points of importance. What, one begins to ask, are the bases of voice and speech and how could these be developed in the arts of drama and life?

Gwynneth Thurburn is one of the few writers I know who has at least left the door open for this kind of speech, voice, sound development. Interestingly enough, she is writing about speech in education more particularly than speech for the theatre.

Gwynneth Thurburn was, until 1968, the Principal of the Central School of Speech and Drama, where she upheld the reputation the place had for voice – that is, the training of the vocal instrument. She was well ahead of the elocutionary school of thought and practice.

As soon as man became a social being he must have begun to experience the need for a method of communication with his fellows other than gestures, noises and grimaces. Facial expression and gesture, though they may on occasion be more eloquent than words, yet lack clarity and precision; it is only by means of words that man can at any moment make known a portion of his consciousness to his fellows with a considerable hope of obtaining their understanding. Hence, of all means of self-expression, speech is the most indispensable. It has advantages over the other arts in that it is always available, for it needs no tool except the voice, and in that at its best it is a very exact means of conveying the speaker's meaning, whether it be a simple statement of fact, a command, or an expression of emotion. Man can, in fact, 'speak his mind'. But as with any other art, to portray the mind truly speech must be good. Bad speech is not clear and gives a distorted version of the speaker's intention. It is therefore ugly.

Beauty depends, in speech as in every other art, on the truthfulness with which the mind is presented, and this truthfulness depends in its turn upon mastery of the instrument. Speech has two instruments, language and voice, and command of both is required if speech is to be beautiful. A lovely voice cannot convey every shade or meaning if the speaker has a very limited vocabulary, nor can a fine mastery of words reproduce the speaker's mind if his utterance is faulty.

Manner in speaking can very easily stand in the way of matter, as may be noticed in the case of a speaker who has some little trick of pronunciation which catches the listener's attention, and becomes exaggerated out of all proportion. In fact, having once noticed the trick, he can hear little else.

It is chiefly to the voice that speech owes its emotional and aesthetic appeal, and yet so ill-trained is the average ear in the appreciation of spoken sounds that often people's pronunciation, their mannerisms and personal peculiarities are noticed, while the quality of the sounds is ignored.

A person's pronunciation may be impeccable according to accepted usage, and yet the voice may still grate harshly upon the ear; or a speaker's individual way of saying certain words may be criticized, while the underlying tone, which may be rich and resonant, passes unnoticed.

Yet as a people it is not true that we are unmusical and have no ear – for an audience will readily detect a singer who is out of tune. The reason for lack of appreciation of the spoken word is that most people use their own voices badly and hear badly-used voices all round them, so that they have never developed the power of distinguishing good from bad.

Before beginning the training of young voices, the teacher should look to his own voice, and ask himself a few questions, because it is impossible to over-estimate the importance of the teacher's unconscious example. Children do not necessarily imitate those who are in authority, for the unconscious influence of the home is always great – but their ears must inevitably be influenced, and their capacity for hearing and producing sounds affected, by what they hear around them every day.

The effect upon a class or audience of the voice of a teacher, lecturer, or actor, cannot be measured – but most people will agree that it is easier to assimilate information that is attractively presented than information delivered in such a manner that it requires an effort to listen at all. Everyone has at some time or other listened to flat, toneless voices, or hard and harsh voices, or monotonous voices, while on the other hand most people have experienced the thrill of listening to a voice which makes the words live.

A speaker of strong personality, with a real message to give, may be able to make his effect in spite of any handicaps of voice and speech from which he may suffer – but the ordinary person requires the full assistance that mastery of his instrument can give.

Does not the quality of voice – provided, of course, that the pronunciation is not so individual or peculiar as to be unintelligible – matter more than the type of speech of any speaker? If sufficient attention is paid to Voice as the instrument of speech, rather than to the Speech itself, many difficulties will be avoided, and the work based on the firm foundation of physiological laws rather than on the shifting sands of personal opinion. Attention to details of pronunciation may, and probably will, be necessary, but such attention alone will lead nowhere; some foundation is required on which to build.

Any tendency to regard speech as an end in itself should be banished at the outset, for it must be remembered that its function is to provide man with a means of communication, both of his own ideas and thoughts, and those of the poets and writers – the people whose work he may seek to interpret.

Two or more people must always be involved – the speaker and the listener – and the second is at least as important as the first. The speaker often thinks he has expressed his ideas quite clearly, only to find that he has been completely misunderstood. What he thinks he says, and what the listener thinks he says, are not always the same thing. That training in listening is as important as training in speaking will be shown later. If there is to be communication, reception must have some relation to expression. There must be common understanding of the words used, and the words must be spoken with clarity, fluency and appropriate phrasing. It need hardly be said that if, in addition to the presence of these factors, the voice has a pleasing quality, the speaker's effectiveness is greatly increased.

Pleasantness is a matter much more of tone and quality in the voice than of the accent or pronunciation of particular words – though the latter must never be entirely ignored, for when individual pronunciation is too peculiar it distracts the attention of the listener from the content of the words.

Fluency depends, technically, upon facility of utterance, because facility prevents both the hesitating and the jerky or staccato style of speaking. On the other hand, intellectually, fluency requires such familiarity with the use of words that the right word is in the right context, while in reading it ensures that the text presents no verbal difficulties.

Clarity and intelligibility are of two kinds, technical and intellectual; clarity of diction, and lucidity of thought. The former, as is fairly obvious, is dependent upon good articulation, audibility and correct formation of sounds; while the latter depends upon the individual's whole mental training.

Inarticulate speech is frequently the result, not merely of poor muscular action, but of a limited vocabulary; and – equally or more important – a limited vocabulary stands in the way of clear thinking, because it must be remembered that language is not only a means of communication but also the vehicle for thought, and after a certain point thought becomes impossible without adequate words.

It is the child and not the teacher who should set the pace. The child should acquire words as he needs them for his thoughts. When that is the case his vocabulary is alive, his thinking clear, and he is able in his speech to make full use of his command of language and obtain full enjoyment from it at each stage of its development.

Command of language for everyday use, important as it is, is not the only function of Speech Training. To be able to express our own thoughts freely and easily is essential, but there are also the thoughts and feelings of others to be interpreted and conveyed. The ability to read or speak prose and verse, using the voice as the medium of interpretation, is also important. In addition to the pleasure to be gained from being able to read and speak well, this aesthetic use of the speech organs is invaluable in training them to perform their functions easily, because concentration is directed to two essential points; first to tone, clarity and continuity, and second to developing the ability to convey an idea or an emotion to the best of the speaker's understanding. The rhythms of good prose and verse, the choice of words and their music, and the ideas contained all play an important part in training appreciation and understanding, and they demand the highest degree of performance from the instrument.

The listener has already been mentioned in passing and it will be well to consider in more detail the effect of hearing upon the production of sound. In these days of perpetual noise – road traffic, trains, wireless sets, road drills and the continuous buzz to be found everywhere – ears are becoming dulled.

Many people speak badly because they do not hear properly. They are accustomed to live and work with so much noise around them that their perception of sound is blunted and many of the finer shades are lost. There are even those, generally to be found among the young, who prefer an accompaniment of sound, and will turn on the wireless before sitting down to work, or play the gramophone as a background to conversation.

The value of silence might very well be taught along with the making of sound. It is only when silence is enjoyed that training in discernment and appreciation of sound are possible. Listening to others and listening to oneself are equally important in the development of a critical attitude towards speech.

Gwynneth Thurburn's book was first published by James Nisbet & Co. in 1939, that is, just prior to the War. The Second World War brought a change of attitudes and an increased development in technology, which placed more emphasis upon microphone technique than vocal projection. Everything became scaled down and the desire was for an easy and natural approach to speech work.

More recent years have seen a return in some quarters to realization of the evocative qualities and creative potential in the human voice. From that point of view, Gwynneth Thurburn's article shows clearly its link with the earlier era, in that she talks of the 'beauty of the voice' and deals with the 'sound' the voice makes rather than discussing the range of sounds it is capable of producing.

Nevertheless, it is a valuable contribution, in that it:
1. sees speech not as a separate subject
2. emphasizes the importance of listening
3. considers the value of voice as an instrument, with awareness of its tones and overtones
4. recognizes the value and need for command of the language
5. relates the study of voice to rhythms of prose and verse
6. underlines the link between silence and appreciation of sound.

It is to be hoped that it will not be much longer before vocal expression again becomes as respectable and lively a pursuit as, in many places, the mastery of movement expression has become.

9 Emotional Involvement in Acting
Constantin Stanislavski

Alongside other innovators in the late nineteenth century, Stanislavski in Russia 'protested against the customers' overacting, against the bad manner of production, against the star system which spoiled the ensemble . . .' Stanislavski worked first as an amateur actor and then as a director and, together with Komisarjevsky, he founded in 1888 the Society of Literature and Art. At this time, there was already a growing dissatisfaction with the artificiality of both production and acting styles. In production there was an attempt at historical truth and in acting Stanislavski emphasized the avoidance of a declamatory style in favour of greater simplicity and naturalism. With Nemirovich Danchenko in 1898, he founded the Moscow Art Theatre. Here, he further developed his ideals, strongly rejecting all sign of theatricality and artificial mannerisms, and other exaggerations. His productions of Chekhov's plays mark the highlight of his achievements in the naturalistic approach to theatre. He was now moving from the external historical truth to the internal truth of emotion and feeling. The creation of character is approached from within as well as externally, and the actor develops psychological truth as part of the role.

Stanislavski had a particular gift for being able to systematize and generalize his experience. He wrote several books outlining his ideas, in the form of annals of an actor. *An Actor Prepares*, published in the U.S.S.R. in 1926, is the best-known of these and tends to overshadow *Building a Character*, particularly as it appeared in English in 1936, while *Building a Character* did not appear in this country until 1950.

Elizabeth Hapgood, who translated both these books, explains that at one time Stanislavski had considered issuing his record of the inner preparations of the actor, and the external technical means of bringing a character to life in one volume, but there was too much material and too little time to edit it, so the two sides of the picture remained separated. In his introduction to *Stanislavsky on the Art of the Stage*, David

Magarshack gives a concise and vivid summary of Stanislavski's approach to acting, based on a lifetime of experience. Here, the concern is less with the techniques of the actor and more with what it is he is trying to achieve, and so I have included in the present volume the chapter from *An Actor Prepares* which concerns itself with truth and falseness in acting.

The chapter has two particularly important aspects to contribute to our inquiry. In the first place, it looks again at the question of truth, debating the relationship between the truth of an actual fact, and the truth of an artistic and imaginative fiction.

Stanislavski echoes Aristotle in pointing out that, on the stage, we are concerned not with what actually takes place, but with what could happen. Acting is a kind of investigation into how a human being would react if the circumstances were real. What gives it truth is imaginative reality, 'the reality of the inner life of the human spirit in a part, and a belief in that reality'.

The other point especially worth noting is the way in which Tortsov, the director, works with the actors. He is not the master puppeteer, superimposing his ideas upon the actors, but stands more in the role of a teacher, who sets up situations in which his actors can make discoveries for themselves. He stimulates questions and argues with his students until they can discover the truth for themselves. Those involved in using drama need to develop and draw upon their inner resources and make clear for themselves the differences and values between truth in life and truth in drama.

'Faith and a Sense of Truth' was inscribed on a large placard on the wall at school today.

Before our work began we were up on the stage, engaged in one of our periodic searches for Maria's lost purse. Suddenly we heard the voice of the Director who, without our knowing it, had been watching us from the orchestra.

'What an excellent frame, for anything you want to present, is provided by the stage and the footlights,' said he. 'You were entirely sincere in what you were doing. There was a sense of truthfulness about it all, and a feeling of believing in all physical objectives which you set yourselves. They were well defined and clear, and your attention was sharply concentrated. All these necessary elements were operating properly and harmoniously to create – can we say art? No! That was not art. It was actuality. Therefore repeat what you have just been doing.'

We put the purse back where it had been and we began to hunt it. Only this time we did not have to search because the object had already been found once. As a result we accomplished nothing.

'No. I saw neither objectives, activity nor truth, in what you did,' was Tortsov's criticism. 'And why? If what you were doing the first time was actual fact, why were you not able to repeat it? One might suppose that to do that much you would not need to be an actor, but just an ordinary human being.'

We tried to explain to Tortsov that the first time it was *necessary* to find the lost purse, whereas the second time we knew there was no need for it. As a result we had reality at first and a false imitation of it the second time.

'Well then, go ahead and play the scene with truth instead of falseness,' he suggested.

We objected, and said it was not as simple as all that. We insisted that we should prepare, rehearse, live the scene . . .

'*Live* it?' the Director exclaimed. 'But you just did *live* it!'

Step by step, with the aid of questions and explanation, Tortsov led us to the conclusion that there are two kinds of truth and sense of belief in what you are doing. First, there is the one that is created automatically and on the plane of actual fact (as in the case of our search for Maloletkova's purse when Tortsov first watched us), and second, there is the scenic type, which is equally truthful but which originates on the plane of imaginative and artistic fiction.

'To achieve this latter sense of truth, and to reproduce it in the scene of searching for the purse, you must use a lever to lift you on to the plane of imaginary life', the Director explained. 'There you will prepare a fiction, analogous to what you have just done in reality. Properly envisaged "given circumstances" will help you to feel and to create a scenic truth in which you can believe while you are on the stage. Consequently, in ordinary life, truth is what really exists, what a person really knows. Whereas on the stage it consists of something that is not actually in existence but which could happen.'

'Excuse me', argued Grisha, 'but I don't see how there can be any question of truth in the theatre since everything about it is fictitious, beginning with the very plays of Shakespeare and ending with the papier mâché dagger with which Othello stabs himself.'

'Do not worry too much about that dagger being made of cardboard instead of steel,' said Tortsov, in a conciliatory tone. 'You have a perfect right to call it an impostor. But if you go beyond that, and brand all art as a lie, and all life in the theatre as unworthy of faith, then you will have to change your point of view. What counts in the theatre is not the material out of which Othello's dagger is made, be it steel or cardboard, but the inner feeling of the actor who can justify his suicide. What is important is how the actor, a human being, would have acted if the circumstances and conditions which surrounded Othello were real and the dagger with which he stabbed himself were metal.

'Of significance to us is: the reality of the inner life of a human spirit in a part and a belief in that reality. We are not concerned with the actual naturalistic existence of what surrounds us on the stage, the reality of the material world! This is of use to us only in so far as it supplies a general background for our feelings.

'What we mean by truth in the theatre is the scenic truth which an actor must make use of in his moments of creativeness. Try always to begin by working from the inside, both on the factual and imaginary parts of a play and its setting. Put life into all the imagined circumstances and actions until you have completely satisfied your sense of truth, and until you have awakened a sense of faith in the reality of your sensations. This process is what we call justification of a part.'

As I wished to be absolutely sure of his meaning, I asked Tortsov to sum up in a few words what he had said. His answer was: 'Truth on the stage is whatever we can believe in with sincerity, whether in ourselves or in our colleagues. Truth cannot be separated from belief, nor belief from truth. They cannot exist without each other and without both of them it is impossible to live your part, or to create anything. Everything that happens on the stage must be convincing to the actor himself, to his associates and to the spectators. It must inspire belief in the possibility, in real life, of emotions analogous to those being experienced on the stage by the actor. Each and every moment must be saturated with a belief in the truthfulness of the emotion felt, and in the action carried out, by the actor.

The Director began our lesson today by saying: 'I have explained to you, in general terms, the part that truth plays in the creative process. Let us now talk about its opposite.'

'A sense of truth contains within itself a sense of what is untrue as well. You must have both. But it will be in varying proportions. Some have, let us say, seventy-five per cent sense of truth, and only twenty-five per cent of sense of falseness; or these proportions reversed; or fifty per cent of each. Are you surprised that I differentiate and contrast these two senses? This is why I do it,' he added, and then, turning to Nicholas, he said: 'There are actors who, like you, are so strict with themselves in adhering to truth that they often carry that attitude, without being conscious of it, to extremes that amount to falseness. You should not exaggerate your preference for truth and your abhorrence of lies, because it tends to make you overplay truth for its own sake, and that, in itself, is the worst of lies. Therefore, try to be cool and impartial. You need truth, in the theatre, to the extent to which you can believe in it.

'You can even get some use from falseness if you are reasonable in your approach to it. It sets the pitch for you and shows you what you should not do. Under such conditions a slight error can be used by an actor to determine the line beyond which he may not transgress.'

'This method of checking up on yourself is absolutely essential whenever you are engaged in creative activity. Because of the presence of a large audience an actor feels bound, whether he wishes to or not, to give out an unnecessary amount of effort and motions that are supposed to represent feelings. Yet no matter what he does, as long as he stands before the footlights, it seems to him that it is not enough. Consequently we see an excess of acting amounting to as much as ninety per cent. That is why, during my rehearsals, you will often hear me say, "Cut out ninety per cent."

'If you only knew how important is the process of self-study! It should continue ceaselessly, without the actor even being aware of it, and it should test every step he takes. When you point out to him the palpable absurdity of some false action he has taken he is more than willing to cut it. But what can he do if his own feelings are not able to convince him? Who will guarantee that, having rid himself of one lie, another will not immediately take its place? No, the approach must be different. A grain of truth must be planted under the falsehood, eventually to supplant it, as a child's second set of teeth pushes out the first.'

Here the Director was called away, on some business connected with the theatre, so the students were turned over to the assistant for a period of drill.

When Tortsov returned a short time later, he told us about an artist who possessed an extraordinarily fine sense of truth in criticizing the work of other actors. Yet when he himself acts, he completely loses that sense. 'It is difficult to believe', said he 'that it is the same person who at one moment shows such a keen sense of discrimination between what is true and what is false in the acting of his colleagues, and at the next will go on the stage and himself perpetrate worse mistakes.

'In his case his sensitiveness to truth and falseness as a spectator and as an actor are entirely divorced. This phenomenon is widespread.'

We thought of a new game today: we decided to check falseness in each other's actions both on the stage and in ordinary life.

It so happened that we were delayed in a corridor because the school stage was not ready. While we were standing around Maria suddenly raised a hue and cry because she had lost her key. We all precipitated ourselves into the search for it.

Grisha began to criticize her.

'You are leaning over,' said he, 'and I don't believe there is basis for it. You are doing it for us, not to find the key.'

His carpings were duplicated by remarks of Leo, Vassili, Paul and by some of mine, and soon the whole search was at a standstill.

'You silly children! How dare you!' the Director cried out. His appearance, catching us unaware in the middle of our game, left us in dismay.

'Now you sit down on the benches along the wall, and you two,' said he brusquely to Maria and Sonya, 'walk up and down the hall. No, not like that. Can you imagine anyone walking that way? Put your heels in and turn your toes out! Why don't you bend your knees? Why don't you put more swing into your hips? Pay attention! Look out for your centre of balance. Don't you know how to walk? Why do you stagger? Look where you're going!'

The longer they went on the more he scolded them. The more he scolded the less control they had over themselves. He finally reduced them to a state where they could not tell their heads from their heels, and came to a standstill in the middle of the hall.

When I looked at the Director I was amazed to find that he was smothering his laughter behind a handkerchief.

Then it dawned on us what he had been doing.

'Are you convinced now,' he asked the two girls, 'that a nagging critic can drive an actor mad and reduce him to a state of helplessness? Search for falseness only so far as it helps you to find truth. Don't forget that the carping critic can create more falsehood on the stage than anyone else because the actor whom he is criticizing involuntarily ceases to pursue his right course and exaggerates truth itself to the point of its becoming false. What you should develop is a sane, calm, wise, and understanding critic, who is the artist's best friend. He will not nag you over trifles, but will have his eye on the substance of your work. Another word of counsel about watching the creative work of others. Begin to exercise your sense of truth by looking, first of all, for the good points. In studying another's work limit yourself to the role of a mirror and say honestly whether or not you believe in what you have seen and heard, and point out particularly the moments that were most convincing to you.'

In continuing the description of his method, the Director illustrated his remarks today by an analogy between acting and travelling.

'Have you ever made a long journey?' he began. 'If so, you will recall the many successive changes that take place both in what you feel and what you see. It is just the same on the stage. By moving forward along physical lines we find ourselves constantly in new and different situations, moods, imaginative surroundings, and the externals of production. The actor comes into contact with new people and shares their life.

'All the while his line of physical actions is leading him through the ins and outs of the play. His path is so well built that he cannot be led astray. Yet it is not the path itself that appeals to the artist in him. His interest lies in the inner circumstances and conditions of life to which the play has led him. He loves the beautiful and imaginative surroundings in his part, and the feelings which they arouse in him.

'Actors, like travellers, find many different ways of going to their destination: there are those who really, physically, experience their part, those who reproduce its external form, those who deck themselves with stock tricks and do their acting as though it were a trade, some who make a literary, dry lecture of a part, and those who use the part to show themselves off to advantage before their admirers.

'How can you prevent yourself from going in the wrong direction? At every junction you should have a well trained, attentive, disciplined signal man. He is your sense of truth which co-operates with your sense of faith in what you are doing, to keep you on the right track.

'The next question is: what material do we use for building our track?

'At first it would seem that we could not do better than to use real emotions. Yet things of the spirit are not sufficiently substantial. That is why we have recourse to physical action.

'However, what is more important than the actions themselves is their truth and our belief in them. The reason is: Wherever you have truth and belief, you have feeling and experience. You can test this by executing even the smallest act in which you really believe and you will find that instantly, intuitively and naturally, an emotion will arise.

'These moments, no matter how short they may be, are much to be appreciated. They are of greater significance on the stage, both in the quieter parts of a play and in places where you live through high tragedy and drama. You have not far to go to find an example of this: what were you occupied with when you were playing the second half of that exercise? You rushed to the fireplace and pulled out a packet of bank notes: you tried to revive the moron, you ran to save the drowning child. That is the framework of your simple physical actions, inside of which you naturally and logically constructed the physical life of your part.

'Here is another example: with what was Lady Macbeth occupied at the culminating point of her tragedy? The simple physical act of washing a spot of blood off her hand.'

Here Grisha broke in because he was not willing to believe 'that a great writer like Shakespeare would create a masterpiece in order to have his heroine wash her hands or perform some similar natural act'.

'What a disillusion indeed,' said the Director ironically. 'Not to have thought about tragedy! How could he have passed up all of an actor's tenseness, exertion, "pathos", and "inspiration"! How hard to give up all the marvellous bag of tricks and limit oneself to little physical movements, small truths, and a sincere belief in their reality.

'In time you will learn that such a concentration is necessary if you are to possess real feelings. You will come to know that in real life also many of the great moments of emotion are signalized by some ordinary, small, natural movement. Does that astonish you? Let me remind you of the sad moments attendant on the illness and approaching death of someone dear to you. With what is the close friend or wife of the dying man occupied? Preserving quiet in the room, carrying out the doctor's orders, taking the temperature, applying compresses. All these small actions take on a critical importance in a struggle with death.

'We artists must realize the truth that even small physical movements, when injected into "given circumstances", acquire great significance through their influence on emotion. The actual wiping off of the blood had helped Lady Macbeth to execute her ambitious designs. It is not by chance that all through her monologue you find in her memory the spot of blood recalled in connection with the murder of Duncan. A small, physical act acquires an enormous inner meaning; the great inner struggle seeks an outlet in such an external act.

'Why is this mutual bond all-important to us in our artistic techniques? Why do I lay such exceptional stress on this elementary method of affecting our feelings?

'If you tell an actor that his role is full of psychological action, tragic depths, he will immediately begin to contort himself, exaggerate his passion, "tear it to tatters", dig around in his soul and do violence to his feelings. But if you give him some simple physical problem to solve and wrap it up in interesting, affecting conditions, he will set about carrying it out without alarming himself or even thinking too deeply whether what he is doing will result in psychology, tragedy or drama.

'By approaching emotion in this way you avoid all violence and your result is natural, intuitive, and complete. In the writings of great poets even the simplest acts are surrounded by important attendant conditions and in them lie hidden all manner of baits to excite our feelings.

'There is another simple and practical reason for approaching delicate emotional experiences and strong tragic moments through the truth of physical actions. To reach the great tragic heights an actor must stretch his creative power to the utmost. That is difficult in the extreme. How can he reach the needed state if he lacks a natural summons to his will? This state is brought about only by creative fervour, and that you cannot easily force. If you use unnatural means you are apt to go off in some false direction, and indulge in theatrical instead of in genuine emotion. The easy way is familiar, habitual and mechanical. It is the line of least resistance.

'To avoid that error you must have hold of something substantial, tangible. The significance of physical acts in highly tragic or dramatic moments is emphasized by the fact that the simpler they are, the easier it is to grasp them, the easier to allow them to lead you to your true objective, away from the temptation of mechanical acting.

'Come to the tragic part of a role without any nervous twinges, without breathlessness and violence and above all, not suddenly. Arrive gradually, and logically, by carrying out correctly your sequence of external physical actions, and by believing in them. When you will have perfected this technique of approach to your feelings, your attitude towards the tragic moments will change entirely, and you will cease to be alarmed by them.

'The approach to drama and tragedy, or to comedy and vaudeville, differs only in the given circumstances which surround the actions of the person you are portraying. In the circumstances lie the main power and meaning of these actions. Consequently, when you are called upon to experience a tragedy do not think about your emotions at all. Think about what you have to do.'

When Tortsov had finished speaking there was silence for a few moments until Grisha, ready as always to argue, broke in: 'But I think that artists do not ride around on the earth. In my opinion they fly around above the clouds.'

'I like your comparison,' said Tortsov with a slight smile. 'We shall go into that a little later.'

At today's lesson I was thoroughly convinced of the effectiveness of our method of psycho-technique. Moreover, I was deeply moved by seeing it in operation. One of our classmates, Dasha, played a scene from *Brand*, the one with the abandoned child. The gist of it is that a girl comes home to find that someone has left a child on her doorstep. At first she is upset, but in a moment or two she decides to adopt it. But the sickly little creature expires in her arms.

The reason why Dasha is so drawn to scenes of this sort, with children, is that not long ago she lost a child, born out of wedlock. This was told to me in confidence, as a rumour. But after seeing her play the scene today no doubt remains in my mind about the truth of the story. All during her acting the tears were coursing down her cheeks and her tenderness completely transformed for us the stick of wood she was holding into a living baby. We could feel it inside the cloth that swaddled it. When we reached the moment of the infant's death, the Director called a halt for fear of the consequences to Dasha's too deeply stirred emotions.

We all had tears in our eyes. Why go into an examination of lives, objectives and physical actions when we could see life itself in her face?

'There you see what inspiration can create,' said Tortsov with delight. 'It needs no technique; it operates strictly according to the laws of our art because they were laid down by Nature herself. But you cannot count on such a phenomenon every day. On some other occasion they might not work and then . . .'

'Oh, yes, indeed they would,' said Dasha. Whereupon, as though she were afraid that her inspiration would wane she began to repeat the scene she had just played. At first Tortsov was inclined to protect her young nervous system by stopping her, but it was not long before she stopped herself, as she was quite unable to do anything.

'What are you going to do about it?' asked Tortsov. 'You know that the manager who engages you for his company is going to insist that you play not only the first but all the succeeding performances equally well. Otherwise the play will have a successful opening and then fail.'

'No. All I have to do is to feel and then I can play well,' said Dasha.

'I can understand that you want to get straight to your emotions: of course that's fine. It would be wonderful if we could achieve a permanent method of repeating successful emotional experiences. But feelings cannot be fixed. They run through your fingers like water. That is why, whether you like it or not, it is necessary to find more substantial means of affecting and establishing your emotions.'

But our Ibsen enthusiast brushed aside any suggestion that she used physical means in creative work. She went over all the possible approaches: small units, inner objectives, imaginative inventions. None of them was sufficiently attractive to her. No matter where she turned, or how hard she tried to avoid it, in the end she was driven to accept the physical basis and Tortsov helped to direct her. He did not try to find new physical actions for her. His efforts were to lead her back to her own actions, which she had used intuitively and brilliantly.

This time she played well, and there was both truth and belief in her acting. Yet it could not be compared to her first performance.

The Director then said to her: 'You played beautifully, but not the same scene. You changed your objective. I asked you to play the scene with a real live baby, and you have given me one with an inert stick of wood wrapped in a tablecloth. All of your actions were adjusted to that. You handled the stick of wood skilfully, but a living child would necessitate a wealth of detailed movements which you quite omitted this time. The first time, before you swaddled the make-believe baby, you spread out its little arms and legs, you really felt them, you kissed them lovingly, you murmured tender words to it, you smiled at it through your tears. It was truly touching. But just now you left out all these important details. Naturally, because a stick of wood has neither arms nor legs.

'The other time, when you wrapped the cloth around its head you were very careful not to let it press on the baby's cheeks. After he was all bundled up you watched over him, with pride and joy.

'Now try to correct your mistake. Repeat the scene with a baby, not a stick.'

After a great deal of effort Dasha was finally able to recall consciously what she had felt unconsciously the first time she played the scene. Once she believed in the child her tears came freely. When she had finished playing, the Director praised her work as an effective example of what he had just been teaching. But I was still disillusioned and insisted that Dasha had not succeeded in moving us after that first burst of feeling.

'Never mind,' said he, 'once the ground is prepared and an actor's feelings begin to rise he will stir his audience as soon as he finds an appropriate outlet for them in some imaginative suggestion.

'I do not want to wound Dasha's young nerves, but suppose that she had had a lovely baby of her own. She was passionately devoted to him, and suddenly, when only a few months old, he died. Nothing in the world can give her any solace, until suddenly fate takes pity on her and she finds, on her doorstep, a baby even more lovely than her own.'

The shot went home. He had barely finished speaking when Dasha began to sob over the stick of wood with twice as much feeling as even the very first time.

I hurried to Tortsov to explain to him that he had accidentally hit upon her own tragic story. He was horrified, and started towards the stage to stop the scene, but he was spellbound by her playing and could not bring himself to interrupt her.

Afterwards I went over to speak to him. 'Isn't it true', I said, 'that this time Dasha was experiencing her own actual personal tragedy? In that case you cannot ascribe her success to any technique, or creative art. It was just an accidental coincidence.'

'Now you tell me whether what she did the first time was art?' countered Tortsov.

'Of course it was,' I admitted.

'Why?'

'Because she intuitively recalled her personal tragedy and was moved by it,' I explained.

'Then the trouble seems to lie in the fact that I suggested a new *if* to her, instead of her finding it herself? I cannot see any real difference', he went on, 'between an actor's reviving his own memories by himself and his doing it with the aid of another person. What is important is that the memory should retain these feelings, and, given a certain stimulus, bring them back! Then you cannot help believing in them with your whole body and soul.'

'I agree to that,' I argued, 'yet I still think that Dasha was not moved by any scheme of physical actions, but by the suggestion that you made to her.'

'I do not for a moment deny that,' broke in the Director. 'Everything depends on imaginative suggestion. But you must know just when to introduce it. Suppose you go to Dasha and ask her whether she would have been touched by my suggestion if I had made it sooner than I did, when she was playing the scene the second time, wrapping up the stick of wood without any display of feeling at all, before she felt the foundling's little arms and legs, and kissed them, before the transformation had taken place in her own mind and the stick had been replaced by a lovely, living child. I am convinced that at that point the suggestion that that stick with a grimy rag around it was her little boy would only have wounded her sensibilities. To be sure, she might have wept over the coincidence between my suggestion and the tragedy in her own life. But that weeping for one who is gone is not the weeping called for in this particular scene where sorrow for what is lost is replaced by joy in what is found.

'Moreover, I believe that Dasha would have been repelled by the wooden stick and tried to get away from it. Her tears would have flowed freely, but quite away from the property baby, and they would have been prompted by her memories of her dead child, which is not what we needed nor what she gave us the first time she played the scene. It was only after she made the mental picture of the child that she could weep over it again as she had at first.

'I was able to guess the right moment and throw in the suggestion that happened to coincide with her most touching memories. The result was deeply moving.'

There was, however, one more point I wanted to press, so I asked: 'Wasn't Dasha really in a state of hallucination while she was acting?'

'Certainly not,' said the Director emphatically. 'What happened was not that she believed in the actual transformation of a wooden stick into a living child, but in the possibility of the occurrence of the play, which, if it happened to her in real life, would be her salvation. She believed in her own maternal actions, love, and all the circumstances surrounding her.

'So you realize that this method of approach to emotions is valuable not only when you create a role but when you wish to relive a part already created. It gives you the means to recall sensations previously experienced. If it were not for them, the inspired moments of an actor's playing would flash before us once and then disappear for ever.'

Our lesson today was taken up by testing the sense of truth of various students. The first to be called on was Grisha. He was asked to play anything at all he liked. So he chose his usual partner, Sonya, and when they had finished the Director said: 'What you have just done was correct and admirable from your own point of view, which is that of exceedingly clever technicians, interested only in the external perfection of a performance.

'But my feelings could not go along with you, because what I look for in art is something natural, something organically creative, that can put human life into an inert role.

'Your make-believe truth helps you to represent images and passions. My kind of truth helps to create the images themselves and to stir real passions. The difference between your art and mine is the same as between the two words *seem* and *be*. I must have real truth. You are satisfied with its appearance. I must have true belief. You are willing to be limited to the confidence your public has in you. As they look at you they are sure that you will execute all the established forms with perfection. They rely on your skill as they do on that of an expert acrobat. From your standpoint the spectator is merely an onlooker. For me he involuntarily becomes a witness of, and a party to, my creative work; he is drawn into the very thick of the life that he sees on the stage, and he believes in it.'

Instead of making any argument in reply, Grisha caustically quoted the poet Pushkin as having a different point of view about truth in art:

'A host of lowly truths is dearer
Than fictions which lift us higher than ourselves.'

'I agree with you and with Pushkin as well,' said Tortsov, 'because he is talking about fictions in which we can believe. It is our faith in them that lifts us. This is a strong confirmation of the point of view that on the stage everything must be real in the imaginary life of the actor. This I did not feel in your performance.'

Whereupon he began to go over the scene in detail and correct it just as he had done with me in the exercise of the burnt money. Then something happened which resulted in a long and most instructive harangue. Grisha suddenly stopped playing. His face was dark with anger, his lips and hands trembled. After wrestling with his emotions for some time, finally he blurted out: 'For months we have been moving chairs around, shutting doors, lighting fires. That's not art; the theatre is not a circus. There physical actions are in order. It is extremely important to be able to catch your trapeze or jump on a horse. Your life depends on your physical skill. But you cannot tell me that the great writers of the world produced their masterpieces so that their heroes would indulge in exercises of physical actions. Art is free! It needs space, and not your little physical truths. We must be free for great fights instead of crawling on the ground like beetles.'

When he had finished, the Director said: 'Your protest astonishes me. Up to now I have always considered you an actor distinguished for his external technique. Today we find suddenly, that your longings are all in the direction of the clouds. External conventions and lies – that is what clips your wings. What soars is: imagination, feeling, thought. Yet your feelings and imagination seem to be chained right down here in the auditorium.

'Unless you are caught up in a cloud of inspiration and whirled upwards by it, you, more than any other here, will feel the need of all the groundwork we have been doing. Yet you seem to fear that very thing and look upon exercises as degrading to an artist.

'A ballerina puffs, blows, and sweats, as she goes through her necessary daily exercises, before she can make her graceful flights in the evening's performance. A singer has to spend his mornings bellowing, intoning through his nose, holding notes, developing his diaphragm and searching for new resonance in his head tones if, in the evening, he is to pour out his soul in song. No artists are above keeping their physical apparatus in order by means of necessary technical exercises.

'Why do you set yourself up as an exception? While we are trying to form the closest kind of direct bond between our physical and spiritual natures, why do you try to get rid of the physical side altogether? But nature has refused to give you the very thing you long for: exalted feelings and experiences. Instead she has endowed you with the physical technique to show off your gifts.

'The people who talk most about exalted things are the very ones, for the most part, who have no attributes to raise them to high levels. They talk about art and creation with false emotions, in an indistinct and involved way. True artists, on the contrary, speak in simple and comprehensible terms. Think about this and also about the fact that, in certain roles, you could become a fine actor and a useful contributor to art.'

After Grisha, Sonya was tested. I was surprised to see that she did all the simple exercises extremely well. The Director praised her and then he handed her a paper-cutter and suggested that she stab herself with it. As soon as she smelled tragedy in the air she got up on her stilts and at the climax she brought out such a tremendous amount of noise that we laughed.

The Director said to her: 'In the comedy part you wove a delightful pattern and I believed in you. But in the strong, dramatic places you struck a false note. Evidently your sense of truth is one-sided. It is sensitive to comedy and unformed on the dramatic side. Both you and Grisha should find your real place in the theatre. It is extremely important, in our art, for each actor to find his particular type.'

Today it was Vanya's turn to be tested. He played the exercise of the burnt money with Maria and me. I felt that he had never done the first half as well as this time. He amazed me by his sense of proportion and convinced me again of his very real talent.

The Director praised him, but he went on: 'Why', said he, 'do you exaggerate truth to such an undesirable degree in the death scene? You have cramps, nausea, groans, horrible grimaces and gradual paralysis. You seem, at this point, to be indulging in naturalism for its own sake. You were more interested in external, visual memories of the dissolution of a human body.

'Now in Hauptmann's play of *Hannele*, naturalism has its place. It is used for the purpose of throwing the fundamental spiritual theme of the play into high relief. As a means to an end, we can accept that. Otherwise, there is no need of dragging things out of real life on to the stage which had much better be discarded.

'From this we can conclude that not every type of truth can be transferred to the stage. What we use there is truth transformed into a poetical equivalent by creative imagination.'

Stanislavski's work is basic to thinking about development in drama within the theatre or education. I personally find the style and manner rather dated, though some people find it easier to digest the theory through this kind of narrative approach. The piece also enables us to see how close the relationship is between the theatre director and the drama teacher.

Stanislavski is working towards a text and is still thinking of the actor as an interpreter. In point of fact, if we get at all a true picture from 'Stanislavski Rehearses Othello', it seems that Stanislavski did most of the interpretation. It is, however, not difficult to apply his approach to other situations and develop it along even more creative lines.

The main points seem to be:

1. a firm belief in imaginative reality helps to make acting convincing.
2. flights of imagination, feeling and thought, have to be linked with skill
3. there is a need for self study, training and discipline
4. the director sets up situations in which actors may make discoveries
5. having made discoveries, there is a period of analysis and general discussion
6. the inner resources of the person are being explored and developed
7. the actors are making discoveries about the very nature of drama and people.

10 Mental Objectivity in Acting
Bertolt Brecht

Bertolt Brecht, 1898–1956, marks another important step in the progress of understanding the movement of theatre from its total pre-occupation with the artificial to its re-establishment as a significant part of community life. He is sometimes seen as being in opposition to Stanislavski but this is to ignore important aspects of both Stanislavski and Brecht.

Even before the First World War, Brecht was concerned with experimental drama and became influenced by German Expressionism. From very early days his outlook was Marxist and he regarded the theatre as a weapon in bringing about social change. He therefore needed to reform the theatre as it existed. In 1926 he was writing that the theatre was a nonsense, because it made no contact with the public. Brecht wanted the theatre to be didactic, but he did not want it to be boring. He constantly refers to the need to get fun out of the theatre, and held that Shakespeare 'wrote things primarily that he and his friends got fun out of'.

The rise of Hitler meant that Brecht had to leave Germany, at first living in Scandinavia, then in 1941 travelling to the U.S.A.; and it is between 1937 and 1945 that most of his major works were completed.

But it is after his return to Germany in 1949, and the establishment of the Berliner Ensemble, his own theatre company, that his influence dates. From this point he devoted himself more to productions of his own plays. Through his theoretic writings his stature as thinker and dramatist became recognized.

The two essays which follow are from John Willett's collection of Brecht writings, *Brecht on Theatre*, first published in England in 1964. The first: 'Theatre for Pleasure or Theatre for Instruction', was not published in Brecht's lifetime, and its date of composition and purpose are not known; it is thought to have been written about 1936, but it was not published until 1957. The second essay: 'A Short Description of a New Technique of Acting' was written in 1940, but not published then.

From these essays, some of the differences between Stanislavski and Brecht can be seen. Brecht is aiming to break away from romantic realism, largely because he feels that the identification between actor and audience which results suggests that the situation is inevitable. Change, however, Brecht maintains, lies in our hands and the theatre can be a powerful influence. However, because Epic Theatre transmutes knowledge into poetry, it can remain enjoyable. Brecht maintains that this requires a fresh approach to acting. Influenced by Asiatic Theatre, he maintains that the actor has to be a more virtuoso performer and be able to distance himself from the role, to avoid ever becoming totally immersed in the role he is playing. In this way, he can remain critical of the character, and his attitudes and actions, and realize more fully their functions in the play.

Both Brecht and Stanislavski stress the importance of the team-work of a group of actors. Both worked in permanent established companies, working over long periods on a single production. What Stanislavski did to reclaim the art and significance of the actor, Brecht did to the art and significance of the theatre in society.

THEATRE FOR PLEASURE OR THEATRE FOR INSTRUCTION

The epic theatre

Many people imagine that the term 'epic theatre' is self-contradictory, as the epic and dramatic ways of narrating a story are held, following Aristotle, to be basically distinct. The difference between the two forms was never thought simply to lie in the fact that the one is performed by living beings while the other operates via the written word; epic works such as those of Homer and the medieval singers were at the same time theatrical performances, while dramas like Goethe's *Faust* and Byron's *Manfred* are agreed to have been more effective as books. Thus even by Aristotle's definition the difference between the dramatic and epic forms was attributed to their different methods of construction, whose laws were dealt with by two different branches of aesthetics. The method of construction depended on the different way of presenting the work to the public, sometimes via the stage, sometimes through a book; and independently of that there was the 'dramatic element' in epic works and the 'epic element' in dramatic. The bourgeois novel in the last century developed much that was 'dramatic', by which was meant the strong centralization of the story, a momentum that drew the separate parts into a common relationship. A particular passion of utterance, a certain emphasis on the clash of forces, are hallmarks of the 'dramatic'. The epic writer Döblin provided an excellent criterion when he said that with an epic work, as opposed to a dramatic, one can as it were take a pair of scissors and cut it into individual pieces, which remain fully capable of life.

There is no place to explain how the opposition of epic and dramatic lost its rigidity after having long been held to be irreconcilable. Let us just point out that the technical advances alone were enough to permit the stage to incorporate an element of narrative in its dramatic productions. The possibility of projections, the greater adaptability of the stage due to mechanization, the film, all completed the theatre's equipment, and did so at a point where the most important transactions between people could no longer be shown simply by personifying the motive forces or subjecting the characters to invisible metaphysical powers.

To make these transactions intelligible, the environment in which the people lived had to be brought to bear in a big and 'significant' way.

This environment had, of course, been shown in the existing drama, but only as seen from the central figure's point of view, and not as an independent element. It was defined by the hero's reactions to it. It was seen as a storm can be seen when one sees the ships on a sheet of water unfolding their sails, and the sails filling out. In the epic theatre it was to appear standing on its own.

The stage began to tell a story. The narrator was no longer missing, along with the fourth wall. Not only did the background adopt an attitude to the events on the stage – by big screens recalling other simultaneous events elsewhere, by projecting documents which confirmed or contradicted what the characters said, by concrete and intelligible figures to accompany abstract conversations, by figures and sentences to support mimed transactions whose sense was unclear – but the actors too refrained from going over wholly into their role, remaining detached from the character they were playing and clearly inviting criticism of him.

The spectator was no longer in any way allowed to submit to an experience uncritically (and without practical consequences) by means of simple empathy with the characters in a play. The production took the subject-matter and the incidents shown and put them through a process of alienation: the alienation that is necessary to all understanding. When something seems 'the most obvious thing in the world' it means that any attempt to understand the world has been given up.

What is 'natural' must have the force of what is startling. This is the only way to expose the laws of cause and effect. People's activity must simultaneously be so and be capable of being different.

It was all a great change.

The dramatic theatre's spectator says: Yes, I have felt like that too – Just like me – It's only natural – It'll never change – The sufferings of this man appal me, because they are inescapable – That's great art; it all seems the most obvious thing in the world – I weep when they weep, I laugh when they laugh.

The epic theatre's spectator says: I'd never have thought it – That's not the way – That's extraordinary, hardly believable – It's got to stop – The sufferings of this man appal me, because they are unnecessary – That's great art: nothing obvious in it – I laugh when they weep, I weep when they laugh.

The instructive theatre

The stage began to be instructive.

Oil, inflation, war, social struggles, the family, religion, wheat, the meat market, all became subjects for theatrical representation. Choruses enlightened the spectator about facts unknown to him. Films showed a montage of events from all over the world. Projections added statistical material. And as the 'background' came to the front of the stage so people's activity was subjected to criticism. Right and wrong courses of action were shown. People were shown who knew what they were doing, and others who did not. The theatre became an affair for philosophers, but only for such philosophers as wished not just to explain the world but also to change it. So we had philosophy, and we had instruction. And where was the amusement in all that? Were they sending us back to school, teaching us to read and write? Were we supposed to pass exams, work for diplomas?

Generally there is felt to be a very sharp distinction between learning and amusing oneself. The first may be useful, but only the second is pleasant. So we have to defend the epic theatre against the suspicion that it is a highly disagreeable, humourless, indeed strenuous affair.

Well: all that can be said is that the contrast between learning and amusing oneself is not laid down by divine rule; it is not one that has always been and must continue to be.

Undoubtedly there is much that is tedious about the kind of learning familiar to us from school, from our professional training, etc. But it must be remembered under what conditions and to what end that takes place.

It is really a commercial transaction. Knowledge is just a commodity. It is acquired in order to be resold. All those who have grown out of going to school have to do their learning virtually in secret, for anyone who admits that he still has something to learn devalues himself as a man whose knowledge is inadequate. Moreover, the usefulness of learning is very much limited by factors outside the learner's control. There is unemployment, for instance, against which no knowledge can protect one. There is the division of labour, which makes generalized knowledge unnecessary and impossible. Learning is often among the concerns of those whom no amount of concern will get any forwarder. There is not much knowledge that leads to power, but plenty of knowledge to which only power can lead.

If there were not such amusement to be had from learning, the theatre's whole structure would unfit it for teaching.

Theatre remains theatre even when it is instructive theatre, and in so far as it is good theatre it will amuse.

Theatre and knowledge

But what has knowledge got to do with art? We know that knowledge can be amusing, but not everything that is amusing belongs in the theatre.

I have often been told, when pointing out the invaluable services that modern knowledge and science, if properly applied, can perform for art and specially for the theatre, that art and knowledge are two estimable but wholly distinct fields of human activity. This is a fearful truism, of course, and it is as well to agree quickly that, like most truisms, it is perfectly true. Art and science work in quite different ways: agreed. But, bad as it may sound, I have to admit that I cannot get along as an artist without the use of one or two sciences.

Whatever knowledge is embodied in a piece of poetic writing has to be wholly transmuted into poetry. Its utilization fulfils the very pleasure that the poetic element provokes. If it does not at the same time fulfil that which is fulfilled by the scientific element, none the less in an age of great discoveries and inventions one must have a certain inclination to penetrate deeper into things – a desire to make the world controllable – if one is to be sure of enjoying its poetry.

Is the epic theatre some kind of 'moral institution'?

According to Friedrich Schiller the theatre is supposed to be a moral institution. In making this demand it hardly occurred to Schiller that by moralizing from the stage he might drive the audience out of the theatre. Audiences had no objection to moralizing in his day. It was only later that Friedrich Nietzsche attacked him for blowing a moral trumpet. To Nietzsche any concern with morality was a depressing affair; to Schiller it seemed thoroughly enjoyable. He knew of nothing that could give greater amusement and satisfaction than the propagation of ideas. The bourgeoisie was setting about forming the ideas of the nation.

Putting one's house in order, patting oneself on the back, submitting one's account, is something highly agreeable. But describing the collapse of one's house, having pains in the back, paying one's account, is indeed a depressing affair, and that was how Friedrich Nietzsche saw things a century later. He was poorly disposed towards morality, and thus towards the previous Friedrich too.

The epic theatre was likewise often objected to as moralizing too much. Yet in the epic theatre moral arguments only took second place. Its aim was less to moralize than to observe. That is to say it observed, and then the thick end of the wedge followed: the story's moral. Of course we cannot pretend that we started our observations out of a pure passion for observing and without any more practical motive, only to be completely staggered by their results. Undoubtedly there were some painful discrepancies in our environment, circumstances that were barely tolerable, and this not merely on account of moral considerations. It is not only moral considerations that make hunger, cold and oppression hard to bear. Similarly the object of our inquiries was not just to arouse moral objections to such circumstances (even though they could easily be felt – though not by all the audience alike; such objections were seldom for instance felt by those who profited by the circumstances in question) but to discover means for their elimination. We were not in fact speaking in the name of morality but in that of the victims. These truly are two distinct matters, for the victims are often told that they ought to be contented with their lot, for moral reasons. Moralists of this sort see man as existing for morality, not morality for man. At least it should be possible to gather from the above to what degree and in what sense the epic theatre is a moral institution.

Can epic theatre be played anywhere?

Stylistically speaking, there is nothing all that new about the epic theatre. Its expository character and its emphasis on virtuosity bring it close to the old Asiatic theatre. Didactic tendencies are to be found in the medieval mystery plays and the classical Spanish theatre, and also in the theatre of the Jesuits.

These theatrical forms corresponded to particular trends of their time, and vanished with them. Similarly the modern epic theatre is linked with certain trends. It cannot by any means be practised universally. Most of the great nations today are not disposed to use the theatre for ventilating their problems. London, Paris, Tokyo and Rome maintain their theatres for quite different purposes. Up to now favourable circumstances for an epic and didactic theatre have only been found in a few places and for a short period of time. In Berlin Fascism put a very definite stop to the development of such a theatre.

It demands not only a certain technological level but a powerful movement in society which is interested to see vital questions freely aired with a view to their solution, and can defend this interest against every contrary trend.

The epic theatre is the broadest and most far-reaching attempt at large-scale modern theatre, and it has all those immense difficulties to overcome that always confront the vital forces in the sphere of politics, philosophy, science and art.

E

SHORT DESCRIPTION OF A NEW TECHNIQUE OF ACTING WHICH PRODUCES AN ALIENATION EFFECT

What follows represents an attempt to describe a technique of acting which was applied in certain theatres with a view to taking the incidents portrayed and alienating them from the spectator. The aim of this technique, known as the alienation effect, was to make the spectator adopt an attitude of inquiry and criticism in his approach to the incident. The means were artistic.

The first condition for the A-effect's application to this end is that stage and auditorium must be purged of everything 'magical' and that no 'hypnotic tensions' should be set up. This ruled out any attempt to make the stage convey the flavour of a particular place (a room at evening, a road in the autumn), or to create atmosphere by relaxing the tempo of the conversation. The audience was not 'worked up' by a display of temperament or 'swept away' by acting with tautened muscles; in short, no attempt was made to put it in a trance and give it the illusion of watching an ordinary unrehearsed event. As will be seen presently, the audience's tendency to plunge into such illusions has to be checked by specific artistic means.

The first condition for the achievement of the A-effect is that the actor must invest what he has to show with a definite gest of showing. It is of course necessary to drop the assumption that there is a fourth wall cutting the audience off from the stage and the consequent illusion that the stage action is taking place in reality and without an audience. That being so, it is possible for the actor in principle to address the audience direct.

It is well known that contact between audience and stage is normally made on the basis of empathy. Conventional actors devote their efforts so exclusively to bringing about this psychological operation that they may be said to see it as the principal aim of their art. Our introductory remarks will already have made it clear that the technique which produces an A-effect is the exact opposite of that which aims at empathy. The actor applying it is bound not to try to bring about the empathy operation.

Yet in his efforts to reproduce particular characters and show their behaviour, he need not renounce the means of empathy entirely. He uses these means just as any normal person with no particular acting talent would use them if he wanted to portray someone else, i.e. show how he behaves. This showing of other people's behaviour happens time and again in ordinary life (witnesses of an accident demonstrating to newcomers how the victim behaved, a facetious person imitating a friend's walk, etc.), without those involved making the least effort to subject their spectators to an illusion. At the same time they do feel their way into their characters' skins with a view to acquiring their characteristics.

As has already been said, the actor too will make use of this psychological operation. But whereas the usual practice in acting is to execute it during the actual performance, in the hope of stimulating the spectator into a similar operation, he will achieve it only at an earlier stage, at some time during rehearsals.

To safeguard against an unduly 'impulsive', frictionless and uncritical creation of characters and incidents, more reading rehearsals can be held than usual. The actor should refrain from living himself into the part prematurely in any way, and should go on functioning as long as possible as a reader (which does not mean a reader-aloud). An important step is memorizing one's first impressions.

When reading his part the actor's attitude should be one of a man who is astounded and contradicts. Not only the occurrence of the incidents, as he reads about them, but the conduct of the man he is playing, as he experiences it, must be weighed up by him and their peculiarities understood; none can be taken as given, as something that 'was bound to turn out that way', that was 'only to be expected from a character like that'. Before memorizing the words he must memorize what he felt astounded at and where he felt impelled to contradict. For these are dynamic forces that he must preserve in creating his performance.

When he appears on the stage, besides what he actually is doing he will at all essential points discover, specify, imply what he is not doing; that is to say he will act in such a way that the alternative emerges as clearly as possible, that his acting allows the other possibilities to be inferred and only represents one out of the possible variants. He will say for instance 'You'll pay for that', and not say 'I forgive you'. He detests his children; it is not the case that he loves them. He moves down stage left and not up stage right. Whatever he doesn't do must be contained and conserved in what he does. In this way every sentence and every gesture signifies a decision; the character remains under observation and is tested. The technical term for this procedure is 'fixing the "not . . . but"'.

The actor does not allow himself to become completely transformed on the stage into the character he is portraying. He is not Lear, Harpagon, Schweik; he shows them. He reproduces their remarks as authentically as he can; he puts forward their way of behaving to the best of his abilities and knowledge of men; but he never tries to persuade himself (and thereby others) that this amounts to a complete transformation. Actors will know what it means if I say that a typical kind of acting without this complete transformation takes place when a producer or colleague shows one how to play a particular passage. It is not his own part, so he is not completely transformed; he underlines the technical aspect and retains the attitude of someone just making suggestions.

Once the idea of total transformation is abandoned, the actor speaks his part not as if he were improvising it himself, but like a quotation. At the same time he obviously has to render all the quotation's overtones, the remark's full human and concrete shape; similarly the gesture he makes must have the full substance of a human gesture even though it now represents a copy.

Given this absence of total transformation in the acting, there are three aids which may help to alienate the actions and remarks of the characters being portrayed:

1. Transposition into the third person.
2. Transposition into the past.
3. Speaking the stage directions out loud.

Using the third person and the past tense allows the actor to adopt the right attitude of detachment. In addition, he will look for stage directions and remarks that comment on his lines, and speak them aloud at rehearsal ('He stood up and exclaimed angrily, not having eaten: . . .', or 'He had never been told so before, and didn't know if it was true or not', or 'he smiled, and said with forced nonchalance: . . .'). Speaking the stage directions out loud in the third person results in a clash between two tones of voice, alienating the second of them, the text proper. This style of acting is further alienated by taking place on the stage after having already been outlined and announced in words. Transposing it into the past gives the speaker a standpoint from which he can look back at his sentence. The sentence too is thereby alienated without the speaker adopting an unreal point of view; unlike the spectator, he has read the play right through and is better placed to judge the sentence in accordance with the ending, with its consequences, than the former, who knows less and is more of a stranger to the sentence.

This composite process leads to an alienation of the text in the rehearsals which generally persists in the performance too. The directness of the relationship with the audience allows and indeed forces the actual speech delivery to be varied in accordance with the greater or smaller significance attaching to the sentences. Take the case of witnesses addressing a court. The underlinings, the characters' insistence on their remarks, must be developed as a piece of effective virtuosity. If the actor turns to the audience it must be a whole-hearted turn rather than the asides and soliloquizing technique of the old-fashioned theatre. To get the full A-effect from the poetic medium, the actor should start at rehearsal by paraphrasing the verse's content in vulgar prose, possibly accompanying this by the gestures designed for the verse. A daring and beautiful handling of verbal media will alienate the text. (Prose can be alienated by translation into the actor's native dialect.)

The attitude which the actor adopts is a socially critical one. In his exposition of the incidents and in his characterization of the person he tries to bring out those features which come within society's sphere. In this way his performance becomes a discussion (about social conditions) with the audience he is addressing. He prompts the spectator to justify or abolish these conditions according to what class he belongs to.

The object of the A-effect is to alienate the social gest underlying every incident. By social gest is meant the mimetic and gestural expression of the social relationships prevailing between people of a given period.

It helps to formulate the incident for society, and to put it across in such a way that society is given the key, if titles are thought up for the scenes. These titles must have a historical quality.

This brings us to a crucial technical device: historicization.

The actor must play the incidents as historical ones. Historical incidents are unique, transitory incidents associated with particular periods. The conduct of the persons involved in them is not fixed and 'universally human'; it includes elements that have been or may be overtaken by the course of history, and is subject to criticism from the immediately following period's point of view. The conduct of those born before us is alienated (*entfremdet*) from us by an incessant evolution.

It is up to the actor to treat present-day events and modes of behaviour with the same detachment as the historian adopts with regard to those of the past. He must alienate these characters and incidents from us.

About rational and emotional points of view

The rejection of empathy is not the result of a rejection of the emotions, nor does it lead to such. The crude aesthetic thesis that emotions can only be stimulated by means of empathy is wrong. None the less, a non-aristotelian dramaturgy has to apply a cautious criticism to the emotions which it aims at and incorporates. Certain artistic tendencies like the provocative behaviour of Futurists and Dadaists and the icing-up of music point to a crisis of the emotions. Already in the closing years of the Weimar Republic, the post-war German drama took a decisively rationalistic turn.

Fascism's grotesque emphasizing of the emotions, together perhaps with the no less important threat to the rational element in Marxist aesthetics, led us to lay particular stress on the rational. Nevertheless, there are many contemporary works of art where one can speak of a decline in emotional effectiveness due to their isolation from reason, or its revival thanks to a stronger rationalist message. This will surprise no one who has not got a completely conventional idea of the emotions.

The emotions always have a quite definite class basis; the form they take at any time is historical, restricted and limited in specific ways. The emotions are in no sense universally human and timeless.

The linking of particular emotions with particular interests is not unduly difficult so long as one simply looks for the interests corresponding to the emotional effects of works of art. Anyone can see the colonial adventures of the Second Empire looming behind Delacroix's paintings and Rimbaud's 'Bateau Ivre'.

If one compares the 'Bateau Ivre' say, with Kipling's 'Ballad of East and West', one can see the difference between French mid-nineteenth century colonialism and British colonialism at the beginning of the twentieth. It is less easy to explain the effect that such poems have on ourselves, as Marx already noticed. Apparently emotions accompanying social progress will long survive in the human mind as emotions linked with interests, and in the case of works of art will do so more strongly than might have been expected, given that in the meantime contrary interests will have made themselves felt. Every step forward means the end of the previous step forward, because that is where it starts and goes on from. At the same time it makes use of this previous step, which in a sense survives in men's consciousness as a step forward, just as it survives in its effects in real life. This involves a most interesting type of generalization, a continual process of abstraction. Whenever the works of art handed down to us allow us to share the emotions of other men, of men of a bygone period, different social classes, etc., we have to conclude that we are partaking in interests which really were universally human. These men now dead represented the interests of classes that gave a lead to progress. It is a very different matter when Fascism today conjures up on the grandest scale emotions which for most of the people who succumb to them are not determined by interest.

Is the critical attitude an inartistic one?

An old tradition leads people to treat a critical attitude as a predominantly negative one. Many see the difference between the scientific and artistic attitudes as lying precisely in their attitude to criticism. People cannot conceive of contradiction and detachment as being part of artistic appreciation. Of course, such appreciation normally includes a higher level, which appreciates critically, but the criticism here only applies to matters of technique; it is quite a different matter from being required to observe not a representation of the world but the world itself in a critical, contradictory, detached manner.

To introduce this critical attitude into art, the negative element which it doubtless includes must be shown from its positive side: this criticism of the world is active, practical, positive. Criticizing the course of a river means improving it, correcting it.

Criticism of society is ultimately revolution; there you have criticism taken to its logical conclusion and playing an active part. A critical attitude of this type is an operative factor of productivity; it is deeply enjoyable as such, and if we commonly use the term 'arts' for enterprises that improve people's lives, why should art proper remain aloof from arts of this sort?

Although we are only meeting Brecht here in translation, it nevertheless seems important to come as close as possible to Brecht's own statements about the nature of epic theatre and alienation.

'Theatre for Pleasure or Theatre for Instruction' seems to have been written somewhere around 1935 or 1936. It may have been prepared for one of Brecht's visits to Moscow or New York: for instance, as a possible contribution to the Conference of Producers to which Piscator invited Brecht in Moscow.

The term which John Willett has here translated as 'alienation' is *Entfremdung*, as used by Hegel and Marx, and not the *Verfremdung*, which Brecht was soon to coin and make famous.

Both the term 'epic theatre' and the term 'alienation' are much used with all kinds of connotations. It is interesting to observe the ways in which the style of Stanislavski and Brecht contrast: even here, we can note Stanislavski's subjective narrative against Brecht's objective concepts.

It is particularly worth noting that:

1. Brecht comments on the relationship between the epic, the narrative and the dramatic (compare these with Aristotle)
2. he points out that it is the increased use of technical aspects of theatre which have helped to make the narrative dramatic
3. he emphasizes the audience's detachment and that of the actor, for critical purposes
4. he insists on the need to make the spectator believe that change in the human condition is possible
5. he calls for an instructive, a philosophic and an amusing theatre, but one based on the simplest form of narrative – the story
6. he sees no reason why a critical detachment need result in negative approach.

SECTION FOUR
Links with the Sub-conscious

11 Drama in Dreams
J. A. Hadfield

Primitive man and the young child have been seen to express and explore their problems and perplexities through the medium of drama. The more sophisticatedly self-conscious man becomes, the more inhibited he is about expressing his ideas through activity, especially that involving imitation and impersonation. The trouble with acting is that it involves the individual totally at the time of communication and, as Jean-Louis Barrault pointed out, the more awareness man has of being observed, the more he tends to hide himself and project what he thinks is the desired image. This can lead to an unwillingness to face up to problems, and so many of these become suppressed into the sub-conscious and find expression only in dreams.

Freud had examined the visual imagery of dreams, aware that it was complicated and, to some extent, inexplicable, often progressing in an apparently illogical way. He saw that sometimes dreams could be interpreted by a process of free association, which lead to discovering some of the meaning of the symbols involved. Throughout his writings, Freud drew readily upon the drama for illustrations of human behaviour and universal traits. Sub-conscious symbolism is sometimes seen in the active drama of the play; sometimes in the passive drama of dreams.

Dreams, like adult dramatic play, seem covertly enacted. It appears that the adult not only dares not act out his experience to others, but dares not act it out for himself. The examination of dreams and the consideration of them in terms of drama can throw some light on the values of symbolism and analogy. J. A. Hadfield reviews various approaches to the dream, and discusses the relationship between the theories of Freud, Adler and Jung.

Hadfield came to psychology after a varied education. He began by taking a degree in arts, then read theology. Some work with William McDougall, the psychologist, led him to study medicine at Edinburgh University. After the First World War, he had a practice in Harley Street, in psychological medicine, and became a lecturer in psychopathology and mental hygiene at London University.

In *Dreams and Nightmares*, he indicates that dreams can be involved in the solution of practical and fairly commonplace situations, as well as in the more complex problems of present-day society. What he has to say in our two selections can illuminate our understanding of links between the conscious and the subconscious in imaginative and dramatic situations.

The function of dreams is, by the mere fact of reproducing an experience and by the repetition of a problem, to stand in the place of the experience; they warn us of the consequences of our action; they point to the causes of our trouble; they reveal the defects in our armour; and they make us face a situation we are trying to avoid. They call our bluff, they will not let us shirk the issues, but insist on thrusting the problem before us until we attend to it, face it, and solve it. They point towards a solution of the problem. Finally, they not only reveal but release hidden potentialities and repressed emotion in our nature, so that we are restored to wholeness. In our sleep we continue to worry out the problems of life as we do in our waking state; but dreams take up more specifically those problems which the conscious mind will not face or cannot solve, and therefore serve a biological function which no other mental process does.

The value of dreams without interpretation

But it may be asked, Can dreams be of any value unless they are interpreted? For if not, how can we say that it is their biological function to solve problems if the dreamer, as in most cases, cannot understand their meaning? The answer is that the dreamer can sense the significance of a dream intuitively although he may not be able to understand it cognitively. No doubt the interpretation of a dream adds enormously to its value, for it then enlists the co-operation of the conscious reason, and is so used in analytic treatment. But quite apart from its interpretation, a dream may have a profound effect upon the dreamer and may be of great therapeutic value.

Dreams, like the other processes of the subconscious mind, get their effects by association, suggestion, and analogy; we 'feel' the effect upon us even without the co-operation of the reason, although, as we have said, they are the better for such co-operation.

Dreams and children's play

This method of working out problems by symbolic representation finds its counterpart in children's play, much of which is found to be concerned with working out the child's own problems by the use of concrete symbols.

In their play, say of fathers and mothers, policemen, robbers, fairies, and animals, they are imagining situations and taking up attitudes (to their 'naughty dolls' for instance) without in the least knowing that they are dealing with their personal problems, that they are trying to adjust their attitudes to their own naughtiness, to the authority of their fathers, to the lack of love from their mothers, to their jealousy of baby brothers, to their own conscience. In condemning the sins of the doll the child is condemning the same sins to which she is prone, without knowing that she is doing so. Children who were bombed out during the war first suffered a period of shock and then began to play at bombing. Why? Was it a wish to be bombed? No! It was because they had been confronted with a problem created by the bombing which bewildered them and they wanted to work it out. The playing at bombing had a double effect, first by acclimatizing them to the situation and then by bringing the situation under their own control as they were able to do in their play. The working out of the problem even on a symbolic plane had the effect of settling the problem in their own minds, so that after a time their personalities were restored to equilibrium – which is precisely what happens in dreams. Moreover, when the child's problem is diagnosed, the play therapist can lead the child to a healthier solution in the play itself by making the characters in the play do certain things and take up certain healthier attitudes which may completely change the child's own behaviour and relations to the baby and the members of its family – and all this without the child knowing in the least that its problems are thus being worked out, without the play being interpreted, and indeed without the child realizing what its problems are. Its problems are solved symbolically in play as they are in dreams. A child's play, like dreams, reproduces unsolved problems and by that means works towards a solution of other problems.

Folk-stories

The same applies to folk-stories and fairy-stories, which have a profound effect on the mind of a child and of a people without their understanding their psychological meaning; that is why a child wants to hear the same story, say, of Little Black Sambo, over and over again, for it means something to him although he may have no conception of what it does mean. The story of Cinderella appeals to the child who feels itself left out, and what child does not at some time? Jack the Giant-Killer appeals to a child's desire to be strong as a corrective to his own present helplessness. Little Red Riding Hood brings him face to face with the problem of a mother or nurse who at one time appears kindly but, like the kindly grandmother, may turn into the angry wolf at any moment. They want these stories over and over again so as to get the problems clear by imagining similar situations and so acclimatizing themselves to their situations and so work towards a solution. It is indeed because we do not understand our deeper emotional problems that we have to work them out by analogy, by myth, and by parable, and that is precisely the function of dreams. It is interesting to note that Christ made this distinction between the automatic effect of the parable and its conscious interpretation, for when he spoke to the people in parables, and afterwards his disciples wanted an explanation, he said, 'Unto you [disciples] it is given to know the mystery of the kingdom of God, but unto them that are without [the people] . . . in parables' (Mark iv:11). To the people he told the parable and left it to produce its own effect, for obviously he was not merely story-telling to the people. He realized that the stories would have a greater effect in the untutored mind without interpretation, for the untutored mind is the subconscious mind. But as obviously his disciples could get the most out of the parables by understanding the meaning and interpretation which he gave, as in this Parable of the

Sower. Dreams are parables, symbolic stories, carrying a deeper meaning, and they have an effect on the mind even when they are not consciously understood or interpreted. The story carries its own moral.

The value of analogy

Another mode of thinking which primitive man shares with the child is
that he argues by analogies. One of the uses of analogies in everyday life
is to make things clear. We say 'it is like', 'it is as if'. Such an analogy is
of course no argument at all, although it is constantly used as such, but
it helps us to understand a difficult or abstruse problem; and the curious
fact is that when we understand something clearly we are apt to take it
to be true – 'I can understand *that*!' we say. When we accept an argument by analogy we are following primitive thinking in accepting that
there is a real connection as well as an analagous one, that 'things that
are similar are the same thing'.

The idea that two things which happen together in time are causally
related is, of course, logically false. Nevertheless, this capacity to bring
things into juxtaposition is the cause of many scientific discoveries which
reason has failed to achieve, for that is the basis of analogy, and analogy
leads to discovery. We have referred to such scientific discoveries as the
work of the subconscious mind. We can now say that it is largely by the
recognition of similarities that the subconscious mind is able to make
these discoveries.

William James said that genius is the capacity to observe analogies.
As we have seen, it is in relaxed states of mind that the mind works by
association of ideas and the recognition of similars; so Newton's discovery came when he was relaxing under an apple-tree and realized the
analogy between the falling apple and the world's suspension in space.
It was an analogy of snakes swallowing their tails which led to the discovery of the benzene ring. There is no logical connection between these
two, but the similarity led to a great discovery. Archimedes discovered
his principle concerning the displacement of water and shouted 'Eureka!'
when reclining in his bath. It is, of course, by the observation of similarities that we are enabled to formulate what we call 'the laws of nature',
for these are based on the observed regularity of events in nature; that in
certain sets of circumstances certain other things invariably follow – for
instance, that solids expand when heated, and that ponderous bodies
always fall to the ground, an observation which is summarized in the

Law of Gravity. When we find apparent exceptions to the rule, that enables us to test or 'prove the rule' – a phrase commonly misinterpreted to mean than an exception in some mysterious way goes to prove that a rule is true.

Dreams are animistic

Another characteristic of primitive man as of dreaming is that he is *animistic*, and to him all things material are living – trees, sun, and storms as well as man and animals. In dreams we find this same animistic tendency, so that even ideas are dressed up in human form, and qualities of character are represented by people possessing those qualities. In other words, in dreams our thoughts, feelings, and attitudes of mind are often personalized, being represented by some person, known or imaginary, who has that quality. Thus our anger may be represented by a man we know who is bad-tempered; our sexuality in the form of a loose woman; our intellectual life by a professor; the healing forces within us as the doctor. More imaginatively our rage may be personalized as a fury, sex as a vampire, and our feelings of revenge projected and personalized as a witch. In fairy-tales even trees take on animistic form and animals take on human form and speech, a trend in human nature which Walt Disney has popularized in his excellent cartoons. The delight that old and young have in these films is largely based on this reversion to an animistic mode of thought. His animals are very human, which is only another way of saying that humans are very like animals. Thus dreams are always playing at charades and acting out ideas instead of putting them in the form of spoken words. Harpo Marx of the Marx brothers represents the non-vocal primitive element in human life with its 'all or nothing' characteristics. He never speaks, but if he wants to light a cigarette he produces a blowlamp from his tail pocket!

Dream as a drama

We have come, therefore, to realize that the dream is a drama in which all the actors represented in the dream are parts of oneself. Our personalities have many attributes; we have our kindly side, our arrogant side, our ingratiating side, our lazy side. These are often in conflict, and therefore create problems in the personality which may be reproduced in dreams. Because of the tendency of the human mind to animism, all these aspects of the personality are personalized, and in the dream may be represented by persons, whether of our acquaintance or an imaginary person of that same character, all having an argument or discussion – as they might in a play. In the dream at the beginning of this chapter, the dreamer's own arrogance was represented by his friend who was 'too big for his boots', and whom the patient had to knock out. In the Prometheus dream the woman representing intuition was an imaginary woman who tells him what to do with the negro representing his primitive self. In a dream described earlier, the policeman represented the patient's moral self or super-ego and the tramp his primitive natural self, and the dream worked out his problem by the interplay of these personalities as in a drama.

So the dream represents a drama in which all the people are dramatis personae, representing, as they do on the stage, certain ideas or types of mind, not the people themselves. In a play, a man of self-sufficient character stands for self-sufficiency in the abstract, a priggish man for priggishness, a prostitute for the sensual part of ourselves, a parish priest for consideration for others. These are all characteristics we ourselves possess and the dream presents a drama in which all these characteristics in us are represented by people fighting it out, debating the question, playing out the problem in dramatic form and therefore tending towards a solution. The value of a theatre is that we see ourselves as we see others; in a dream we see ourselves as our subconscious sees us. In treating patients, the technique of psycho-drama, in which the patients play out certain roles, is used for much the same purpose.

As the dream turns thoughts, ideas, and emotions into people representing them, so in our dream interpretation we need to reverse the process and find out what those people stand for and so discover what they stand for in ourselves. This tells us what is the nature of the conflict within our soul and what solution the soul offers.

Let us now look at a dream to illustrate the function of the dream as a drama.

This patient was outwardly a kindly, ingratiating, helpful person, who had had his own personality crushed out of him by a childishly jealous father. Fear of his father, especially when backed by his mother, who felt she must be 'loyal' to the father (and thus did an injustice to the son), made him ingratiating but aloof. His problem was that he wanted affection, but he had had to repress that in favour of a detached and pompous attitude which he had taken over from his father. But this attitude left him without friends and, because of the repression of his aggression, with an inability to work. All his conscious efforts to work and to be sociable were of no effect at all. How does he solve that one? He dreams: 'I was in my house and saw two boys looking through the glass, wanting to come in to see my friend Fred. I did not want to be seen by them, but I realized that I had been seen and so let them in. They were not certain that they would be welcomed by Fred. I let them in and then there was a girl there whom I embraced – it makes me want to cry now in speaking about it – the idea of her tenderness and of my being welcomed.' The interpretation: his shutting himself in the house and not wanting to be seen represented his detached attitude towards people which resulted from his treatment in early childhood. Fred and the girl he embraced are in fact man and wife, an affectionate couple and friends of his. Fred he had regarded as a kind of father, friendly, as he would like his father to have been, but also detached and aloof like his father. Fred therefore represented the aloof side of his personality. The two boys who wanted to be sociable and friendly represented that other part of his personality which wanted to break down his aloofness and be friendly: the 'two' the intensity of his need for friendship. But he was dubious as to whether Fred, his aloof pompous side, would welcome the expression of his need for affection. However, he does open the door and admits the friendly spirit into his personality. Immediately he does this he is overcome with affection as represented by his embracing the girl. Friendship once released immediately develops into love and affection. The girl represents love and the tender side of his nature, something more than sex and more than mere friendliness which is represented by the boys. This tenderness which he had always longed to express is now released, so much so that in speaking of this affection and love in the dream he is filled with emotion. The dream brings together all these sides of his personality and works out in the form of a drama a readjustment of his personality: it shows him throwing off his detached aloof self, admitting friendship in the first place, and thereby releasing the affection and tenderness in his nature which he had so long repressed. Let it be noted that quite irrespective of any interpretation, the effect of the dream was in fact to release this tenderness: 'It makes me want to cry!' he says.

Freud is inclined to stress the more objective interpretation, Jung the subjective. According to a Freudian interpretation, Fred would stand for his father (who is none too friendly) and the woman he embraces, his mother – an Oedipus situation of a sexual incestuous nature embodying a wish-fulfilment. But the patient was in fact alienated from his mother, since she had let him down by agreeing with his father. If the woman were taken to be the mother, the dream then might represent a reconciliation with his mother, a wish-fulfilment of restoration to his mother. A Jungian interpretation might be that the female form is his *anima*, his femininity and tenderness, the suppressed part of his personality, the opposite of his masculine independence and detachment, and the dream would be interpreted as compensatory. From the practical point of view, the upshot is the same – the release of his repressed emotional need for affection.

Thus, by regarding the dream as a drama, and the persons in the dream as the dramatis personae representing characteristics in ourselves, we may discover the nature of our problems, and by watching the actions of the people in this drama we may discover what our subconscious mind suggests as to a solution of our problems.

This is an extract from *Dreams and Nightmares*, first published in 1954. In Chapter IV of this book, on the function of dreams, Hadfield considers the way in which dreams stand for experience and how, through this substitution, they help towards the understanding of a problem. In Chapter VI, on the construction of the dream, he discusses the value of analogy and argues in what sense dreams can be considered as drama.

Sometimes Hadfield's interpretation of dreams seems rather slick, but his outlines help us to see a method being applied. This kind of thinking is an important contribution to our understanding of the subconscious element in acting. It relates to Margaret Lowenfeld's consideration of children's play and is relevant in relation to Moreno's explanation of psycho-drama. Clearly it is important to realize that the last word has not been said on dream interpretation or psycho-drama.

Hadfield makes us aware of several basic concepts. Note particularly:

1. that dreams, like drama, have many functions
2. their value is on an intuitive level, even when the full cognitive significance of the dream drama is not immediately appreciated
3. Hadfield's linking of children's play and folklore
4. the value of pictorialization and personification of our subconscious anxieties and feelings
5. the value of symbol in the understanding and clarification of the

more complex aspects of our living – insight through analogy leading to further discovery

6. the importance of elements which are animistic (it reminds us of Jean-Louis Barrault and E. K. Chambers)

7. the difficulty in interpretation; sometimes it increases its value and application – the act is more expressive than the word

8. that dreams are slightly less valuable than improvisation since the recall is less certain and it is not possible for other people to observe dreams – in improvisation others can assist in examination and analysis.

12 Drama as Therapy
J. L. Moreno

The discovery of aspects of the subconscious, through spontaneous dramatic situations, has been developed by Dr J. L. Moreno in an approach to therapy which he calls 'Psycho-drama'. Here, Dr Moreno explains his own background and the principles and methods of his approach. He indicates the important differences between his group approach, in which the patient acts with others in a theatre, against the psycho-analytical approach developed by Freud, where the patient is alone on the analyst's couch.

Moreno is working with people who are, more or less, deeply disturbed, but his comments about the values and methods of role-playing are just as important for more normal people. His aim is remedial, but some of his methods are easily extended to broader investigation. Dr Moreno himself makes frequent reference to Aristotle's views and indicates how these can be developed, and the way in which catharsis is of value to the actors as well as the auditors. The therapy which takes place through drama is based on a controlled environment. For, as he indicates, it is far better that expression should find its outlet in a laboratory situation where any dangers can be diverted. His statement that 'the function of the role is to enter the unconscious from the social world and bring shape and order into it' could well be applied to dramatic work in any of the approaches we have so far discussed. Drama is a valuable way of gaining further insight into the complex human situation.

Historic background

There were in 1914 in Vienna two antitheses to psychoanalysis; the one was the rebellion of the suppressed group versus the individual; it was the first step beyond psychoanalysis, 'group psychotherapy'. I introduced this particular name to underscore that it concerned itself first of all with a 'therapy' of the group and not merely with sociological or psychological analysis. The other was the rebellion of the suppressed actor against the word. This was the second step beyond psychoanalysis, the 'psychodrama'. In the beginning was existence. In the beginning was the act.

Principle – The merely analytic and verbal method of group psychotherapy very soon led to difficulties.

As long as group psychotherapy was practised only in situ, that is, within the family, the factory, etc., where life is lived, in all dimensions of the present, in action, in thought and speech, as monologue, dialogue, or drama, the psychomotor element of the organism and the creative meaning of the encounter remained unconscious and uninvestigated. When, however, the moment came to move from a natural to a synthetic place – for instance, from the family to the clinic – it was necessary to restructure life in all its dimensions in order to carry out therapy in the actual meaning of the word. All relationships which occur in everyday life had, therefore, to be constructed anew; we had to have a space in which the life of the family could be lived in the same fashion as it occurred in reality as well as symbolically. The bedroom, the kitchen, the garden, the dramatis personae of the family – father, mother, child – the discussions, conflicts, and tensions between them just as they occur in everyday life, all that which is taken for granted and remains unconscious had to be reconstructed but reduced to the truly symbolic elements. What before appeared as problematic and unfortunate became an asset. Group psychotherapy was forced to enter into all dimensions of existence in a depth and breadth which were unknown to the verbally oriented psychotherapist. Group psychotherapy turned into action psychotherapy and psychodrama.

The role concept

One of the most significant concepts in this new theoretical framework is the psychiatric role concept. What we psychodramatists did is (a) to observe the role process within the life context itself; (b) to study it under experimental conditions; (c) to use it as a method of psychotherapy (situation and behaviour therapy); and (d) to examine and train behaviour in the 'here and now' (role training, spontaneity and behaviour training).

The term 'role'

Role, originally an old French word which penetrated into medieval French and English, is derived from the Latin 'rotula'. In Greece and also in ancient Rome, the parts in the theatre were written on 'rolls' and read by the prompters to the actors who tried to memorize their part by heart; this fixation of the word role appears to have been lost in the more illiterate periods of the early and middle centuries of the Dark Ages. It was not until the 16th or 17th centuries, with the emergence of the modern stage, that the parts of the theatrical characters were read from 'roles' or paper fascicles. In this manner each scenic 'part' becomes a role.

Role is thus not by origin a sociological or psychiatric concept; it came into the scientific vocabulary via the drama. It is often overlooked that modern role theory had its logical origin and its perspectives in the drama. It has a long history and tradition in the European theatre from which I gradually developed the therapeutic and social direction of our time. I brought it to the U.S.A. in the middle twenties. From the roles and counter-roles, the role situations and role conserves developed naturally their modern extensions: role player, role playing, role expectation, acting out, and finally, psychodrama and sociodrama . . .

Definition and constructs of the role

The role concept cuts across the sciences of man, physiology, psychology, anthropology and binds them together on a new plane. The theory of roles is not limited to a single dimension, the social. The psychodramatic role theory, operating with a psychiatric orientation, is more inclusive. It carries the concept of role through all dimensions of life; it begins at birth and continues throughout the lifetime of the individual and the socius. It has constructed models in which the role begins to transact from birth on. We cannot start with the role process at the moment of language development, but in order to be consistent, we must carry it through the non-verbal phases of living. Therefore, role theory cannot be limited to social roles, it must include the three dimensions – social roles, expressing the social dimension; psychosomatic roles, expressing the physiological dimension; and psychodramatic roles, expressing the psychological dimension of the self.

Function of the role

'The function of the role is to enter the unconscious from the social world and bring shape and order into it.' The relationship of roles to the situations in which the individual operates (status) and the relation of role as significantly related to ego has been emphasized by myself.

Everybody is expected to live up to his official role in life, a teacher is to act as a teacher, a pupil as a pupil, and so forth. But the individual craves to embody far more roles than those he is allowed to act out in life, and even within the same role one or more varieties of it. Every individual is filled with different roles in which he wants to become active and that are present in him in different stages of development. It is from the active pressure which these multiple individual units exert upon the manifest official role that a feeling of anxiety is often produced.

Every individual – just as he has at all times a set of friends and a set of enemies – has a range of roles in which he sees himself and faces a range of counter-roles in which he sees others around him. They are in various stages of development. The tangible aspects of what is known as 'ego' are the roles in which he operates, with the pattern of role-relations around an individual as their focus. We consider roles and relationships between roles as the most significant development within any specific culture.

Role is the unit of culture; ego and role are in continuous interaction.

Role playing, role perception and role enactment

Role perception is cognitive and anticipates forthcoming responses. Role enactment is a skill of performance. A high degree of role perception can be accompanied by a low skill for role enactment and vice versa. Role playing is a function of both role perception and role enactment. Role training in contrast to role playing is an effort through the rehearsal of roles, to perform adequately in future situations.

Fundamental rules

Psychodrama was introduced in the United States in 1925, and since then a number of clinical methods have developed – the therapeutic psychodrama, the sociodrama, the axiodrama, role playing, the analytic psychodrama and various modifications of them.

The chief participants in a therapeutic psychodrama are the protagonist, or subject; the director, or chief therapist; the auxiliary egos; and the group. The protagonist presents either a private or a group problem; the auxiliary egos help him to bring his personal and collective drama to life and to correct it. Meaningful psychological experiences of the protagonist are given shape more thoroughly and more completely than life would permit under normal circumstances. A psychodrama can be produced anywhere, wherever patients find themselves, in a private home, a hospital, a schoolroom, or a military barracks. It sets up its 'laboratory' everywhere. Most advantageous is a specially adapted therapeutic space containing a stage. Psychodrama is either protagonist-centred (the private problem of the protagonist) or group-centred (the problem of the group). In general, it is important that the theme, whether it is private or collective, be a truly experienced problem of the participants (real or symbolic). The participants should represent their experiences spontaneously, although the repetition of a theme can frequently be of therapeutic advantage. Next to the protagonist, the auxiliary egos and the chief therapist play an important part. It is their responsibility to bring the therapeutic productivity of the group to as high a level as possible.

The protagonist, in order to get into the production, must be motivated consciously or unconsciously. The motive may be, among other things, self-realization, relief from mental anguish, ability to function in a social group. He is frustrated, let us say, in the role of father or any other role in life itself, and he enjoys the feeling of mastery and realization by means of psychodrama which gives him symbolic satisfaction.

Resistance

The term resistance is used here in an operational sense. It means merely that the protagonist does not want to participate in the production. How to overcome his initial resistance is a challenge for the therapist's skill.

He may send an auxiliary ego to play the 'double' of the protagonist. The double usually places himself back of the patient and begins to soliloquize. He gets the protagonist to participate in the soliloquy and perhaps to admit the hidden reasons he has for refusal. This technique is a 'soliloquy-double technique'.

The chief therapist himself may use another technique – the 'soliloquy technique of the therapist'. He may sit on the side of the stage and begin to soliloquize about as follows: 'I know that Jack (the patient) doesn't like me. I don't see what other reason he would have for not co-operating.' The patient might fall in with this and say, 'It isn't you I don't like. It is this woman in the front row. She reminds me of my aunt.'

Another method is to let the patient (A) step back into the group and start with another patient (B) and then call patient A back to be an auxiliary ego in any episode to B, for instance acting as his father, a policeman or a doctor. This is the 'patient's auxiliary ego technique'. A, who did not want to present his own problems, may be willing to help another member of the group present his.

A further method of breaking resistance is the 'symbolic technique' starting on a symbolic production so that fear of private involvement is eliminated as a cause of resistance. The director addresses the group thus: 'There is a conflict between husband and wife because of certain irregularities in the behaviour of the husband. He may be a gambler, a drunk, or whatever. They have an only child, a son, who is uncertain on whose side he should be.' At this point the director turns towards the group and asks, 'Who wants to take the part of the husband, of the wife, or of the son?' These roles being non-committal of the private lives of the members of the group, the director may more easily provoke some of them to participate.

Another 'resistance remover' is the use of significant relations existing between members of the group. The director, for instance, knows that there is a rivalry between two individuals, A and B. He may invite them to fight it out on the stage: 'Let the group evaluate who is fair and who is unfair.'

Another method is to utilize 'leader tensions' or 'ethnic hostilities', for instance, of refugees versus Americans, Puerto Ricans versus the Negroes in the group.

An effective technique to break resistance is to use comical themes or caricatures in order to arouse the sense of humour of the members.

Last but not least, particular attention should be given to resistance which is directed against the 'private' personalities of the chief therapist or of the auxiliary egos. In such cases, the therapist or auxiliary egos may have to be replaced, and it may even be necessary to restructure the group itself so as to meet the needs of the patient.

It is up to the resourcefulness of the director to find clues to get the production started and, once it is started, to see that it grows further along constructive lines. The causes for patient's resistance may thus be summarized as being private, social, or symbolic.

Therapeutic, controlled acting out

The psychodramatist argues as follows: 'Why not let him act out these hidden thoughts and strivings as an alternate to an "analysis" of his resistance?' The patient on the couch, for instance, may be a woman who suddenly has an urge to get up and dance, or talk to her husband whom she suspects of being disloyal to her, or, ridden by a feeling of guilt, she may want to kneel down and say a prayer. If these activities are forbidden to the patient, certain elements which are upsetting him do not come to the fore and cannot be explained and treated. But if the patient knows that the acting of his hidden thoughts and strivings is tolerated by the therapist, he will display them. The therapist, in turn, will be able to utilize the forthcoming material to the advantage of the patient. If, for instance, the patient plans a suicidal attempt the next day, and if he is permitted to portray this attempt within the framework of a therapeutic session, the therapist may prevent the acting out in life itself. But if he makes non-acting out a rule, the patient may kill himself the next day, and so he may not return to the next psychoanalytic hour, except in the form of an obituary note from the relatives. If acting out does take place during the session, and if the episode is not properly carried out by the therapist, this, of course, also can be harmful to the patient. So the crux of the matter is that acting out be tolerated and allowed to take place within a setting which is safe for execution and under the guidance of therapists who are able to utilize the experience.

The whole problem of non-involvement goes back to the original attitude of many of the early psychoanalysts – fear of direct love or direct hostility, their fear of acting out of the patients towards them and their own acting out towards the patients. The confusion here is particularly increased by the different meanings of the term 'acting out'. When I introduced this term (1928) it meant acting that out which is within the patient, in contrast to acting a role which is assigned to a patient by an outsider. It did not mean that they should not be acted out because they camouflage a form of resistance of the patient (psychoanalytic view). I meant just the opposite – that they should be acted out because they may represent important inner experiences of the patient which otherwise remain camouflaged and difficult if not impossible to interpret. In psychodramatic thinking, acting from within, or acting out, is a necessary phase in the progress of therapy; it gives the therapist an opportunity to evaluate the behaviour of the patient and gives the patient a chance to evaluate it for himself (action insight).

But if natural behaviour is persistently prohibited, the psychodramatic effort is in danger of deteriorating to a game of words, a parlour game without feeling and with reduced therapeutic value. In order to overcome the semantic confusion, I suggested that we differentiate two types of acting out: irrational, incalculable acting out in life itself, harmful to the patient or others, and therapeutic, controlled acting out taking place within the treatment setting. An illustration of therapeutic, controlled acting out is in the following Magic Shop Technique. The director sets up on the stage a 'Magic Shop'. Either he himself or a member of the group selected by him, takes the part of the Shopkeeper. The shop is filled with imaginary items, values of a non-physical nature. These are not for sale, but they can be obtained by barter, in exchange for other values to be surrendered by the members of the group, either individually or as a group. One after another, the members of the group volunteer to come upon the stage, entering the shop in quest of an idea, a dream, a hope, an ambition. They are expected to come only if they feel a strong desire to obtain a value which they cherish highly or without which their life seems worthless. An illustration follows: A depressive patient, who was admitted in the course of 1948 after a suicidal attempt, came to the Magic Shop requesting 'Peace of Mind'. The shopkeeper, Justus Randolph, a sensitive young therapist, asked her, 'What do you want to give in return? You know we cannot give you anything without your willingness to sacrifice something else.' 'What do you want?' the patient asked. 'There is something for which many people who come to this shop long', he replied, 'fertility, the ability and willingness to bear children. Do you want to give this up?' 'No, that is too high a price to pay, then I do not want peace of mind.' With this she walked off the stage and returned to her seat. The shopkeeper had hit a sensitive spot. Maria, the protagonist, was engaged but she refused to get married because of deep-seated fear of sex and childbirth. Her fantasy pre-occupations involved images of violent suffering, torture, death, etc., in the act of childbirth.

Spontaneity

My operational definition of spontaneity is often quoted as follows: The protagonist is challenged to respond with some degree of adequacy to a new situation or with some degree of novelty to an old situation. When the stage actor finds himself without a role conserve, the religious actor without a ritual conserve, they have to 'ad lib', to turn to experiences which are not performed and readymade, but are still buried within them in an unformed stage. In order to mobilize and shape them, they need a transformer and catalyst, a kind of intelligence which operates here and now, hic et nunc, 'spontaneity'. Mental healing processes require spontaneity in order to be effective. The technique of free association, for instance, involves spontaneous acting of the individual, although it is restricted to speaking out whatever goes through his mind. What is working here is not only the association of words but the spontaneity which propels them to associate. The larger the volume of word association is, the more significant and more spontaneous is its production. Other conditions being equal, this is true of all other methods designed to assist in mental cures. In psychodrama particularly, spontaneity operates not only in the dimension of words but in all other dimensions of expression, such as acting, interacting, speaking, dancing, singing, and drawing. It was an important advance to link spontaneity to creativity, the highest form of intelligence we know of, and to recognize them as the primary forces in human behaviour. The dynamic role which spontaneity plays in psychodrama as well as in every form of psychotherapy should not imply, however, that the development and presence of spontaneity in itself is the 'cure'. There are forms of pathological spontaneity which distort perceptions, dissociate the enactment of roles, and interfere with the integration on the various levels of living.

Catharsis

Catharsis, as a concept, was introduced by Aristotle. He used this term to express the peculiar effect of the Greek drama upon its spectators. In his Poetics, he maintains that drama tends to purify the spectators by artistically exciting certain emotions which act as a kind of relief from their own selfish passions.

The concept of catharsis has undergone a revolutionary change once systematic psychodramatic work began in Vienna in 1919. This change has been exemplified by the movement away from the written (conserved) drama and toward the spontaneous (psycho) drama, with the emphasis shifted from the spectators to the actors.

In my treatise, the Spontaneity Theatre (Das Stegreiftheater), published in 1923, the new definition of catharsis was: 'It (the psychodrama) produces a healing effect – not in the spectator (secondary catharsis) but in the producer-actors who produce the drama and, at the same time, liberate themselves from it.'

There have been two avenues which led to the psychodramatic view of mental catharsis. The one avenue led from the Greek drama to the conventional drama of today and with it went the universal acceptance of the Aristotelian concept of catharsis. The other avenue led from the religions of the East and the Near East. These religions held that a saint, in order to become a saviour, had to make an effort; he had, first, to actualize and save himself. In other words, in the Greek situation the process of mental catharsis was conceived as being localized in the spectator – a passive catharsis. In the religious situation the process of catharsis was localized in the actor, his actual life becoming the stage. This was an active catharsis. In the Greek concept the process of realization of a role took place in an object, in a symbolic person on the stage. In the religious concept the process of realization took place in the subject – the living person who was seeking catharsis. One might say that passive catharsis, is here face to face with active catharsis; aesthetic catharsis with ethical catharsis. These two developments, which heretofore have moved along independent paths, have been brought to a synthesis by the psychodramatic concept of catharsis. From the ancient Greeks we have retained the drama and the stage, from the Hebrews we have accepted the catharsis of the actor. The spectator has become an actor himself.

Mental catharsis cannot be always attained on the reality level, to meet all the situations and relationships in which there may exist some causes for disequilibrium. But it has to be applied concretely and specifically in order to be effective. The problem has been, therefore, to find a medium which can take care of the disequilibrating phenomena in the most realistic fashion, but still outside of reality; a medium which includes a realization as well as a catharsis for the body; a medium which makes catharsis possible on the level of speech; a medium which prepares the way for catharsis not only within an individual but also between two, three, or as many individuals as are interlocked in a life-situation; a medium which opens up for catharsis the world of phantasies and unreal roles and relationships. To all these and many other problems, an answer has been found in one of the oldest inventions of man's creative mind – the drama.

The Director

From the point of view of production, the significant relation between psychodrama and the dream has been often emphasized. Lewis Mumford said on one occasion, 'Psychodrama is the essence of the dream.' It is correct that in both cases we deal often with fantastic productions in which the protagonist is profoundly involved; just as in a dream, so a psychodrama appears to be an exposition of unconscious dynamics. But it may be appropriate to point out some fundamental differences. The characters in a dream are hallucinated phantoms. They exist only in the dreamer's mind, and they vanish as soon as the dream is over. But the characters in a psychodrama are real people. The dreamer can go on dreaming the most fantastic things without any resistance from his dream characters, his dream characters and the whole plot being his own production. In a psychodrama, however, the auxiliary egos playing roles frequently resist the reveries of the protagonist, they talk back and fight back and modify the course of the plot, if necessary. There is counter-resistance, one may say, propelled toward the protagonist from all sides. They may for exploratory and therapeutic reasons 'interpolate' resistance of all sorts, contrary to the protagonist's design. The protagonist in a psychodrama is never as alone as the nocturnal dreamer. Without the counterforces which the auxiliary egos and the members of the group inject, the opportunities for the protagonist to learn would be very much reduced.

The general rule of directing is to depend chiefly upon the protagonists to provide the clues as to how to carry on the production. The first clue of a hallucinating patient may be: 'I hear my father screaming.'

Th: 'Where does the voice come from?'
P: 'It comes from behind the wall.'
Th: 'Is your father alone?'

P: 'No, he is with my mother, they are fighting.'

A clue may be or may not be found, but if it is, then the episode is acted out.

The director instructs two auxiliary egos to experiment with the portrayal of father and mother and the conflict between them.

The father sits down.

'No', the protagonist protests, 'He is not sitting, he is walking up and down.'

P: 'No, he doesn't hold his head up. He coughs and spits like this.'

He tries to show the auxiliary ego how.

The protagonist may ask over and over for new modifications; if he protests too much he may be asked to take the part of the father himself. Now he gives 'his own interpretation' of the hallucinated father as he perceives him. Here we notice that 'straight' role playing can be insufficient, and we see why psychodramatic techniques need to be introduced. It is (1) to get the protagonist into deeper action by involving him more in his own experience, and (2) to make his hallucinations become more tangible either through his own enactment of them or by an auxiliary ego's enactment. Our hypothesis is that if such experiments are made at the time when hallucinations are active, controls are interpolated in the patient's mind, conditioning barriers, which become particularly important as a reservoir of preventive measure in case of later relapses. If he should have a relapse, the previous episodes of similar hallucinations will return to him associated to 'controls', not as much in his memory as in his behaviour, and these preventives will return with them and reduce the violence of the new attack.

The patient may, of course, use even psychodrama itself as a means of resistance. But the psychodrama director has the opportunity to intervene with various techniques so as to hinder the protagonist from 'not playing the game' and using the psychodramatic situation itself as a screen for non-co-operation.

Conclusions

Behaviouristic schools have been limited to observing and experimenting with 'external' behaviour of individuals, leaving out major portions of the subjective. Many psychological methods, such as psychoanalysis, Rorschach, and TAT, went to the other extreme, focusing on the subjective but limiting the study of direct behaviour to a minimum and resorting to the use of elaborate systems of symbolic interpretation. The psychodramatic method brings these two extremes to a new synthesis. It is so designed that it can explore and treat immediate behaviour in all its dimensions.

Because we cannot reach into the mind and see what the individual perceives and feels, psychodrama tries, with the co-operation of the patient, to transfer the mind 'outside' of the individual and objectify it within a tangible, controllable universe. It may go the whole way in the process of structuring the world of the patient up to the threshold of tolerance, penetrating and surpassing reality ('surplus' reality), and may insist upon the most minute details of episodes in physical, mental, and social space to be explored. Its aim is to make total behaviour directly visible, observable, and measurable. The protagonist is being prepared for an encounter with himself. After this phase of objectification is completed, the second phase begins; it is to resubjectify, reorganize, and reintegrate that which has been objectified. (In practice, however, both phases go hand in hand.)

The psychodramatic method rests upon the hypothesis that, in order to provide patients, singly or in groups, with a new opportunity for a psychodynamic and sociocultural reintegration, 'therapeutic cultures in miniature' are required, in lieu or in extension of unsatisfactory natural habitats. Vehicles for carrying out this project are (1) existential psychodrama within the framework of community life itself, in situ, and (2) in neutral, objective, and flexible therapeutic theatre. The latter represents the laboratory method in contrast to the method of nature, and, is structured to meet the sociocultural needs of the protagonist.

This extract is from the introductory section of Moreno's book *Psycho-Drama, I* which was first published in 1946.

Doctor Moreno is a little pre-occupied with his own desire to establish himself as the father of this approach to psychology and drama. Nevertheless, his discussion is fascinating in the way in which it links Aristotle's work with present psychological approaches.

It seems especially relevant in that:
1. Moreno points out that psycho-drama is an acting out in imaginative and controllable situations rather than in a reality
2. he suggests drama for a restructuring and reordering of situations
3. drama is an involvement in activity rather than a passivity
4. it is purposeful

5. he indicates some of the values of the techniques as well as the dangers
6. it is a means of linking the sciences and sociology, philosophy and psychology
7. Moreno claims that 'role is the unit of culture'
8. it is easy to see the relationship between this and Hadfield's work; there are important similarities and important differences
9. drama is a laboratory where situations can be controlled and spontaneity developed to the point of creativity.

SECTION FIVE

Search for Drama in Education

13 **Drama as Playmaking**
Caldwell Cook

Before the First World War, Henry Caldwell Cook published his book *The Play Way*. As a young, idealistic graduate from Oxford, Cook was given a post as a teacher of English at the Perse School in Cambridge, under the headmastership of A. L. Rowse. Dr Rowse gave him plenty of scope and encouraged him in developing The Mummery, a large room rebuilt on the principles of the Elizabethan theatre, where the boys could act out their own improvised plays based on poetic narrative and dramatic literature. Caldwell Cook had to find his own way; or rather, he responded to the youngsters in his classes, who helped him to discover an activity method which gave enough freedom and discipline for them to extend their range and powers of expression.

At the outset of his book, he makes his position clear:

'The natural means of study in youth is play, as any one may see for himself by watching any child or young animal when it is left alone. A natural education is by practice, by doing things, and not by instruction, the hearing how, as you may see in the flight of a young bird. And telling can only be the servant of trying, not its substitute. Certainly preliminary advice and warning might save us from many a sore trial, but we rarely profit by any experience other than our own. The burnt child dreads the fire, but the child that has only been warned is still to be burnt. Therefore wild oats are more approved by men of the world than moral lectures. But instead of leaving a child to gain wisdom by painful as well as pleasant experience, it is well to let him try as much as he can for himself under guidance. It would not be wise to send a child innocent into the big world; and talking is of poor avail. But it is possible to hold rehearsals, to try our strength in a make-believe big world. And that is Play.'

His book is a record of much of the work that he did with the boys at the Perse School. He was a teacher of English, who discovered that the dramatic approach was one of the liveliest and most helpful to those he taught and when he writes about his experiments, he sees his work and approach as having implications for the whole of education. His style and some of his attitudes belong to the period of his writing, but a remarkable amount of what he has to say is still in, and even ahead of, the stream of educational thought today. While he emphasizes the literary value of the dramatic work, he is well aware also of the personal values the drama has for those taking part.

It is, I think, a mistake to encourage boys to invent the story and characters for themselves. They will be too apt to lay the scene in the cellar of a London bank, or in a Wild West cañon, or in the boarding house of a public school; and to choose for their protagonist a detective or a bushranger, or one of those caricatures of boyhood who strut and fret their hour in magazines written for schoolboys, and then are heard no more. This side of the boys' interests should not by any means be neglected in school-work. But we have always found place for the crude expression of this youthful taste in preliminary exercises, and in 'asides' from the main business. In the oral exercises, for instance, with which our study of prose composition began – soliloquy, description, narrative, and dialogue – the boys were not only permitted but encouraged to choose subjects which had an immediate interest for them. There were at first no restrictions. The main purpose was that the boys should exercise themselves in 'oral composition' of some kind, until they should become ready speakers. Early practice was not hampered by an exacting literary taste; nor was self-expression at first conditioned by the quest of 'art forms'. But after a time the boys came to feel the inadequacy and superficiality of their exercises based upon the commonplace. They were then easily persuaded to use craft in selection and condensation. They began with some feeling to say things with an artistic intention, and to express where before they had been content to describe. The soliloquy of a man in a dentist's chair, or the description of a crowded railway station, were all very well as first exercises; but these preliminaries were succeeded by prose studies which had the merit of style. . . .

The same course should be followed in playmaking. Boys should not be plunged at once into the deeps of an expressive art without some preliminary paddling on the margin. A boy's desire to try his hand at some new thing without tiresome direction (expressed in the words 'Let's have a go!') may be allowed free play before sober and studious business is put under way.

'Let's have a go!' is the right spirit in which to undertake any enterprise of play. It is far more healthy for the beginner that he learn his earliest adjustments of balance empirically at the risk of (and better still at the cost of) a few real sprawls upon the hard ice, than that he sit secure and idle, and admire the evolutions of his skilled instructor.

After a series of preliminary exercises, a few free kicks, a few nasty sprawls, the pupil returns to his master – ready now for the instruction to begin. But not, I hope, at all apologetic for having adventured on his own account, tried his hand at the new instrument – had, in fact, his 'go'. For it would be a grave mistake for a teacher (in the arts at all events) to fancy that the pupil's venture had only served to convince him of the supreme necessity of reliance upon his instructor. The pupil has certainly found the need of a teacher, but he has also discovered many another thing of value. He has discovered not only difficulties but potentialities, not only the need of instruction but a consuming desire for it.

When an important play is afoot, the experiment of inventing your plot is so difficult and attended with so much risk of disaster that it is wiser to follow the example of Chaucer, Spenser, Shakespeare, Milton, and all our other great poets, and found your story upon the firm rock of some traditional tale. . . .

Having borrowed their story, take what you have need of, and set aside the rest. You may add, divide, and multiply. But you must start by borrowing. The creative skill of the stealers and their choice in theft are the test of their Promethean virtue.

In taking an existing tale as the story of their play, the boys will find that they have in hand a core of substance. Persons and events exist already; characterization and plot, those twin deities of the drama, have been wed together in the tale for perhaps five hundred, perhaps two thousand years; and in making their play, with what additions and modifications soever, the boys are but making one more version of a tale that has outlived, or rather lived through, a thousand versions. The tale has been bandied about until nothing but the essentials (and perhaps a few of the latest accretions) remain. On the other hand, a new plot, conceived yesterday, and thrown down today into the ring to be wrought upon by a group of urgent playmakers, each anxious to have his say, each eager to insist upon this modification or that, will be knocked to pieces in an hour or two. It has no essential being, no core.

The sources of tales fit for playmaking are inexhaustible, for we have all the treasury of mythology and all the fairy tales and folk legends to draw upon. The teacher's taste, knowledge, and experience are naturally of great weight in the selection; and a group of boys under one master will show a preference for a certain type of story which the pupils of another master will find quite foreign to their taste. A man gifted with an appreciation of Hindu mythology could easily engage the interest of his boys in the exploits of Krishna and tales from the Mahabharata. The Egyptian Book of the Dead, also, would make a great morality play. But, since the making of a play demands the close and careful work of the boys for a considerable length of time, it is wiser to associate the subject with some of their regular school studies, in Greek, Latin, French, or English literature, and in history.

A play should be in hand for at least a term, and it will do nothing but good to keep it building throughout the school year. The historical period in which the play is set is of importance in a hundred ways. It may either be determined by the courses of history and literature going on at the time; or, if it is done on a large enough scale, and time can be found for good reading in many books, the playmaking circle might include in itself the study of the history and literature of the period. . . .

The Bible has always been one of the great sources of inspiration in English literature; and many of the stories in the Old Testament make excellent material for playmaking. In the style of the Bible narrative the boys would have before them the very purest and most beautiful of English prose.

There are two points I should like to make with regard to style. One is that boys cannot do any satisfactory work in connection with style, in the more restricted sense, before the age of fourteen or thereabouts; and the other point is that the quest of style in the wider sense of the term may begin in mere child's-play, for it includes many diverse activities. Style is not all book-study.

First, then, consider the possibilities of imitation. A boy must read the masterpieces of literature, some very thoroughly and some very often. Then he may take some distinctive styles and deliberately set himself to write in imitation. But he must take them one at a time and, during the period of this practice, must scrupulously avoid mixing the characteristic elements of one style with those of another. Bible English is in a style which any boy can recognize whenever he hears it. He must, then, school himself to write in this style until his fellows on hearing him read his exercise can say, 'That is like nothing but the Bible'. Style is to be learnt, if at all, by example and experiment rather than by rule and prescription.

The method of 'learning Shakespeare' through acting the plays instead of only through a reading and discussion of them, and the method of performing parts in history and of declaiming orations, especially if due attention is given by the master to the clear enunciation of words and to the free and open delivery of the speeches, will do much to foster the pupil's appreciation. . . .

With his acting of Shakespeare goes miming, to the furtherance of free movement and expressive gesture. For we English, as Milton would say, dare not take our hands out of our pockets in the cold air, and are 'exceeding close and inward' with all our movements. At this time also comes his chief practice in playmaking, for the fuller understanding of Shakespeare's dramatic craftsmanship. At this time his writing may still be good by chance, through natural genius and childish inspiration; but it can scarcely yet be good through conscious art, for his sense of style as it may be learned is only beginning here. He will sometimes strive after effect, and produce many monstrosities, the correction of which must chiefly be looked for in his close imitation of the best writers.

At this age (which more or less begins the age of puberty) it is necessary for his bodily welfare, no less than for the perfection of his mind, that his schooling should be as much as possible in active pursuits and bodily exercises in the open air; and as little as possible indoors, sitting still, or in long-continued reading. Therefore, this age is the fittest time for the making and acting of plays, especially those of a martial and heroic character, and for dancing. At this age also he first begins to understand music, and his taste can be formed to know and partly to appreciate what is good, through glees and madrigals, processional chants, folk-songs, choir-singing, and playing some instrument. In all this he can take part. But he should also hear much good music performed by an orchestra, and on the organ, in school and out.

In school the first step in playmaking is to find your story and to have it read and told, and reread and retold, until it is thoroughly familiar to everyone who is to take a share in the playmaking. Discussion then follows. It is impossible to lay down any rule respecting the order in which the various matters should be taken, or the method in which the discussion should be conducted. I have found the system very successful which at this juncture frankly admits 'The debate is now open to the House'. A whole lesson at a time can profitably be given up to an informal discussion and exchange of views among the boys. Many talk at the same time. There is, so far as I can see, no reason why six or seven persons should not be speaking their views all at once, provided that it is not necessary for every one to hear every speaker. There is so much to be said that the boys soon split up into little groups according as their chief interest lies in the adaptation of the story, or the working out of the characters, or the allotment of the parts, or the staging, or the provision of make-shift costume and properties, or the actual writing of provisional parts in the form of notes giving cues and a rough suggestion of the dialogue. The class at this stage of the playmaking has in fact resolved itself into a number of sub-committees 'sitting' all in the same room. That is why there is such a noise. I have seen whole lesson-whiles devoted to this busy argument.

There is merry laughter, some scolding, and much debate. Several boys are walking about; a few perhaps are illustrating to one another on the platform a bout or a death or a method of harangue or of capture – doing it in action as they will do it before the duke. One perhaps sketches a plan on the blackboard. Some sit in the desks while others stand before them or lean over their shoulders. They are gathered in working groups, putting their brown heads together for the making of their play; and the room is full of an industrious chatter. A visitor entering suddenly might fancy that he had come by mistake into a classroom of the old school in the absence of the master; for the noise of allowed play sounds at first just like the noise of disorder. But if you listen you will find that it is articulate. The master is present, and is perfectly satisfied with the discipline. He visits the groups in turn at their requirement, and spends his advice according to need; though he might easily find enough of interest and value to occupy him in one sub-committee throughout the period.

The next stage in the playmaking is the preparation of notes by the boys, partly in school during this informal discussion, but chiefly as a series of homework in the evening. These notes represent, as it were, the 'finding' of each member of a sub-committee. Those who have been working upon the adaptation of the story will draw up as homework an outline of the scenes, such as I have given for the dramatization of Bible stories in the earlier pages of this chapter. Those who have given their chief attention to the characters will sketch out the part of some principal person, or make a little study of the place to be filled by a number of minor parts. Others will actually write parts for the principals in the chief scenes, giving them all their cues, all the stage-directions, and the openings of their most important speeches.

In order to follow out as far as possible the craftsmanship of Shakespeare it will be advisable for the boys to jot down on their parts, either beforehand in preparation or during the early rehearsals before the play is actually written, all the stage directions, all the important movements they have to make, and all the properties required at certain junctures. Then when the play is finally written the makers will, as far as possible, mention or allude to these things actually in the lines to be spoken. Some reader may overlook the importance of this suggestion. But the embodiment of all the action and the material in the words written to be spoken is an essential part of playmaking on this system. It is one of the chief characteristics of workmanship which – to make all clear in a verbal quibble – distinguishes the playwright from the playwriter.

With young folk under fifteen you must at this point begin to act your play if you wish to get any life into the composition. Of course it is an amorphous thing at this time. The speeches are partly read from notes and partly composed impromptu on the spur of utterance. The action is interrupted from time to time by the onlooking playmakers, by the master, and by the actors themselves. The understanding is that during the early composition rehearsals there may be as many interruptions as are necessary. If the matter of inquiry or suggestion can be settled at the moment, by adoption or rejection, it is so settled; but if it should involve longer discussion or repeated trial, or elaborate changes, or much re-casting and rewriting of what is already done, the matter is postponed to a later and special discussion period.

Those chosen to act the amorphous play in the composition rehearsals may not be the ones who will eventually play the parts. But it is of course a good plan to settle as soon as possible upon the actual cast, because once you have a player before you in actual being you can build your created character to fit him; or he and his part can grow up together in the making. This suggestion may surprise some reader who has always regarded characters in a play as the absolute creations of the artist's invention. But just as a character when played gains or loses by the individual interpretation of the actor, so may a character in the making be modified, shaped, and influenced by reference and approximation to a living model.

After the acting there is more discussion, and after the discussion more acting. And all the time there is many a child among you taking notes, and busily thinking out the speeches, and fashioning his draft lines. The purpose of acting the play from the very first is that the boys may see the story in rough dramatic form. Then they can trim it and shape it, and finally write it. The discussions are of two kinds – first, the informal exchange of ideas among the boys, and secondly, the lessons of the master; in the course of which the boys – as in lessons everywhere – may ask for information or raise difficult points for discussion.

The master in these lessons can teach the rules and proprieties of the art of dramatic poetry so far as suits the age of his boys. They should have notebooks and write down what they learn about action, construction, characterization, and diction, with a multitude of examples, for a rule is both understood and remembered best in an example. Even boys of ten could be taught to understand and to observe many rules and proprieties which the modern playwriters of London would be the better for knowing. At first the things taught will be simply practical, such as the way of making your play to suit a given stage, the use of the traverse, advice about exits and entrances, about light and dark, about crowds, processions, 'business', and so on. Later on the boys will be taught the meaning and force of certain literary and dramatic conventions, the distinction of styles, the power of tradition. But the teacher should never be so engrossed in his lecturing as to forget 'the play's the thing'.

It would be dangerous to draw up any scheme of playmaking lest any one should be tempted to stick to the letter of it. So a mere list shall be given here of the activities of boys and master which result in a finished play:

   i.   Reading and telling of the story.
   ii.   Informal discussion.
   iii.   Sub-committee stage.
   iv.   Preparation of rough notes.
   v.   Acting in the rough.
   vi.   Master's lessons.
   vii.   Discussion of special points.
   viii.   Careful fashioning, shaping and writing.
   ix.   Careful acting, as in rehearsal.
   x.   Final revision of text of speeches.
   xi.   Performance with all due ceremony.

The sub-committees really exist throughout the playmaking, for there will always be groups of boys interested in one branch of the work more than in another, and more able than the other boys to do the work connected with it. Thus there are the plot-managers, the actors, the poets, the producers, the craftsmen, and so on. But one boy may fill several of these functions. Sub-committees should not be formally appointed, for this would lead to specializing, and specializing is not desirable here.

Words for the songs in the plays should be composed by the boys. The music can be borrowed from the folk-song collections, where there are scores of melodies grave and gay. If the master is himself a musician he can compose simple settings for boys' voices. But it will be best of all if he can teach the boys to compose their own music. There is all too little music in English schools. For simple and beautiful dances there could be nothing better than the country dances deciphered by Mr Cecil Sharp from Playford's English Dancing Master (1650) and taught by The English Folk Dance Society. Our playboys have danced many of these and also the Morris and sword dances. But boys cannot do the country dances without girls. If you haven't any girls you must borrow some, as we did.

Poetry for me has never been a thing set apart from everyday life and work. Those teachers who make it their business to treat literature only as a thing to be studied, and never new-made; as some framed thing by a great master, hung up for the pupil to appreciate; who feel that literature has a place only in the lecture-room and the library, and is to be approached only in the fit attire of a scholar's cap and gown in the daytime or in a dressing-gown and slippers at night – such men will be shocked at this rude and unscholarly way we have of associating literature with things done and things still to do; this shirt-sleeve manner of approach, that will read the best books, not only by the quiet lamp on a study table, but also by the guttering candlelight of the tiring-house. There is yet another possible light in which to read literature. It is the too often misleading will-o'-the-wisp lantern borne hither and thither by that lover of the preposterous, Robin Goodfellow, a knave to all night wanderers, but the very darling of simple folk, and a familiar of the fairy king himself.

The clear distinction between our view and that of our scholarly friends is that, while they are content to study literature we aspire to make it. According to the spirit of the Play Way, poetry should be, as it were, an occupation song, at once the inspiration, the accompaniment, and the finest expression of play. When our drama has been wrought then it may be written. And the same is true of our national history. For those of us who have been present throughout the whole process of playmaking, the shirtsleeve period is so intimately a part of the work that we cannot truly say afterwards whether we love more the literary achievement of our work in the finished book of the words, or the piece of our life which is embodied in those words; the flavour of old play which they hold, the recollection of our doings and dealings behind the scenes, and of the traffic of the stage at rehearsals.

The playboys are quite at ease upon the stage. In fact one is at pains during the last rehearsals (in preparation for a public performance) to school them not to break away from their divine parts whenever it occurs to them to make some comment or inquiry – to ask or suggest 'Wouldn't it be better if I did so-and-so?' After a term or so of active playmaking it would even at times be difficult for me to say for certain when a boy was speaking in character and when he was speaking in his own person, for the little tricks and ways of a lad get into his part, and the feelings and sayings proper to a part grow to the lad. There are also whimsical ways of quoting, and current tags of speech, and even a sort of communal manner of thought which always grows up in a company of close friends. After a while it is not possible to be definitely sure whether you are in the play or not, whether the figure that accosts you in the tiring-house is speaking in propria persona or trying on you, to see what you think of it, an addition to his part which occurred to him but now on the stage. I do not mean that such a blend of boy and part, of player and character, is possible under any conditions of 'school theatricals'! No. It is a consummation devoutly to be wished, but one which is only attainable when you as a company are making your own play, when the master knows his boys almost as well as their parents know them, and when everyone can feel that his fellow's heart is in the work even as his own. The playmaster at the centre of such a play activity finds himself in a whirl of the real, the make-believe, the conventional, and the humorous elements – and even if he could disintegrate them, he would not know which he best appreciated.

I would appeal for a very high standard to be set in all playmaking. We should be earnest and serious, not only when we take for our material stories which are bound up with an ancient tradition, but in connection with any theme which has in itself some native dignity. I would go further, and say that as teachers of literature we should resolutely decline to countenance in our presence any show upon a school stage which is not sound in art and unimpeachable in taste. We should hold ourselves responsible as keepers and guardians of a valued tradition, and feel in honour bound to insist upon the finest regard for good literary quality in the subject-matter and in the treatment of all our plays.

The Play Way was first published by Heinemann in 1914. The foregoing is from his chapter on Play-Making. In spite of the style, there is much sound and valuable practice set out here. The progression he recommends is from sprawling and limited psycho-drama to shaped and polished plays which can be shared with an audience. Cook is not a theatre man, he is a teacher of English, and it is from this standpoint that he writes.

He advises:
1. begin with free play – free expression 'exercises'
2. in play-building, use an existing story (value of folk and fairy tales)
3. take at least a term on play-making projects

4. that imitation is valuable in creating a style
5. integration of 'English' and 'Drama' activities
6. using much group work
7. continued development in creative activity and selection, shaping and communication
8. use of the 'stage', though his is only a couple of steps high from the floor and is the 'open' (not proscenium arch) variety
9. with older children there is value in sharing the work with an audience.

14 Drama as Challenge
Dorothy Heathcote

Working from the Institute of Education at Newcastle-upon-Tyne Dorothy Heathcote has developed her own approach to drama in education. She comes from Yorkshire and was trained at the Bradford Civic Playhouse School, under Esme Church, shortly after the Second World War.

Dorothy Heathcote's dynamic personality often proves a great asset in stimulating the child's response to situation and mood. She tends to like to work with the whole group or class as a unit and will often help the situation by taking part herself, like a Moreno-style director. She places a good deal of emphasis upon social drama, seeing the prime value of the drama in the 'living through' situations and the insight there is to be gained from them. The statement which follows has not previously been published, but is from a kind of manifesto issued by the Institute to those taking its One-Year Diploma Course in Drama in Education. It forms a very stimulating discussion on the nature of drama taking Kenneth Tynan's definition, 'Theatre and Living' from *Declaration* the collection of essays published in 1957 as its text. For drama to be worthwhile, it needs to concern itself with conflicts significant to the lives of those taking part. It needs to involve them in feeling.

It is generally acknowledged by teachers in most of our educational establishments that the Arts offer children certain experiences which other subjects cannot give. With regard to music, the plastic arts, and painting, the work of Cizek, Herbert Read and, for example, the B.B.C.'s work in music and movement have established music and painting in our schools. Teachers feel they understand these mediums at least sufficiently well to try them out. Because these art forms may be preserved, music on the tape-recorder, art on our walls, teachers can see their results and make evaluations of this kind of work. With regard to drama, however, because it is such a transient medium, incapable of real preservation beyond the moment of its creation, it has not yet become established as a teaching aid in our schools. Teachers do not feel, except perhaps a very small minority, that either they understand this medium, its techniques, its possibilities or that they know how to apply the medium to a child's development. There has been much emphasis in past years on the value of dramatics in a child's growth; but there has been very little attempt to examine the nature of dramatic activity in relation to the nature of the child's changing needs as he matures.

The Oxford Dictionary defines drama as 'a stage play, dramatic art, play-like series of events' and dramatic as being 'forcible, theatrical and striking'. The Greeks used the word drama with a rather different meaning, i.e. 'to live through' and it is in the latter context that we should consider drama and a child's growth. Kenneth Tynan defines his personal meaning of drama in *Declaration* as 'Good drama for me is made up of the thoughts, the words and the gestures that are wrung from human beings on their way to, or in, or emerging from a state of desperation'. He further defines a play as being 'an ordered sequence of events that brings one or more of the people in it to a desperate condition which it must always explain and should, if possible, resolve'. In these two sentences lies the key to the essential nature of drama. The teacher's role in education surely is to provide learning situations. At times he may instruct, but in the main he is concerned with the growth of the personality to whom he offers facts and information and skills as they are required. Therefore, his main way of teaching, if we are concerned with maturity rather than factual knowledge in education, is in the provision of situations which challenge the energies, the intelligence and the efforts of the children in his class. It is as a releaser of energy that drama is valuable to him. This, to a large extent, is not fully understood by teachers who, through no fault of their own, but simply because their own experiences of drama lead them to consider the finished product, and the energies of the participants tend to be directed towards this finished product and the contribution to the growth of the child is pushed to the background. This does not happen so much in music and painting because rarely are these activities carried out with an audience in mind. A child may hang his painting on the wall and so complete the creative process. He may stand his model on the window-shelf and look at it and live with it and perhaps later discard it. To a certain extent his music can be created and enjoyed without necessarily involving an audience. But somehow the creative urge in drama cannot be completed without an audience to participate in what is at once its birth and its destruction. So, it is easily seen that the emphasis will be placed upon this final situation and this is rightly so. However, if our purpose is to release the energy then we cannot afford to work only to the finished product. Certainly we must make opportunity for the product to be concluded, probably with an audience, however small, but we must not overlook the fact that it is the making of the drama which is going to contribute most to the growth of the child. Therefore, we are concerned not with rehearsal for the event, but with 'living through'.

Drama is a means of learning, a means of widening experiences even if we never act in a play or stand upon a stage. It is a human instinct to have 'a willing suspension of disbelief' (attributed to Coleridge). That from the moment we open a book, or our ears and eyes, we are willing to discard all prejudices, all pre-knowledge and wait for the story or the play to take control of our imaginations and *for the time* we believe in the action. We follow the cowboy on his horse and feel the tension as he nears the place of ambush. We seek to know in the beginning of the film who will be the hero, the heroine and the villain. We see in the glimpse of the revolver in the drawer, forthcoming violence and wait for it, believing in it, exactly in the same way as does a child. To dramatize is instinctive.

It belongs not to the artificiality of the first night theatrical production, to the so-called 'practices for the night' in a school production, to the painted books on the stage flats and the wine-gum jewels on the ladies costumes; it lies in the nature of a man to at once escape from his own existence and to learn from the events he sees, reads and hears about by sharing the emotions conjured up by the author. We are thereby given fresh acquaintance with mankind. We are offered a further opportunity for insight into human actions and feelings and some of this which we share is brushed off on to our own lives though we may not fully understand this. When the New York audiences wept three gallons of tears during Arthur Miller's play *Death of a Salesman* no one knew, least of all those men and women who wept, what knowledge had entered their lives, what awareness and sensitivity had been given to them. When the Greeks on the hillsides watched the stories they knew 'lived through' yet again, who knows what strength was given to them by this re-acquaintance with their myths, this new look at the warp and the weft of their heritage. Michael Ayrton says, 'I do know that we live by myth, inventing it when necessary, returning to it with satisfaction when it seems useful' (*The Testament of Daedalus*). When we have had acquaintance via the story-tellers, the poet, the author and the playwright with the emotions and situations of other men, who knows what energies may be released in us for greater sensitivity, greater comprehension, new knowledge of our society and other men (and even of ourselves) and of new awareness of our relationships with those near to us in the community in which we live. It is this which must concern us when we consider drama in our schools. The teacher's role is to harness drama to his own needs. To use it in the way in which it will most aid him in challenging children to learn. Its purpose will never vary, but the activity will vary as the child matures. In the young child there is need for play (which is real work) for feeding to young children the myths, the legends, the fairy stories, the real events around them and the opportunity for making these the basis of their own dramatic play. This playing out of situations challenges the child's social attitude, his verbal control and language ability, his unselfishness, his physical energies and his imagination as he 'lives through' the situations of interest to him. He learns to understand them in his own way. He relates them to his experience and makes them comprehensible in the light of his experience. Therefore, the teacher's role in this situation is that of feeder, whether of stories or of ideas. His task is to create a permissive atmosphere in which deep involved play may take place. As the child grows and his ability to verbalize becomes stronger there may be less need for the playing out and more need for a challenge towards the verbalization and real planning of the situation. The shape of the story will become much more important than erstwhile and it can be seen that though children are still using their own words to express the emotions aroused by the story and their own gestures and actions, greater demands will be made upon their ability to organize their material. So gradually Tynan's second sentence is being incorporated. 'The play is an organized sequence of events.' We are already over the barrier from the so-called informal side to the so-called formal side. We have been challenged not only to feel, but to organize our feelings into some kind of expression. In other words, we have challenged the children first to feel and comprehend, then to make their knowledge clear to themselves. We have challenged their language, both emotional and intellectual, because in any play-making situation, language demands vary considerably. Sometimes the language required is based upon emotion, at other times the language will be social as the children discuss the pros and cons of their play and come to terms with their own different ideas upon the matter in hand. At yet other times, the language challenge will be towards clarity of expression. So we have challenged children not only to play out their ideas, but to organize them. This is surely educational. At a later date still these children need challenging further, possibly to become interpreters of someone else's writing and, though at any time in their school life they may have been challenged to show their playmaking to others, they have not yet been challenged to interpret another person's writing. This challenge must come when they are ready to meet it, and, of course, it is understood that certain children will never be ready to meet it. For example, the educationally subnormal child who may never reach the stage of interpretive work. As soon as children are ready to be challenged to interpret and as long as teachers realize that before interpretation can happen, 'living through' must be achieved, then the children are using theatrical art and this means that their eyes and observation should be turned towards the theatre for they are working in the direct way of the theatre as soon as they concern themselves with an audience and a play.

Therefore, we have now progressed through playing for ourselves, in order that we may better understand the world and make acquaintance with it and the heritage and legends of it, towards learning to create within a group and finding language to communicate to each other in that group, and now towards the interpretation of other people's ideas of the world which leads us to our own understanding of the world and to our awareness of the place of the theatre or the television or the film or the novel or the poem in our world. In other words, our eyes have turned outwards to the place of the arts in the world of the adult. It should be possible to give the arts the same consolidated position in our classrooms as we have given at present to the skills of reading, writing and the sciences. If only we can give our teachers real insight into the nature of the arts, they will be working in, and sufficient techniques to enable them to work with the children with some measure of success; if we can train teachers to be themselves sensitive and to use the arts in their own lives and achieve a measure of continuity of experience through these teachers for the children in the classroom, then who knows what success we may have in educating children to become sensitive, aware, mature citizens, able not only to see the world from their own viewpoint, but through the eyes of others.

Three factors must concern us in training teachers to use the Arts. These factors are not necessarily different from, or opposed to, factors required in the sciences. In fact, there is probably a very close relationship.

1. Attitudes.
2. Knowledge of the subject.
3. Techniques of teaching.

Attitudes: in drama the teacher in a way suffers a reversal of his usual role, which is that of one who knows. In mathematics he knows the answers to the problems. He can read better than the children, he has more experience of the application of mathematics and, in general, he knows much more than the child. In drama, this is not so. He may have more life experience to draw upon, having lived longer, but when it comes to the interpretation of ideas it is the child's viewpoint which is important, not the teacher's. The child is not measuring up to a pre-set situation, he is discovering through the situation of the play. Therefore, he is not asking the teacher for the answer, he is offering the teacher a viewpoint and in return the teacher may offer another one. Neither one will be right or wrong. Each will differ because the two people concerned are different. For some reason this attitude is a difficult one to engender. The role of onlooker, guider, is somehow a very difficult one for the teacher, partly because his training leads him to feel he must know in advance of his pupils; that his role is that of the instructor and that there may be some loss of face in admitting to a younger person that that person's viewpoint may carry equal weight with that of the teacher. Once, however, this barrier is overcome and teachers are induced to leave their pedestals, generally grown from fear in the past (fear of inspectors, fear of not measuring up intellectually to their jobs, fear of ridicule in the eyes of the children), it will be seen that this situation, whereby the child is challenged to bring as much as the teacher into the classroom, develops on the teacher's part at a very special advantage. It brings with it a new relationship which can be best likened perhaps to that of the Renaissance painter with his school of students or sculptors like Mestrovitch working with his students on one monument to the dead. This relationship of the teacher offering to the children his extra life experience and the children offering to the teacher their own fresh way of looking at things can readily be seen will be of tremendous advantage to both. Not only does it free the child to bring himself to the situation rather than the personality he thinks the teacher expects, but it offers the teacher a freedom which he cannot possibly obtain in the role of the 'all knowing'. This new relationship brings with it certain instinctively-felt disciplines which children will not cross. One very rarely finds children in this relationship to the teacher being rude or lacking class discipline, because each recognizes the strength of the other in the situation. This attitude, which we in the Newcastle Institute feel to be of the most supreme importance, will colour all the teacher's school life. This attitude will encourage the children towards greater maturity, greater courage in expression and carrying out of ideas and a more realistic approach to adult life. It produces trust, self-knowledge, care for others, integrity and an ability to respond freshly to each situation. If we can engender in teachers, through dramatics, the idea that they are releasers of ideas, rather than interpreters of ideas, we have some chance of success.

With regard to knowledge of the subject, we must aim to give teachers as thorough a grounding as we may in the actual dynamics of drama. The heart of this lies in Kenneth Tynan's first sentence and if we can carry them through from this first basic conception of dramatics being first feeling, then the selection and expression of those feelings, to all the techniques which they will require in the understanding of the presentation of the theme to children, through to the final stage production for parents, etc., phase, then they will be equipped to exploit the energy giving factors of the attitudes section.

Following this real knowledge of the medium, we can feed to teachers the necessary techniques, knowing that they will not be misled into using those techniques blindly because they achieve results which are acceptable to headmasters, parents, etc., but will use them as and when required, and not lose sight of their aims for the particular class with which they are concerned.

Now let us examine the demands made upon the actor, whether he be child or professional in the adult theatre, when he works upon a play which has already been written. First, a written play is someone else's creation. The author 'lived through' the experience as he wrote the play. He wrote it from his own experience, the ideas released by these experiences, the people and events he has met and has been attracted to or repelled by, his own intelligence, his own emotional responses to these events and to these characters. In this respect, the written play is already complete. One man's energies have been released. Already he has created something; he has 'lived through' it. The actor meeting this script can only glimpse the author's intention through the medium of 'worn out words'. For words do wear out. Their meanings change with fashion. A good example is 'I couldn't care less', which now is given a very light-hearted interpretation and the real meaning has been worn away. So the actor converts the 'worn out words' and must re-breathe life into them. Michael Ayrton, in his book *The Testament of Daedalus* (Methuen, 1962) says, 'to make a thing is to touch dead things and to breathe on them', and the words of a play lie dead until the actor breathes upon them. To bring them to life he has only the same elements as the author had when he first created the play, i.e. his experience of life and his reflections upon life, his observation, which in the actor, as in all creators, is acute, his memory, his kinaesthetic ability, his sensitivity and his intellectual powers. Therefore, the actor must seek behind the written word to find the dynamic thought and emotion, using only the above factors. Having done this, he must, again using only his personal experience of things seen, read and felt, create another personality based upon his interpretation of the author's intention. This personality will be made up of fragments of observation, memory and experience remembered and recalled as needed. Having done this, the actor must then speak the lines left to him by the original playwright as if they were just conceived spontaneously and at the same time he must remember that it is not what he says, but what he listens to and responds to which is most important, i.e. the actor's medium may be said to be that of the pause between the words spoken where the emotional response of the audience is drawn into the play, and the actor is as much a listener, a responder, as a speaker. In other words, he 'lives through' each time he makes fresh acquaintance with the play. Rehearsals offer the actor two opportunities. One opportunity lies in making his acquaintance with the author's intention. He never practices for tomorrow, as we often expect the child to do; he 'lives through' today's rehearsal in order that tomorrow will have fresh life and new insight. The other opportunity offered by rehearsal is that having felt a situation or an emotion, the actor must then select, using his memory, his kinaesthetic ability and his acute observation, the appropriate gestures, movements, responses from 'living through' that he has conjured up during acquaintance with the play. Having done this, the actor is now equipped to put his feelings aside, his 'living through' and concentrate on the expression of that feeling. Because the actor's task, once he has conjured up the feelings, emotions and character, must be to balance the play, to evolve the play's expression, so that the audience who have paid their money and their time, feel the play and 'live through' at performance. This, as can readily be seen, is a very complicated structure. It may be summed up thus. An actor feels, out of his feelings he conjures his techniques to express the feeling and in performance before an audience he does not feel; every movement, every gesture, every modulation of voice is calculated, almost coldly, in order that the audience gets its money and its time's worth; because the audience pays its money to feel, to 'live through', to share. If we are going to use play production as a medium of education, it is absolutely essential that teachers understand the fundamental nature of this work and the demands which it makes upon children. These demands are not insurmountable and provided emphasis is laid upon the fact that play production means 'living through' rather than of showing to, then it is not wrong for children to interpret plays. A barrier has grown up and people have taken sides. The two teams are the advocates of the so-called informal dramatics, whose creed is that children shall use their own language always, versus those who consider the so-called formal production is best. One glance at Kenneth Tynan's remarks quoted earlier will show that there is no reason why these two teams should necessarily be opposed. If our purpose in education is that children shall learn by doing as much as by listening to, then both these fields of activity, the so-called formal and the so-called informal are only two views of the same thing. Whether a play is to be taken from a book or conjured from the children's own experience, depends not upon a teacher's beliefs, but upon the child's needs and abilities. A child of seven years old is not yet ready to be an interpreter of other people's ideas; a child of seventeen should be working as an interpreter. So it is in the light of the child's needs that our selection is made and our programme planned.

Returning once again to Kenneth Tynan's definition, the heart of successful dramatization, so that children are involved and concentrating and being made to think and use their energies, physical and mental, lies in the word 'wrung from'. Much of the confusion which teachers have with regard to drama lies in the fact that it is so intransient. They can hear when a musical instrument is tuned properly; they recognize the need for this and it's as easily apparent when the tuning is wrong. The same applies to paint and clay where it is easy to perceive wrong mixing of paints, wrong size of brush, etc., and this can easily be put right. In drama, the equivalent of too liquid paint or badly tuned instruments is not easily apparent and one of the first essentials for teachers is that they learn in dramatic terms 'how to mix the paints'. The clue lies in Tynan's first sentence, that drama is concerned with people whose normal tenor of life has been disturbed and who are either about to be or are already involved in emotional disturbances. The playwright in the adult theatre knows this; far too often the playwright for schools ignores this. Drama, then, is concerned with the thoughts, words and actions which people are driven to use because they can do no other, and it is this which in education, if carefully used, will release the energies of our children. This is the reason for putting the word drama on a time-table in a school curriculum.

Like Caldwell Cook, Dorothy Heathcote sees drama in a broad educa-tion setting. It is impossible to consider drama without involving more general educational principles. While for the most part she would go along with views of drama expressed by Peter Slade and Brian Way, she also recognizes the value of performance and accepts that, in the proper context, acting for others can extend the art and its communication. Similarly, she sees no need for there to be any conflict between the drama which employs a text and that which works without it.

Particularly note her attempt to:
1. return to basics of the subject – attitudes, knowledge and teaching techniques
2. underline the value of the 'doing' in drama, rather than the end product
3. reiterate the naturalness of acting
4. emphasize that drama is concerned with topics which draw upon feelings
5. show that acting moves from a living through to organizing and to effectively expressing (a recreating process)
6. point out the importance in living through and sharing experiences.

15 Drama as a Study
Glynne Wickham

Glynne Wickham is not only a theatrical historian, but he has even himself become part of theatrical history. In August 1960, he became Professor of Drama at the University of Bristol. This was the first time that anyone had held a Chair of Drama in Britain. He went from Oxford to Bristol University as Assistant Lecturer in 1948, and since then has steadily built up a Department of Drama which today with its finely equipped Vandyke Theatre, stands as a model for most other universities.

Professor Wickham has undertaken a history of *Early English Stages*, *1300–1600*, covering a range as wide as the works of E. K. Chambers already referred to, and challenging many accepted viewpoints.

Here is part of Glynne Wickham's inaugural lecture, in which he discusses the unique opportunities which exist at Bristol with its strong link between University Drama Department, the Bristol Old Vic Theatre Company, and the Bristol Old Vic Theatre School. Professor Wickham also reviews the problems facing the establishment of drama in a world of science.

The Bristol University Department of Drama has been fortunate in the interest shown towards it by the Press. Some might say that it has attracted a quite unwarranted degree of Press publicity: others that such notoriety has only been occasioned by the fact that the department was unique. Speaking for myself, I think it is more likely that Bristol, in voting the department into existence, happened to give form and substance to something which in a multitude of vague, unexplored, and unexpressed ways was becoming of interest to people too numerous and too widespread to count except as readers of newspapers. There have been signs – portents, if you like – to support this view. The post-war growth of festivals is one of them: not only the big commercial undertakings – Edinburgh, Aix, Venice, Cannes, Salzburg – but student festivals, both national and international. Another is the number and range of plays that people have encountered for themselves, thanks to a public service system of broadcasting in this country. One municipality, Coventry, has gone so far as to take full financial responsibility for building and maintaining a theatre on behalf of its citizens; and Nottingham is about to follow suit. Other theatres, for the first time in living memory, enjoy limited subsidy from the Exchequer via the Arts Council. Perhaps most important of all, the whole English theatre is once again permitted to speak its mind freely on any subject it cares to handle; four hundred years of religious bigotry and political prejudice, as represented in the censorship of the stage imposed by the governments of the first Queen Elizabeth, have been at last rolled away by those of the second Elizabeth; and already no other country in the world can boast as formidable an array of notable young writers for the stage as England at this moment – two of them, happily, associated with this place.

Bearing this in mind, it is in the order of things rather than surprising that drama should have reacquired a measure of respectability in academic life. Yet it is ever at moments like this, when struggle encounters a temporary success, that celebration can become the bride of complaisance. In the thirteen years of teaching experience that lie behind us, my colleagues and I have had time and opportunity to conduct a thorough exploration of the subject in the manner of a geographical survey. A first viewing of the terrain revealed a landscape dominated by lofty peaks – Sophocles, Shakespeare, Schiller, or Strindberg (to take only those with sibilant affinities). Yet it was objected to us that these features were under close enough survey already in departments of language and literature for our attention to be redundant.

We switched our attention from plays and dramatists to places of performance, to the great theatres of antiquity with their perfect sight-lines and astonishing acoustics – Epidaurus, Aspendus, Orange – to the charm and elegance of theatres in the baroque style – Bayreuth, Schonbrunn, Drottningholm, our own Theatre Royal – or to the intricate complexities of the modern opera house. And again it was objected that these matters were already taken care of by archaeologists and architects. We turned our gaze to stage machines and scenery, to perspective settings, and to the varied possibilities of lighting them by candle, by limelight or by electricity, and so to the further optical developments that led to the filming and televising of the acted play; only to be advised that such matters lay within the preserves of science. Experiments in acting and other practical activities of the theatre, brought protests that such work was better conducted by artists and craftsmen in a vocationally slanted academy than within the contemplative atmosphere of university studies. There remained the study of audiences. What persuaded them to support the theatre at the box-office, to champion its survival against the attacks of its detractors, to prefer one dramatist to another, and to accord actors at one and the same time the status of royalty and near-criminals? Yet these preoccupations, we were told, were not ours either, but those of the economists and social historians, the psychologists and psychiatrists. Drama, in short, was not a subject: simply a collection of fragments, more or less interesting, and all peripheral to sounder disciplines already in existence. And here the horse jibbed: for, as Eugene O'Neill once observed, 'dramatists were psychologists – and good ones at that – before psychology was thought of'. Improving upon O'Neill, we noticed that audiences had been patronizing theatres all over the world long before social history and economics became fashionable subjects. Somewhere in all this careful fencing of special preserves and hedging about of proper and improper interests, was something suspiciously timid, parochial, and inbred – something to be challenged as itself wholly improper to a university because a contradiction of its very name, nature, and function. One might as well say that mathematics was no subject because its many aspects were already well enough looked after in a variety of engineering and science disciplines. Here, under our noses where drama was concerned, we were meeting face to face that fragmentation of knowledge, that artificial divorcing of one aspect of a subject from another, implicit in specialization, that division of society against itself that results in anarchy and is known as barbarism. The charge levelled against drama of being 'no subject' had the ominous appearance of being derived from either plain ignorance or from fear lest its admission might do some damage to the fences and hedges erected around the countless precious allotments and ignore the prominent notice, 'Trespassers will be prosecuted'.

It is pleasant to be able to record that in this university the penalty threatened for any infringement of this notice has been more honoured in the breach than the observance. The Drama Department has every reason to be grateful for the number of Joint Schools, the help received both from the Department of Physics in elementary optics and acoustics, and from lectures in the language departments where foreign drama is concerned, as also from the instruction in practical aspects of the subject provided by the Bristol Old Vic School and Theatre Staff: all of which testifies to the existence in this place of a broadly humane and co-operative spirit. Nevertheless, one important result of admitting drama as a subject in this university has been to focus attention sharply upon the amount of specialization that exists within faculties and upon the barriers which this specialization has created, dividing one department from another and cutting off one faculty from another. I choose to raise this issue because neither of these factors has helped in any way to define the new subject in the manner which ensured that the teaching of it should be to the maximum advantage of its students. Some people will doubtless object that students have no right to expect any consideration beyond being informed that the subject exists, and that they have opportunity to study it. This attitude, however, if acceptable in an age when higher education was a privilege reserved for the very few, is no longer tenable at a time when students, from the age of eleven onwards, are being trained to regard a university education as the factor which determines economic and social status in later life.

Sir Francis Bacon once boasted that all knowledge was his profession; and indeed the range of his mental activities has amazed scientists as well as students of letters ever since. Yet, however much may have been added to the world's stockpile of knowledge in the four hundred years since his birth, few scientists today have any knowledge of how to prevent the fruits of specifically scientific discoveries being used to plunge mankind into an unparalleled chaos of suffering, destruction, and new-barbarism.

Even fewer arts graduates know enough about the modern scientific subjects or processes to which they owe their present standard of living to be trusted with responsibility for the peaceable government of mankind in a world where the individual has committed the control of his agricultural and industrial economy, of his communications, and even of his bodily and mental health, to scientists. In this world of science and related technology, the right hand has effectively ceased to know what the left hand is doing – the world in fact of Mr Harold Pinter's plays or Eugene Ionesco's. It is against this background that I have to ask myself what the study of drama offers to prospective students. Of what possible value can it be to them? Is it just another subject to which they must become slaves? Or may it be a subject which can advance them in the art of living and qualify them to lead others in that art? In our concern for the sanctity of our respective specialities, are we to continue to ignore, with fastidious politeness, almost every issue of serious consequence to the student, from the future of television and the Commonwealth to Africa and the H-bomb, and rest satisfied with giving him a gilt-edged ticket to present to the Labour Exchange? Is drama to be another special subject of special interest to the special few, or can it cater simultaneously for the genuine specialist inquirer, and for those who are not yet equipped to do more than acquire a general cultural background but form an increasingly large proportion of university entrants? The demands of specialization in arts subjects already impose upon the sixth-form pupil as well as upon the undergraduate fantastically congested lecture timetables and reading lists. While these demands themselves narrow his mental horizons, they also eliminate the possibility of effective counterbalance, since the student is given neither time for, nor direction in, any studies, humane or scientific, other than his own speciality. Thus, instead of preparing himself to understand his own society, its traditions and its prospects, he is systematically isolated from it, insidiously dragooned into becoming, as a graduate, part of a governing class, whose background he does not fully understand or necessarily approve, and cut off from that larger part of society whose dreams and struggles propelled him into the University in the first place. Disappointment, bewilderment, and frustration, are the products, and 'Lucky Jim' the representative.

Can drama in the undergraduate curriculum offer us more than this? If not, then I believe we are wasting time and money in admitting it to our prospectus. It would be pleasant to be able to state that in seeking the answer, guidance was forthcoming from the example of other subjects: but it is not. For even where evidence exists of one arts discipline endeavouring to understand and assist its neighbour (as in the many Joint Schools in this University), in general the right hand of arts subjects, far from being concerned to understand what the left hand of science is doing, often appears to have no deeper interest in its gestures than that of a brother who seeks to prevent a sister from obtaining two sweets when he has only one. Up to the present time, drama has simply copied the other disciplines in arts and science in advertising in the faculty prospectus a number of obligatory examinations. And in doing this it has been our aim to show the outside world that the subject was as respectable as its neighbours. In this objective I think we can fairly claim to have been successful. But is this to be the end of the matter? Are we to be satisfied with a replica of something which most of us agree to be inadequate and out of date? Complaints, according to *The Times*, have recently come from Edinburgh that 'lectures in some departments are little more than versions of a textbook'. At Birmingham, a student told a correspondent of the same newspaper: 'I have been completely disillusioned about what a University is since I came here: I thought it would be doing so many things on such a high plane. Instead I found myself on a course which was so technical and so extensive that all the people in the department were completely wrapped up in their own subject.' Some adventurous undergraduates at Oxford have recently focused public attention on these matters by rather unorthodox and perhaps unfortunate methods; but it is hard to refrain from the comment 'not before time'. I can well remember being compelled myself to attend a course of lectures on bibliography and thinking that this measure of obligation must portend something more than usually worthwhile – only to be told at the start of the first lecture that 'a book, may, roughly, be defined, as a gathering of leaves', and treated thereafter to a host of such pedagogical platitudes. Warned in this way that obligatory attendance could as easily camouflage flatulence as revelation, I am aware that incorporation of a subject within a faculty prospectus can just as easily disguise a costly form of escapism as advertise a path to wisdom.

Which is it to be for Drama?

Lacking any obvious lead from within the university, the suggestions which I have to make by way to answer cannot but be personal. They are, however, based upon thoughts which have arisen directly from the experience of teaching the subject and from discovering in the course of that teaching what potential the subject contains for the students who read it.

The most exciting single discovery to have emerged from this thirteen-year survey is the way in which drama can treat of Western civilization as a single homogeneous tradition, not like English literature beginning more than half-way through, not artificially divided on a geographical basis like modern languages, not split in two like the self-contained worlds of modern and ancient history, more fortunate than music in that there is no lack of notation from Greece or Rome, happier than classics in being still alive and practised among us here and everywhere. Continuity is its hall mark, the actor its standard bearer, buildings and designs its baggage train, its comic and its tragic masks the expressions of mankind's encounters with his gods, his concern for his fellow-men, and his strictly selfish interest in himself. Like some miraculous chameleon, the history of European drama reflects the alternating humility and arrogance of the human mind in its relations with the supernatural and in its contemplation of itself.

A discovery scarcely less important than this image of continuity within our European heritage, which a study of Western drama offers, is the dawning understanding that dramatic traditions within the Eastern world follow similar patterns of birth, growth, decay, and re-birth to those in the West, having remarkable affinities at many points with our own. And who knows what we in this materialistic and techno-logical age may regain from such contact with a society which, busy as it may be in industrializing itself, has nevertheless preserved a much more humble approach to nature than our own? May not the safeguard to the tyranny of science perhaps lie there? A tyranny as alarming in the hold which it has taken on men's minds, as those of religious bigotry and feudal serfdom which we have at last thrown off.

The third discovery of experience is one which the scientist may well regard as too simple to warrant mention, but which in arts subjects has been forgotten or suppressed – the discipline implicit in practical work. Exercises in the control of voice and body, in the creation of a setting or a costume (design and construction), the attempt to write a play, or a radio or film script (enforcing a close observation of other people) or the struggle to co-ordinate actors and craftsmen (all of them wilful and human) into the coherent pattern of a play in action – these things are not to be written off as so much time mis-spent. It is a remarkable fact that no student reading drama as a subject here has failed in his degree exams because of an over-indulgence in practical work. Some critics have argued that such work encourages a vocational approach, destroy-ing or inhibiting genuinely academic study: others have criticized a practice which, by seeking to inform rather than to qualify, serves only to elevate what is amateur and esoteric at the expense of what is professional and realistic. That both such risks exist is undeniable; but in raising such objections both types of critics are over-looking a certain good in their concern for a risk of evil. What matters is that within arts discipline the hands can be reunited with the heart and with the head: the whole human personality working as a co-ordinated entity. It is no coincidence that modern psychiatry has discovered a therapeutic value in dramatic activity. All drama, Western and Oriental, African and Latin-American has sprung spontaneously from the fears and joys of the heart; it has been modified, adapted, formalized into religious rituals and civilized by varied forms or genres imposed upon it by the intellect; yet always it has been practised by the speaking, sing-ing, dancing, gesticulation, informed, disciplined, and co-ordinated body. And I refuse to believe that any student today is the worse for having experienced life fully through his mind, his emotions, and his body, even when temporarily confined within a university.

These then are the contributions which drama as a subject can make to the life of a university. It can present the past to its students as a single living and continuous whole. In the present it provides a means of investigating the links connecting Western civilization with that of the East. And in its creative aspects it links past and present to the future. In short, it can provide a forum for the examination and discussion of the human condition, its relationship with its gods, and its interest in itself, collectively and individually, as revealed in its social values.

Arts departments in this country have for the most part dispensed with creative ability. They have relied upon an emotional interest or intellectual curiosity in the student serving as a magnet to attract him to the subject, and have then directed all their attention (once the student is their captive) upon disciplining his intellect within the confines of the subject with an almost total disregard for the emotional and creative aspects of his personality. These have been left to find a fitful outlet in extra-curricular activities to which we pay lip-service when exhorting students to lead a full life in the Union or Hall of Residence and frown upon whenever we meet together to discuss his academic progress. The result is to be seen in a welter of analytical criticism which is predominantly destructive, and in the apathy, the indifference, the complacency, and downright dullness of so much of university life. I would go further and say that our students in comparison with American students, whatever their respective intellectual attainments, are frequently made to seem emotionally immature and often painfully gauche.

Science and engineering subjects, by contrast, however much we in arts departments may deride their vocational nature, at least make some provision for their students' creative capacities and interests.

We are on safer ground if we complain that the scientist or engineer in his concern with man's material environment is dangerously careless in his lack of concern for man's human condition.

Either way, however, it is clear that arts and sciences no longer make the same assumptions about their students nor the same demands of them: to that extent, therefore, they no longer talk the same language. And if we who teach in a university do not share a common approach to what we are supposed to be doing, how can we expect our students, as graduates in responsible positions, to talk a common language in respect of the world and its government? The example of division, of bickering, and of shut doors which we set them, they carry into life.

It is here precisely that I would commend the wisdom of those men who admitted drama as a subject into this university, for I believe that it has something of value to offer both arts and sciences. Knowing no frontiers in time past and no boundaries of nationality or creed, it offers a microcosmic image of human purpose and attainment in a form that is convenient to study. For arts, in particular, it not only widens horizons which have become narrow through the constant pressure of specialization, but introduces an element of practical and creative craftsmanship which at present is the prerogative of the science student in his lab, or left to the vagaries of chance in the Union. To science it offers the easiest of paths into the realm of other arts subjects which, if not much frequented by a student while he is struggling against the clock of his degree timetables, has at least been opened up for him to explore later in life when leisure is available. To one and all, arts man, scientist, graduate-duke, and non-graduate-dustman, it offers a forum for the study and discussion of moral values – one of the few surviving forums left to us where the duke's interest and the dustman's can be discussed, not individually and separately, but as mutually related within the framework of society – a commonweal, national and international. Any lingering tendency for the auditoriums of theatres to be respecters of persons is now offset by television. In former times theology was reputed Queen of the Sciences on this account. It was within these terms of reference that Marlowe and many another Elizabethan thought philosophy divine. Today, for better or worse, scientific knowledge has given us a world where what is single and unified in nature has been arbitrarily split asunder, and where the contrasts implicit in nature have been virtually eliminated. The electric-light switch abolishes the distinction between day and night. The sharp contrast of town and country disappears daily in the creeping sameness of suburban sprawl. And in countless homes the binding power of human feeling is either spread thinly on causes remote enough to be only vaguely understood – famine relief in the Congo, flood victims in China, the R.S.P.C.A. – or else it is concentrated upon such microscopic social units as the family circle or the immediate and often wholly selfish wants of the individual. It is not that we as individuals have lost our capacity for interest in moral values, but that the complexity of the life made available to us by a hundred years of applied science and exacerbated by the confusion of two world wars eroded our sense of corporate responsibility with nature, to a point where each individual is in danger of abdicating it to some mythical person or organization other than himself: having forgotten how to love God, there are many signs that we are also forgetting how to love our neighbour. And this has ever been the acid test of disintegration and degeneracy within a society. It also happens to be something upon which drama focuses attention: for when all is said and done, dramatic art is not plays, not theatres, not scenery, but actors and audiences – a living, vital, communal relationship – there to mirror for society, and all the individuals who together compose that society, mankind's relationships with his gods and with his fellow-men at that particular point in time. Great drama is the produce of greatness in a people – a concern for God, for society, and for the individual, as acutely mirrored on the stage as it is reflected in the auditorium. Shakespeare could discuss government and politics in his histories, love and its mysteries in his comedies, and the consequences of darker human passions in his tragedies: and he could do this not only with his aristocratic patrons but with the rankest of stink-ards, the fellows with grounded judgements and no formal education, who paid their penny to stand in the yard. The Globe stage and audi-torium was Elizabethan England in miniature, just as the Theatre of Dionysus was Athens. In the same way the Colosseum provides a faithful reflection of the values by which Rome lived in the imperial epoch; itself a breathtaking feat of engineering science, the spectacles presented in it nevertheless reflecting as accurately the person for Rome's fall. I hardly need to stress the comparison that could be made with the modern miracles of cinema and television and the uses to which they have been put.

The playwright Robert Bolt has stated the matter in another way and in words notable enough to be worth quoting.

'The Deluge, being an Act of God, threw little light on human nature . . . An atomic war would be an act of Man, and if, as seems probable, Man destroys himself, it will be because, on balance, Man prefers to; because his hatred of life is stronger than his love of life, because his greed, aggression and fear are stronger than his self-denial, charity and courage. Because, in short, of his nature.

I am aware that the question of Man's nature is an old one, that has been moving up on Man ever since the Renaissance when Man began to move away from God. But because the bomb enables Man for the first time to realize irreversibly whatever fantasies of evil he may have, we . . . are the first generation which cannot dodge the question . . .'

This mirror of moral values in society – of man's interest in himself, of his regard for his neighbour, and of his respect for his gods – is the quintessence of drama as an academic subject: for it is this balance between the three (or lack of balance) in any society which distinguishes one civilization from another. It is the particular quality and purpose of dramatic art to reflect it. Bertholt Brecht puts the point in the simplest possible way in a poem addressed to an actor.

> 'Do not step too far
> From the everyday theatre,
> The theatre whose stage is the street.
> Look – the man at the corner re-enacting
> The accident.
> Thus he gives the driver at his wheel
> To the crowd for trial.
> Thus the victim, who seems old,
> Of each he only gives so much
> That the accident be understood.
> Yet each lives before your eyes
> And each he presents in a manner
> To suggest the accident avoidable.
> So the event is understood
> And yet can still astound,
> For the moves of both could have been different.
> Now he shows how both could have moved
> To circumvent the accident.
> This witness is free from superstition.
> Never to the stars
> Does he abandon his mortals
> But only to their own mistakes.'

This, I submit, is important enough to suggest Joint Schools of the future in partnership with theology, philosophy, history. Bridges more-over exist within the subject of anthropology, to medical psychology, to archaeology, to music, to the fine arts, and of course to literature and languages. The growth of perspective scenery, founded on geometry and optics, and culminating in cinema and television (with all that involves in terms of electricity and the related techniques of sound broadcasting) provides similar bridges to science and engineering subjects.

In short, I ask you to think of drama as a discipline centred upon the comparison of moral values – theological, social, and individual – and equipped at its frontiers with launching sites for a great variety of journeys into other disciplines. Drama, I submit, far from being 'no subject', is in fact a subject with remarkable integrating power which can relate the ancient world to the present day, which can bring critical appraisal into direct contact with creative experiment, which can provide the arts man with a lively introduction to scientific thinking and the scientist with as lively a reflection of his own human condition.

Drama has acquired a long enough and a distinguished enough history behind it to be recognizable in the twentieth century as an academic subject in Sweden, Germany, Austria, Belgium, Italy, the United States, and now in Britain: but it behoves us at the same time to remember that it always was and still is a living art. Yet we live in a time when theatre companies, along with orchestras, have become the victims of chronic financial anaemia. If we believe in the past, therefore, is it not time we began to practise what we teach? Whether we like it or not, whether we are aware of it or not, the Church and the aristocratic layman have handed the torch of patronage to us. Responsibility for the care of the artistic heritage of the past and for there being any part of the future has passed to the universities. The private patron has died with the past: industry is often a generous and well-intentioned successor, but cannot be expected to have the knowledge available within a university. Gone is the time when it sufficed to note the colour of Maecenas' gown and criticize its texture. Now we have to wear it.

This is a problem which Americans and peoples of the commonwealth have already had to face in a much more acute form than we have: and if, as I believe, they have found an answer, then we should at least be humble enough to consider it while we still have time. I refer to the admission of practising artists (with or without degrees themselves) to the lawns and classrooms of the campus. They do not come as outsiders to deliver a single lecture and dash away again, but live there and are available to answer students' questions – not in that nightmare five minutes after a lecture, but day in day out – whenever the need is felt. Painters in residence, composers in residence, printers, singers, actors, writers. Results vary enormously. The principle itself is still debated.

Many academic people object that the strong vocational element within these subjects creates a pressure towards an undesirable vocationalism in other subjects. Many professional critics outside the universities object that these activities encourage a vast amateurism at the expense of professional standards. Where drama is concerned I would agree. Nevertheless, but for the universities and schools, America today would be without a theatre – every actor, writer, and designer of distinction being university trained. I would add further that almost every innovation of importance in the whole long history of European theatre has been made by highly educated amateurs. The professional theatre can hardly describe itself as in the pink of condition at the moment, and maybe the moment has come for another shot in the arm from the amateurs. If so, why not from the universities? In my view the duty of the universities to drama as a living art today should be to provide generous and tolerant patronage for critical thinking about the theatre and creative experiment in it. Attempts to do more than that carry with them grave risks of vulgarizing the university and debasing theatrical art.

What is already quite clear in America is that a student society which learns to accept creative artists in its midst as part of a normal landscape instead of as strangers, as frightening outsiders from another planet, is in a far better position to find use for art and artist in its maturity than are our arts faculties in Britain, where both the fine and the practical are still relegated in most universities either to the extremist limits of the timetable or to the no-man's-land of the vacations. Is it any wonder that, schooled in this way, we come in our maturity to accept ugly buildings, the closing of theatres, and the destruction of natural beauty in the countryside with little more than a murmur?

At least there are some modest signs of a gradual awakening to this responsibility for patronage. Music has come to be accepted in most British universities. Architecture and the fine Arts have established a firm footing here and there. Drama has made a start. Yet where writers are concerned, while every American university of any calibre can run a daily newspaper worth reading, we in Bristol have a struggle to publish two issues in a month. In America, of course, geographical isolation makes the need more urgent, or at least more keenly felt; but that does not excuse the lack of good writing here. It simply reveals that our students have nothing to say and that we have failed to stimulate them into finding anything.

It is my hope that the presence of a Fellow in Playwriting and the existence of New Theatre Magazine within the Drama Department, will do something to redress the balance: but if we are to do our duty to drama as an art as well as to drama as a critical discipline, then we must do more than that. Here in Bristol I hope it will prove possible to strengthen our association with the Old Vic Company and School, and with the Little Theatre, and with the two broadcasting centres in the region. If medical students can be obliged to walk the wards of hospitals, or law students to sit in law courts and solicitors' chambers, I see no reason why students of drama should not occasionally be seen in theatres and in studios. And the same holds for staff. Better that both should occasionally be exposed to a little professional proficiency than cocooned perpetually in an esoteric atmosphere where amateur standards are transfigured into absolutes. If then we in Bristol do not exploit the remarkable facilities for co-operation with those many and varied interests in drama which exist in this city and with which history and luck have endowed us, we shall be judged by history as having thrown away a unique opportunity.

So alongside of higher degree candidates, I want to extend an equal welcome to post-graduates whose interest is avowedly vocational. Writers, producers, managers, critics, teachers – anyone who has proved himself or herself to be an able undergraduate here or elsewhere, and who knows what he wants to do with his life, will be welcome to join us for one year. The Certificate in Advanced Practical Studies, which I hope the university will agree to sanction in the near future, would be open to any graduates, whether in arts, science, or engineering subjects, who could convince us that their careers lay in the theatre, in films, television, or any other field where a humane approach allied to practical proficiency is at a premium. And in judging of this proficiency we would call upon the professional opinion available to us at the Old Vic, The Theatre School, and the B.B.C. In this way we could have confidence that the certificate was as acceptable a token of creative ability to professional practitioners as our higher degrees were guarantees of academic standing and capacity. And lastly, I would hope to see the example of our earlier Rockefeller Lectures extended to enable selected artists of distinction to reside among us from time to time so that the discipline of experience may inform the discipline of study, and vice-versa. These, for me, are the proper paths for drama in a world shaped for us by science, and in which Man has come to regard himself as his own master.

If these paths are considered by you or by others to be no more than ideal dreams, well, let it be so. If these dreams fail to find fulfilment, then as Troilus put it:

'Hector is dead; there is no more to say.'

But should they be realized, then I think something will have been achieved for which not only the university but the city will be the richer. Adapting the title of the Carmen Basiliense, so splendidly set to music by Benjamin Britten as the Cantata Academica, and applying its ancient words to ourselves:

'Nos autem cuncti hoc festo die
Ex animi sententia
Optamus et precamur . . .

We therefore together on this festive day
Wish to pray with all our heart
That a free academy may thrive
In a free community
For ever the ornament and treasure
Of illustrious Bristol.'

This lecture was given in 1960 and since then there have been Drama Departments opened in Manchester, Birmingham and Hull Universities and many more Universities are appointing Fellows and/or Lecturers in aspects of theatre and drama.

Professor Wickham shows clearly both the dangers and the opportunities, not only of drama in the University, but of drama in the world of science.

Note especially:
1. his pleas that drama should advance the art of living
2. his emphasis on the value of drama as a means of uniting the study in aspects of our civilization
3. the importance of practical work alongside intellectual discussion and thought
4. as a means of further uniting science and art – it is not plays, not theatres, not scenery, but a communal relationship between actors and audience that counts most
5. the importance of opportunity for creativity in an academic institution.

SECTION SIX

Search for a New Drama in the Theatre

16 Drama and Happenings
Charles Marowitz

The word 'happenings' first impinged upon the imagination of English theatre-goers at the Edinburgh Festival Drama Conference in 1960; what made the impact was not so much the point and purpose of the event, as that amongst the things which happened a nude lady was pushed on a trolley across the auditorium.

Charles Marowitz took an active part in that Edinburgh Conference and has been concerned with the happenings movement both before and since. He has been working in the theatre in this country since 1956 though he is a New Yorker and his special contribution has been in experimental work and the introduction of new writers. With Peter Brook he directed the Royal Shakespeare Theatre of Cruelty season at the L.A.M.D.A. Theatre.

In 1968, Marowitz opened his own theatre, 'The Open Space', which is a roomy basement in the Tottenham Court Road. His version of *Hamlet*, which he calls a 'collage' is one of his particularly memorable experiments.

Antonin Artaud, John Cage, Dada Kurt, Schwitters, 'Merz', Rauschenberg, Cunningham – these are some of the components. The word itself first appeared in 1959 when Alan Kaprow presented an 'event' at the Reuben Gallery in New York and entitled it '18 Happenings in 6 parts'. Prior 'happenings' had taken place as early as 1952, when, for instance, John Cage, Charles Olson, Robert Rauschenberg and Merce Cunningham lectured, danced, played musical instruments and made assorted noises at an experimental concert at Black Mountain College in North Carolina.

Artaud's rough blueprint appeared in *The Theatre and Its Double*:
'. . . the theatre (must be) contained within the limits of everything that can happen on a stage, independent of the written test.

'. . . to link the theatre to the expressive possibilities of forms, to everything in the domain of gestures, noises, colours, movements, etc., is to restore it to its original direction.

'. . . the spectator is in the centre and the spectacle surrounds him . . .

'. . . in this spectacle, the sonorization is constant: sounds, noises, cries are chosen first for the vibratory quality, then for what they represent.'

The American 'Happenings', mostly the work of painters like Alan Kaprow, Claes Oldenberg, Jim Dine, George Brecht, are extensions of action-painting and constructions. Painters, following their natural instincts, were led – by a logical progression – to the theatre. The same was true for certain electronic composers.

For John Cage (he taught many of the east and west coast exponents and is the major contemporary influence), there is no longer any dividing line between music and theatre. One inevitably fuses into the other.

There is no pat definition with which one can explain away 'Happenings'. The field is too wide, the phenomenon too new for anyone to even attempt a 'theory'; and besides, the repudiation of 'theory' is the one point on which most happeners invariably unite. In some cases, it is an attempt to refresh the senses of sight and sound by placing familiar activities into unfamiliar contexts. (Recently, at the Better Books basement in Charing Cross Road, Jeff Nuttall and Bruce Lacey created just such a Happening, the main feature of which was a grisly surgical operation carried out on a calf's intestines wedged into a girl's prop-stomach.)

It can also be a way of triggering awareness in situations where custom and routine have obscured the true nature of events. (This was true of the Edinburgh Happening at the 1963 Drama Conference; here, a series of actions were so rigged as to deliver an indictment upon egotism and sophistry parading as 'seriousness' and 'intellectualism'.) In most cases,

Happenings work from a 'score' which is as detailed and prescribed as a musical score. Although they incorporate the spontaneous and 'improvised', they are not executed off-the-cuff. In every case, they are 'prepared for' (as opposed to 'rehearsed'); sometimes for as long as five and six months. Although some get repeated (never in quite the same way), they are largely expendable and regarded as such. Their real impact lies in their personal repercussion; in the 'myth' they leave behind them.

So much for background. For almost a century the theatre has been trying to theorize its way out of a cul-de-sac. Gnawing away at everyone's bones has been the desire to 'get out of', 'break away from', 'transform' or 'revolutionize' the theatre, and invariably these desires were analysed in terms of architecture. To some, the open-stage was a panacea; to others, arena-staging promised Tao; others propagandized more extraordinary shapes and sizes, but always there was this wriggling to escape the confines of the 18th century shoe-box which, ironically, is the prevailing shape of the modern theatre.

The practices of the Happeners have cut right through these tedious arguments. They have made theatre in streets, public squares, boiler-rooms, basements, department stores, forests; on buses, building sites, bridges, rooftops. They have by-passed all our musty old arguments about 'art', 'aesthetics' and 'architecture' by saying that 'an environment' is a theatre, and 'social behaviour' is drama; that in certain dramatized situations 'people' are actors, and the rush of social events, mise-en-scene. This hacking-off of that umbilical cord which has linked Aeschylus and Sophocles to Beckett and Brecht is the most revolutionary piece of surgery anyone has ever attempted.

Obviously, if one pushes this concept to its logical conclusion, the line between life and art gets obliterated. Which, for many Happeners, is exactly what is intended. Mark Boyle, one of the most brilliant creators of Assemblages in the country, claims that, in his view, the job of the artist is to remove his function. For Boyle, it is fraudulent to put a frame around a portion of life thereby appropriating it for 'art'. He envisages a point where everyone will have cultivated the artist's awareness of shape, colour, texture and beauty. For Boyle, Happenings need no invited audiences because everywhere there are people, there are happenings, and everywhere there are people and happenings, there is art. It's a wildly idealized view, but if one methodically unbends the muscles of the mind, one can see what he means. Imagine a society where people hear sounds and see sights with the crispness and clarity that narcotics confer. It's not us, and it's not now, but it's as legitimate a Utopia as a properly-functioning Welfare State or a world where the principles of anarchy, properly applied, produce freedom instead of chaos.

Happenings, like jazz, like certain kinds of assemblages, like a few quasi-improvised plays, combine the free and the ordered; the pre-arranged and the immediate. And in these combinations, a new kind of reality (part-real: part-fake) emerges. An artist builds a chair; a person sits on it; he becomes part of the design. An actor baits a member of the audience; the audience member responds; the play incorporates the incident and moves on. In *The Bedsitting Room*, because the Lord Chamberlain had cut out eight minutes of text, Spike Milligan reserved eight minutes of 'free time' at every performance. It was filled differently each night; depending on the urges and preoccupations of the night.

In Ulm there is a theatre that performs a detective-thriller which stops its action just before the end, invites members of the audience to guess who is the murderer and then, improvises a conclusion based on the suggestions. At a recent Happening in London, a disturbance involving The Alberts was staged in the street. The audience, packed into hired buses drove past the scene never absolutely certain whether what they were seeing from their windows was actual or contrived. As they continued their journeys, they discovered more and more 'happenings' in the street; all of these were, in fact, fortuitous. A fascinating kind of confusion ensues. Are we members of an audience watching scenes 'laid on' for us, or simply eye-witnesses at accidental events? The *Guardian* reviewer found that Happening a total waste of time. The *Financial Times* critic said that after it was over, he found 'happenings' everywhere he looked, and had begun, in fact, to look. Both reactions are absolutely accurate; each bespeaks a different degree of perception. A critic who reviews a 'Happening' simultaneously delivers a verdict on his own sensibility. He sees as much as he sees – not merely what is presented.

What Brechtian theatre has made abundantly clear in recent years is that one of the most dynamic factors in any stage-performance is the theatre-ritual itself; the existence of an audience that comes to a playhouse with certain prescribed attitudes and anticipations. For certain writers (Ionesco in *The Bald Prima Donna*; Gelber in *The Connection*) this pre-factor is an integral part of the whole process and can be engaged directly. Brecht (who was also preoccupied with audience-awareness) used the drama to demonstrate, and then gave the audience breathing-spaces in which to assimilate what had been seen. But he never challenged the audience's right of assembly; never invaded its clearly-defined domain.

The Happeners take a much more radical view. The 'imaginative collaboration' of an audience which fantasies itself into an action is for them insufficient. The whole concept of 'audience' is odious; people trapped in a formal tableau for a period of two hours, unnatural. (Who has not sat in a theatre watching the ghoulish spectacle of several hundred vacant faces stacked row upon row?) For them, there is a necessary circuit between the doers and the done-to, and nothing the doers do can have any great significance unless it actively engages those in whose midst it is taking place.

So long as we narrowly define theatre as 'plays' and bleat about 'the romantic drama', 'the realistic drama', the 'theatre of the absurd', we will simply move from one part of the maze to the other. But if we can extend our view of what, legitimately, the theatre can be, then we inherit an entirely new range of possibilities. I do not say – as the wild ones do – that we replace the theatre wholesale and spawn events in Trafalgar Square; my own contention is that for the theatre to survive, it has to be extended, and a sweeping overhaul of theatre-attitudes is the best way to effect this.

The portents are already there: some of the most exciting plays of the last few years have either been 'Happenings' or reminiscent of them. *The Connection* – seen by its author and by a large part of its New York audience as a stream of unfolding behaviour. *The Brig*, a brutal ceremony that is probably being played out in much the same way on improvised stages in Viet Nam and South Africa. The *Marat/Sade*, as base a long-winded polemical discourse; in the English production converted into a series of living tableaux, enlivened by sounds, movements, shapes and colour.

Today Happenings are for the theatre what Cubism was to art, or atonalism to music; an alternative route; a new, relatively-unexplored, outlet. To ignore it is to be anal-retentive about the 19th century; to embrace it may shatter some of our most treasured aesthetic concepts but it may also usher in a whole new world of sensation.

This article first appeared in *Plays and Players* in 1963, and is valuable in emphasizing the importance of Antonin Artaud, whose influence in present-day theatre is considerable but difficult to assess.

Marowitz also makes the link between Brecht, Cage, Milligan and others, all of whom have shown this anxiety to keep their drama fresh. It is worth recalling that:

1. there is a re-emphasis upon spectacle and noise and a particular desire to use these spontaneously
2. several present-day groups, such as The Living Theatre, Bread and Puppet Theatre and The People's Show, use happenings as part of their performance and productions
3. there is an attempt in all this to remove the traditional comfort and to replace it by the physical, the tactile, the near-violent, so that instead of easy communication we get impact
4. although Marowitz claims that happenings are an attempt to break with the past, it is clear that what he means is that there is a return to the basics of the past drama – before it became part of literature.

17 Search for a New Drama/*Albert Hunt and Michael Kustow*

an account of the growth of a collective theatre presentation, US, about the war in Vietnam and life in England. It was first produced at the Aldwych Theatre by the Royal Shake-speare Company, under the direction of Peter Brook.

It is perhaps in the following account of the way in which the Royal Shakespeare Company developed their documentary, stimulated by the Vietnam War, that we can most clearly appreciate the growing link between approaches and uses of drama in education and those in the theatre.

This is an example of a project undertaken by one of our most eminent national companies, but similar kinds of projects have been going on for some time now by local theatre companies, often using regional material to build a documentary.

Not only is Peter Brook one of the Directors of the Company, but his influence has also been felt in free-lance productions and in film direction which he has undertaken in recent years. There is a dynamic quality about anything he undertakes, even though at times I feel the material becomes subordinate to his firm and theatrical direction. The project which is here narrated by two people who were associated with its growth is the kind which some professional actors at least find very difficult, because it takes away the usual security of text and places the emphasis on creativity.

Before this, the Royal Shakespeare Company had spent some time preparing a project called 'Strike', which, thwarted by many difficulties, never got off the ground. We have yet to see the same courage and sense of experiment undertaken by the National Theatre.

Albert Hunt at present works in the Department of Liberal Studies at Bradford College of Art: Michael Kustow is Director of the Institute of Contemporary Arts in London. Both young men have a sense of commitment in all that they tackle and continue to explore ways in which drama is related to current events and attitudes.

NARRATIVE ONE: Albert Hunt

In the article in *The Times* a few weeks after *US* opened, Irving Wardle, suggesting that the second act of the play negated everything that had been said in the first act, asked how far the members of the team that made *US* had been aware from the first of Peter Brook's strategy. The implication was that Brook himself had a master plan; that from the beginning he knew clearly and precisely what he wanted to say; and that he only collected around himself a number of talents in order to manipulate them for his own purposes.

The argument, at first sight, is plausible. It was certainly true, as Irving Wardle knew, that some of the members of the team felt that the play's final statement was not what they had originally intended. But to suggest that Brook planned this from the beginning is to misunderstand the whole process of work through which *US* was made. *US* was, above all, a search. It was a collective search by a group of people who wanted to say something true and honest and useful about a subject we all felt was very important – the Vietnam War. The statement that was eventually made in the Aldwych Theatre on October 13, 1966, may not have satisfied all of us. But it was a statement that had grown out of a process of work, and not one that had been conceived in Brook's mind before the process began. And the possibilities opened up by the process are more important that the limitations of the show that was finally produced.

For me, the process began at a meeting between Brook, Reeves and myself at Brook's house the previous December. At that meeting Brook talked of two subjects which were very much on his mind. The first was the Vietnam War – not so much the war itself as what we, in London, could do about it, and how an awareness of the war could affect our lives. He talked about this in direct, practical terms. If you said you cared about Vietnam, how did this affect the way you spent your day? He talked of a well-known actress who, he said, rationed her day out – so many hours for rehearsal, so many hours for writing to M.P.s or Newspapers, or helping in demonstrations. Was this an adequate way of responding to what was happening in Vietnam? If not, what would be adequate?

The other question that was in Brook's mind that night was a very simple one from the Bhagavad Gita: 'Shall I fight?' Apparently simple, that is. For it was easy enough to give, in the abstract, a negative answer. But the fact was that, in Vietnam, people were fighting. Simply to wash one's hands of this and utter moral precepts seemed to all of us a useless gesture. And yet the question was there and had to be confronted. Brook wanted to create a show in which this question would be raised in terms of the war in Vietnam.

He felt, too, that the show would have to be made in a new way. Reading through the scripts that came into the Royal Shakespeare Company, he was brought up against the fact that no individual playwright, working alone, seemed able, at the moment, to handle a direct statement of this size. Brook said that perhaps the conditions were not right; that a Shakespeare could only have emerged out of a situation in which groups of actors and writers had established a common language. Our job was not to produce a King Lear, but to start on the work of forging a language. The theatre ought to be able to speak about a subject as central as the Vietnam War; no play existed that was in any way adequate; in working together we should try to create circumstances in which such a play could be written. (It is important to realize that even in this early stage it was fully understood that we should be heavily dependent on a writer. A writer of some weight would, we hoped, be involved in the process from the start – taking part in our discussions, working over material we should provide him with, later sitting in with the actors and finding material in rehearsals.)

We began to read all we could lay our hands on about Vietnam. By far the most useful documents we found were the records of the Fulbright Committee Hearings on Vietnam and China. There was a striking phrase by one of the key witnesses, Dr Fairbank: 'Great nations on both sides are pursuing their alternative dreams.' We began to see the war as a collision of dreams. And there was a piece of dialogue from the hearings that increasingly summed up our response to this material:

SENATOR FULBRIGHT: None of us has an answer. I am afraid not.
GENERAL GRIFFITH: I am afraid I do not have.
SENATOR FULBRIGHT: None of us has an answer.

What emerged above all from the Hearings was the awareness, in the United States, that the administration had drifted into a situation which most people bitterly regretted, but that nobody could see the way out. In these circumstances, to stand on a stage and simply demand American withdrawal seemed both impertinent and inadequate. We had somehow to confront the real, complex situation. The question was: how? We studied Happenings and talked about ways of involving the audience physically. At Bradford, with the students of the Art College, we invented a ritualistic game. From the ceiling, there hung a structure, built on two cross-pieces that would spin round if it were touched. Hanging from this structure were dummy bodies, tin cans that made noises, brightly coloured balloons, sheets of pink cellophane, rubber tyres. If anybody collided with these objects, the whole structure whirled round and up and down in colour and movement.

Through this constantly moving structure, five players felt their way, with paper bags over their heads. The bags made them look weird and helpless. Two carried blue flags, two carried red, and one, wearing a bag decorated with stars and stripes, carried a stick. The player with the stick hunted for the others. When he caught anybody he raised his stick. A referee, wearing a frock coat and a black bowler, blew his whistle; everybody froze; the referee led the victim to the front of the stage; and another player, pushed through a door at the back, had taken his place. The hunter never knew whether he had caught a red or a blue.

The game was a complete dramatic event in itself. But the paper bags found their way into rehearsal, and even into the first night: the alternating sequences of noise and silence pointed towards an overall pattern.

Meanwhile, the more we gathered material, the more intractable that material seemed to be. One afternoon, Mitchell, Reeves and myself listened to two American L.P.s of popular songs about Vietnam.

We were all of us saturated by newsreels and reports and television programmes. Horrors no longer had any effect on us. But in a theatre, in in a ritualized situation, it might be possible for us to see the horrors in a fresh way. He didn't expect the show to convert anybody, but possibly something in the show would plant a seed to change, so that when people were later confronted by situations, they might begin to react in a different way . . .

Nevertheless, by the time rehearsals began in July, we still seemed to have very little in the way of actable material. We had two or three pages of ideas we'd jotted down, a document about the war for the actors to read aloud, a few speeches from Charles Wood and a poem by Mitchell. But from now on the work moved into another dimension. Previously we had read and talked. Now, the ideas were to be explored collectively by the actors through their bodies. For the next few weeks, the actors were to be central in the process of work.

July 4

We all met the actors for the first time in the ballroom of Bourne and Hollingsworth in Gower Street. Most of the actors had worked with Brook before, either in the Theatre of Cruelty, or on Marat/Sade. Several had recently been with the Marat/Sade in New York.

To the actors, that first meeting must have been an unnerving experience. The physical arrangement of the room made matters worse. The actors sat in a semi-circle facing a long table. We sat behind the table, facing the actors. We must have looked like intruders, violating the privacy of rehearsal . . .

Very hesitantly, the actors began talking. Once they had started, they felt America was more violent than England, but the examples they gave were not very convincing. They talked about taxi drivers who shouted, and about the violence they felt on the streets at night. But there was nothing specific, and certainly nothing more violent than one can see in the streets of a northern town like Bradford. One felt only that outside the theatre the actors had never had much experience of violence . . .

After lunch, the actors were divided into two groups, about a dozen in each group. One group stayed to work on improvisations arising out of that morning's discussions. These first improvisations did give a line to work on, and the experience could be deepened through rehearsal.

At the end of the day, Brook said he had an idea for a final image in the show. After all the noise and violence there would be a silence. And in the silence there would be released – a butterfly.

July 5

In our pre-rehearsal discussions, we had talked a lot about Happenings. The aim of many of the Happenings we had examined was clearly to shock people into a new kind of awareness, something that the show itself was intended to do. At the same time we knew that, given the condition of having to produce a show for the Aldwych, which might run for some time, we should need something more tightly structured than a Happening. We wanted somehow to catch the immediacy of a Happening while having a fixed, dramatic structure.

On the second day of rehearsal, the actors were presented with a long article from the *Tulane Drama Review* issues on Happenings. Bob Lloyd and Glenda Jackson read the article aloud.

'The Director of a music concert would not allow me to perform Composition 1960 number five. Diana said maybe the reason the Director of a music concert would not allow me to perform Composition 1960 number five was that he thought it was not music. Composition 1960 number five is the piece in which the butterfly is turned loose in the performance area.'

The article contained a discussion about evil. 'Dennis Johnson wrote to me "Do you think there is too much Evil in the world? John Cage thinks there is just the right amount. I think there is too much world in the Evil."' After the reading, the actors discussed the article. We tried to analyse the connection between the society that had produced Happenings and what was going on in Vietnam.

But at this point we were stuck. Apart from the obvious statement that both Happenings and the war were the products of American society, there seemed to be very little to say. And then Mike Williams suddenly demonstrated the kind of theatre language we were looking for. He found an image which made the connection in concrete terms. He put a chair on a table, crumpled some paper and took a match. Then, speaking very simply the words of the letter about the butterfly piece, he climbed on to a chair, and pretended to drench himself in petrol. As he reached the words 'Isn't it wonderful to listen to something you normally look at?' he struck the match.

The image suddenly pulled together the two worlds, so that they commented on each other. It did not say simply that Happenings were trivial, and that the real Happening was to burn yourself to death. The words revealed the immolation as a dramatic event – and the action placed the words in a wider context. It was this kind of revelation that we were looking for when we placed the material about Happenings in the middle of a discussion about burning in Act Two of the finished production. But I don't think we ever in the end achieved anything as clear and penetrating as this very early, suddenly discovered act.

July 6, 7, 8

In the first two days, our search for a language had developed in three main directions: exploring American life through naturalistic improvisations; investigating American popular myths; and looking at the intellectual world of the Happenings. During the rest of the first week, these directions were developed.

The work on Happenings produced the most finished piece of work that week. A group played out a number of New York intellectuals trying to stage a Happening. They never reached the Happening, and in their failure they caught at an image, a group of people struggling with their own ineffectiveness. It was a superficial image, and unfair to the creative energy that goes into a successful Happening, but it was true in so far as it reflected a sense of impotence and in-group isolation. But the limitations were ruthlessly exposed as soon as Brook asked them to turn the scene into an English drawing-room on Sunday afternoon. The result was broad, unfunny cliché.

July 11

One small incident suddenly called attention to the thinness of the work. At the start of one of the raids, the chair thrown as a signal nearly hit one of the actors. He reacted spontaneously, flinching instinctively from the real threatened pain. Then, when the chair missed, he became a Vietnamese villager again, simulating a wound.

For me, this exercise raised a whole set of questions that were never, I think, answered. Brook had said, again and again, that we must somehow find a language of communication that went beyond our deadened responses to the newsreels and television documentaries. Yet how could these actors begin to compete with those shots of the children whose face s had been turned to crust? All we had to offer in this show was ourselves – ourselves in London, not being burnt with jellied petrol. We – or rather the actors – could not convincingly simulate bombed villagers. They could only confront a particular audience on a particular night with their own, unblistered bodies. Whatever was communicated finally would come, not through a skilful imitation of pain, but through that confrontation. To this extent, each performance would be a Happening. The flinching from the thrown chair said more to me about Vietnam that morning than any of the tortured gestures of the actors. It was this quality of immediacy that we should have to look for.

July 12

Brook had already talked about the limitation of this form of communication. He had produced Peter Weiss' oratorio, about the concentration camps, *The Investigation,* as a Sunday night reading. It has been seriously done and Weiss had, of course, shaped the material much more dramatically than we had done in this document. But Brook felt that all the evening had achieved, in the end, was to demonstrate to the audience that they, too, could come to accept atrocity as boring. For the first twenty minutes, he said, you were shocked; then you began to get bored; in the end you waited impatiently for the catalogue of horror to end. We could never communicate to an Aldwych audience in this way. (Anyway, for a performance like that, he pointed out realistically, we should never have an audience to communicate to.)

But after reading, Brook began to explore the ways of forging the documentary material into the language we were looking for. He worked with Ian Hogg on words and phrases from Johnson's Omaha speech. Ian Hogg changed the age of the speaker, first making him older, as if he were approaching his death-bed, then younger, so that the reading became bright and open. Finally, he tried it as if it were a scene from Beckett, reading the speech from three hundred years on. The phrases came over with great force and clarity. 'Therefore, choose life, that thou and thy seed shall live.' Brook discovered a way of communicating directly through what was, intrinsically, undramatic material.

July 13–19

For the first time, Brook showed the way in which his mind was working towards a collage of different elements. He began with a horror comic scenario Mitchell had written, 'Zappman'. He worked through the story in very short scenes, then began to inject other elements into it. First, the group were Americans improvising a Happening; then they moved into the exercise showing air-raid wounds; then into the first scene of the comic strip. At the end of this scene, Ian Hogg, lying on the floor as a dead G.I., did part of Johnson's Great Society speech as an old man. Then the scene went back to wounds again, and then into the second comic strip scene, with Bob Lloyd zapping the Cong, and then turning into Kennedy . . . This mixing of elements was to become part of the pattern of *US*.

Meanwhile, work continued on the American material. A small group tried out a read of Ginsberg's poem, 'Wichita Vortex Sutra'; a new improvisation, 'The Great Masturbator', was built around the Andy Warhol character; another group improvised a storm, and yet another began to plan a Happening. Through these exercises, the basic language was being formed and sharpened. But there was still one major problem that we had scarcely touched. How were we to say anything about a peasant culture when none of us knew anything about peasants? Were we simply to ask the actors to imitate Vietnamese peasants rather badly? And was not this pointing once again to the basic truth that our real material was these actors confronting that audience in the Aldwych Theatre – and that our language would have to be based primarily on this existential fact?

July 21

If we were to find a language to communicate to other people, we must first be able to look honestly at ourselves. Throughout rehearsals, this proved to be very difficult. We all of us – the actors included – had a number of easy responses to the material we were studying. How to get through these responses until we were confronted with what we really experienced?

The difficulty became clear when Brook began working on a torture scene. He used four actors, with the rest sitting round in a group watching. He asked those watching to give their immediate, spontaneous reactions to what they saw, first as if they were watching Americans carrying out the torture, and then as if they were the inhabitants of a bombed village, watching an American airman being tortured.

Most of the responses were the ones that might be expected. They were, for the most part, conventional expressions of disgust. A few of the spectators were able to sympathize with the desire of the Vietnamese villagers for some kind of revenge: none of them seemed to have any sympathy at all for the American position. In discussion afterwards, I asked a girl who had been revolted by what she had seen what she would do if she were an American officer in a village, whose men were being shot off, and who was convinced that the Vietnamese in front of him knew who the killer was. Would the officer not have a primary responsibility to try and save the lives of his men? She replied honestly enough that she could not imagine herself as an American officer.

I felt that the situation needed exploring in this way: as it was the watchers were simply reacting in disgust to actions taken out of context. But what was perhaps more interesting was the zest with which those actions were performed. Both the torturers and the tortured played the game with a lot of imaginative vigour, simulating, realistically, blows to the windpipe and the testicles, with the victim groaning and screaming in agony.

The tortures were sickeningly convincing, and most of us watched them with fascinated attention. What was revealed was the gap between that we pretend to feel, and the disturbing impulses inside. Much later, when we had moved to Conmar, we played a version of the blindfold game the students in Bradford had invented. On that occasion, everybody threw themselves with great gusto into the business of frightening those who could not see – and afterwards everybody sat around again, telling each other how torture was disgusting.

And yet – the instinctive, disgusted response to torture was healthy and genuine. It is a long step from teasing somebody you know in rehearsal, to torturing a prisoner. But it was important for each one to confront the germs of cruelty in himself as a first step towards understanding.

The stage was, in fact, being set for the arrival of Grotowski, who was to relate physical work to a willingness to look inside oneself honestly. From this point onwards, most of this exploration was left until Grotowski arrived.

July 25

Brook talked again to the actors, summing up the work of the previous three weeks. He pointed out that every fragment was self-contained and that the putting together would come later. At the moment, they must apply themselves seriously to each separate piece of work. Such a method would go on for several weeks before they began to see anything taking shape.

The actors must be aware that they were trying to create a new language of acting, by collecting bits and pieces from everywhere. The actor must dig inside himself for responses, but at the same time must be open to outside stimuli. Acting was the marriage of these two processes.

This was the last week before Grotowski was due to arrive, and also the last that Joe Chaikin would be with us. The actors spent most of the week improvising the American material. When they played through a Doris Day story 'Blueberry Pie', they demonstrated the advances in control they had made over the last few weeks. They succeeded in producing moments of pure emotion while being beside themselves with laughter. They had at least broken through the faintly patronizing attitude they had shown at the beginning.

What had been achieved in these first four weeks? The rudiments of an acting style had been created – the actors were now able to move much more flexibly from one mood to another. A language of theatre, based on a bringing together of many different elements was being tentatively formed. And most of the material that was to go into the first act had been thrown up in rehearsal at one time or another.

What was still lacking was a sense of disciplined control by the actors, either physical or emotional. What was needed, after all the exploration of different styles, was a tight concentration on one particular area.

This was what we were hoping for from Grotowski when this first period of rehearsal came to an end. The work he was going to do with the actors would inevitably determine the way the material we already had would be shaped and organized.

The actors were ready for the next step in the process of searching.

NARRATIVE TWO: Michael Kustow

Monday, August 1

At this point in rehearsal, having conducted a first foray into the company's knowledge and images of America, Vietnam and Asia, Brook decided to shift the focus inwards for ten days. Jerzy Grotowski, director of the Polish Teatr Laboratorium at Wroclaw, had been invited to work

SEARCH FOR A NEW DRAMA 197

with our actors, putting them through an intensive course of the exercises and training with which his own actors have reached great physical and spiritual skill. Grotowski arrived with Ryszard Cieslak, one of his leading actors. We were all very intrigued by what Grotowski would do. Some of us had seen his explosive and blasphemous production of Marlowe's *Dr. Faustus*, and had witnessed the taxing exercise and stern, almost monastic discipline of his 'theatre-laboratory' in Poland. All of us recognized a remarkable authority in this pale-faced man, dressed in black, habitually wearing dark glasses.

What followed in the next ten days is difficult to describe, because it took place on such a private, naked level, because it was in every sense a workshop, a consulting-room, a confessional, a temple, a refuge, a place of reflection, but reflection conducted not only with the mind, but with every fibre and muscle of the body.

Brook wrote an article for the Royal Shakespeare Club newspaper, *Flourish*, which summed up Grotowski's impact on all of us at this stage:

Grotowski is unique.

Why?

Because no one else in the world, to my knowledge no one since Stanislavski, has investigated the nature of acting, its phenomenon, its meaning, the nature and science of its mental-physical-emotional processes as deeply and completely as Grotowski.

He calls his theatre a laboratory. It is. It is a centre of research. It is perhaps the only avant-garde theatre whose poverty is not a drawback, where shortage of money is not an excuse for inadequate means which automatically undermine the experiments.

In Grotowski's theatre, as in all true laboratories, the experiments are scientifically valid because the essential conditions are observed. In his theatre there is absolute concentration by a small group, and unlimited time. So if you are interested in his findings you must go to a small town in Poland.

Or else do what he did. Bring Grotowski here.

He worked for two weeks with our group. I won't describe the work. Why not? First of all, such work is only free if it is in confidence, and confidence depends on its confidences not being disclosed. Secondly, the work is essentially non-verbal. To verbalize is to complicate and even to destroy exercises that are clear and simple when indicated by a gesture and when executed by the mind and body as one.

What did the work do?

It gave each actor a series of shocks.

The shock of confronting himself in the face of simple irrefutable challenges.

The shock of catching sight of his own evasions, tricks and clichés.

The shock of sensing something of his own vast and untapped resources.

The shock of being forced to question why he is an actor at all.

The shock of being forced to recognize that such questions do exist and that – despite a long English tradition of avoiding seriousness in theatrical art – the time comes when they must be faced. And of finding that he wants to face them.

The shock of seeing that somewhere in the world acting is an art of absolute dedication, monastic and total. That Artaud's now hackneyed phrase 'cruel to myself' is genuinely a complete way of life – somewhere for less than a dozen people.

With a proviso. This dedication to acting does not make acting an end in itself. On the contrary. For Grotowski acting is a vehicle.

How can I put it? The theatre is not an escape, a refuge. A way of life is a way to life. Does that sound like a religious slogan? It should do. And that's about all there was to it. No more, no less. Results? Unlikely. Are our actors better? Are they better men? Not in that way, as far as I can see, not as far as anyone has claimed. (And of course they were not all ecstatic about their experience. Some were bored.)

But as Arden says:

> For the apple holds a seed will grow.
> In live and lengthy joy
> To raise a flourishing tree of fruit,
> For ever and a day.

Grotowski's work and ours have parallels and points of contact. Through these, through sympathy, through respect, we came together.

But the life of our theatre is in every way different from his. He runs a laboratory. He needs an audience occasionally. In small numbers. His tradition is Catholic – or anti-Catholic; in this case the two extremes meet. He is creating a form of service. We work in another country, another language, another tradition. Our aim is not a new Mass, but a new Elizabethan relationship – linking the private and the public, the intimate and the crowded, the secret and the open, the vulgar and the

magical. For this we need both a crowd on stage and a crowd watching –
and within that crowded stage individuals offering their intimate truths
to individuals within that crowded audience, sharing a collective
experience with them.

We have come quite a way in developing an overall pattern – the idea
of a group, of an ensemble.

But our work is always too hurried, always too rough for the development of the collection of individuals out of whom it is composed.

We know in theory that every actor must put his art into question
daily – like pianists, dancers, painters – and that if he doesn't he will
almost certainly get stuck, develop clichés, and eventually decline. We
recognize this and yet can do so little about it that we endlessly chase
after new blood, youthful vitality – except for certain of the most gifted
exceptions, who of course get all the best chances, absorb most of the
available time.

The Stratford Studio was a recognition of this problem, but it continually ran up against the strain of a repertory, of an overworked
company, of simple fatigue.

Grotowski's work was a reminder that what he achieves almost
miraculously with a handful of actors is needed to the same extent by
each individual in our two giant companies in two theatres 90 miles
apart.

The intensity, the honesty and the precision of his work can only
leave one thing behind. A challenge. But not for a fortnight, not for once
in a lifetime. Daily.

Monday, August 15

Over the week-end, Brook, Hunt and Reeves have gone through all the
material we have explored, and decided (certainly influenced by the fiery
commitment which Grotowski had succeeded in drawing from our
actors) that BURNING, the act of burning oneself, could become the
central image of the play's action. They discussed ways of working
outwards from this naked act, bring in history, politics, communications, all the other facets of the war.

On Monday, Brook spoke to the company. 'We are now entering the
third stage of our work. In the first, you opened up as many fields as you
could, ranged as widely through our knowledge and ignorance and
images as you could. With Grotowski, you explored deeply and intensely

a very focused, tight, personal area of commitment, your own bodily commitment as actors. Now in the third stage, we shall broaden our scope again. But the intense personal exploration will continue – I don't want anyone to feel that the last ten days' work with Grotowski have been a summer school, a refresher course having no direct contact with our subject. No, this personal search – and I know many of you have found it painful – will continue. So once more I say that if anyone wants to pull out now, they can do so.' Nobody did.

Tuesday, August 16

We began, very stumblingly, to assemble together into playable units the 150-page pile of material we had accumulated from research and stage one of our work.

The question of a playwright had become critical, and now been resolved. We had always intended to involve a playwright in the entire rehearsal process, hoping that writer and actors could be mutually beneficial, and that in particular, the writer might delve more deeply when confronted by actors' work which was unsupported by an existing script. Our original playwright, Charles Wood, had been unable to escape from commitments to a film, and after an agonizing period with no playwright at all, we welcomed Denis Cannan into the team. He sat in on our gradual assemblage of the documentary and improvised material which we hoped would form an Act One. It was to Cannan that we were looking for Act Two.

Friday, August 19

We read out loud the Chinese Document, Hunt's compilation of material from largely communist and nationalist sources. We broke at lunchtime, and Brook, Hunt, Stott, Peaslee, Sally Jacobs, Reeves, Mitchell, Cannan and Kustow went to St. James's Park for a working picnic a stone's throw from Buckingham Palace.

On the way to the park, Denis Cannan turned to me and said, 'What I'm working towards in my thinking about the second act is this feeling I have that we all want extreme situations, that we yearn for invasion, apocalypse. Because they simplify our tangled lives.' This proved to be the germ of Glenda Jackson's final speech.

In the park, we decided on the immediately stageable sections of the

Chinese document: the Lament of the Soldier's Wife, Vietnamese legends and poems, the revolutionary car ride.

Saturday, August 27

Run-through of all material assembled over previous fortnight. After an hour and three-quarters, the run-through had still only reached the beginning of the History of Vietnam section. We were afraid of making a five-hour show. Cannon, asked for his reaction to the run-through, said he saw Act One centring on man and his predicament, while Act Two should focus on man and his nature. A very existentialist discussion took place, with Cannan quoting from Sartre's 'Portrait of an Anti-Semite', which he was using to clarify his ideas about Mark's character. Brook went off to look at Cannan's suggested twenty-minute scene about an English boy who wanted to burn himself.

Tuesday, August 30

In the tiny backroom at the Donmar Rehearsal Theatre were: Brook, Hunt, Reeves, Mitchell, Kustow, Cannan and Mark Jones. A very delicate exercise was about to take place, based on the situation of Cannan's proposed final scene. 'You are in Grosvenor Square', said Brook to Mark Jones, 'with your petrol-can and your matches. You have come to burn yourself.' Mark started to make preparations. Along came Cannan working off a clipboard of questions. He stopped Mark in mid-stream, and probed the reasons for his action, the effect he hoped it would have, what he thought of other people and their capacity for change.

It was a sustained, John-Whiting-like assault on Man's (and Mark's) presumption, using harsh anecdotes and Socratic dialectic to try to undermine Mark's resolution. But it didn't connect with the pitch of utter decision which Mark had achieved, the dogged, almost animal like honesty with which he held to his choice. Against this impervious sincerity, even the sharpest flints of Cannan's arguments could not pierce.

Mitchell then tried to sway Mark. 'Can't you see that it's self-sacrifice? Have you really tried every other possible route?'

Hunt read Mark a list of the many people who had committed suicide by fire in Britain over the past two years, for reasons that were pathetic, foolish, mad, or just plain inexplicable. Mark's reaction was that, however others cared to interpret it, he knew his motives, and in that sense at least was untroubled.

Brook sat down on the floor with Mark. Very close to him. 'Look me in the eyes. What is cruelty? Unlimited exercise of power over others. Do you have power over other people? Do you have power over yourself? Aren't you being cruel to your own flesh by setting it on fire? Aren't you alive? What is you? There is something called life and it's there in you. Have you the right to destroy it? What you want to do to yourself is what the world is doing to itself. You want life for the world, why don't you allow yourself to live? If you stop now, one less act of cruelty has taken place. It takes more courage to face the situation than to burn yourself. It takes the same kind of courage for the superpowers involved in this war to back down from their prepared positions.'

Mark put his head in his hands. There was silence for five minutes. The exercise had lasted nearly two hours. We all sat still. I was very aware of the different kind of contact Brook had made with the actor compared with the others. Brook's questioning had been much more physical, much closer to a confessional.

We tried to discuss the results of this exercise afterwards. Hunt feared the sense of a soothing catharsis which such an intense trial-by-fire-and-argument, would generate. Brook said the silence at the end must be 'an open mouth, not a shut eye'. 'Commitment is a changing relationship, like a love affair; not a deal, like a bad marriage. And let's not overestimate the potential effect of the show. An analyst has one person on the couch for maybe twelve years: we have 1000 people on the equivalent of Waterloo Station for three hours. We must work like acupuncture: find the precise spot on the tensed muscle that will cause it to relax. If we succeed, we won't end the war or anything drastic like that, but one person out of one thousand might act differently because of what they experienced in the theatre that night.'

Saturday, September 3

Sally Jacobs, still struggling with ideas for set. Her first proposal had been that the entire action took place over and around the body of a huge fighting man, a stage-sized soldier. This made too rigid a statement, however, and was modified into a huge combat-man dummy, hanging over the proscenium arch. Now Sally proposed a second idea: that the stage should be a vast rubbish-dump, with fragments of aeroplane fuselage, bent wings, and scraps of newscuttings and comics strewn over the floor.

Friday, September 9

Reading of Denis Cannan's draft second act – at this stage a twenty-minute scene between Mark Jones, Glenda Jackson, and Clifford Rose, as a Buddhist monk. It had a prickly electric effect at this first reading, and when Peter asked us to comment immediately after, we couldn't manage very much. We all felt that it was too short, and that the girl character wiped the floor with Mark too conclusively. We worried about the inarticulateness of Mark. Were we in danger of sticking in a cleft stick? Mark's utter commitment to burning rendered him literally speechless and left him apparently at the mercy of Glenda's self-hating.

Saturday, September 10

Run-through of Act One and read-through of Act Two for Peter Hall, Jeremy Brooks, and other RSC associates. Peter Hall's comments: 'The seriousness and breadth of Act One are very impressive; it will certainly hold for close on two hours. And the tight focus of Act Two makes just the right counter-balance. I'm not sure about the flip quality that occasionally invades the acting – there's a danger of becoming camp as soon as you stop being studiously naturalistic. Even if you are playing with a toy gun you must treat it as real. All the material about the USA is richer, more complex, than the material from Vietnam.' (Reflection: we will always find American experience closer to our own than Vietnamese.)

'I want you to think about silence, think about it in relation to our audience. They will come in, take their seats, and wait – with a sort of curious, expectant silence, waiting to see what we can unfold about a war and a political situation about which they have come to conclusions. Our job in this performance is to lead our audience – and ourselves – from one kind of silence to another: the silence of genuine concern, not just attentiveness, indignation, despair, impotence.

Friday, September 23

After the first run-through on the Aldwych stage, the team gathered to discuss the whole balance of the show. Brook: 'The object of Act One is to make people feel that something must be done about Vietnam. In Act Two, Mark and Glenda are the two poles which contain the spectrum of all who feel deeply about the war. The link with Act One must be through Mark – we must see the events through his eyes.' We decided to park Mark at the side of the stage, receiving the war through the imagery of TV and transistor, and only attempting (incoherently) to intervene at the end of the act.

Thursday, September 29

Peter Brook broke rehearsals early (at 4.45 p.m.) and called all of us into the back room of Donmar.

'You have really begun, in the past two days, to create the kind of burning, the kind of relating to every part of the show, that I talked about on Monday. This gives us a real possibility of making something that grows out of the group. You have begun to find the approach that can lead us towards that other kind of silence. But don't let anyone imagine we shall therefore stop questioning and opening this up – we shall do so if possible even more intensively than before.

'The second thing I want to tell you is this: Lord Cobbold, the Lord Chamberlain (without whose permission no play could at this time be performed in England) has telephoned George Farmer, Chairman of the Governors of the RSC about US. He rang George Farmer on his fishing holiday in Scotland to tell him that in his opinion this show was "bestial, anti-American and communist", and that he would be very grateful if Mr. Farmer would exercise his influence to prevent it. He said he could not allow the show – the entire show. George Farmer is flying down from Scotland in the morning, and we will do a run-through for him and Peter Hall in the afternoon, so that he knows exactly where he stands before he goes to see the Lord Chamberlain.

'No one must breathe a word about this outside this room. I don't have to tell you that the slightest murmur in the Green Room and it will be all over town. And it mustn't yet. This will be a very real exercise, to keep this news completely within the group.'

There was then a discussion among the team. It was agreed that Michael Kustow and Jeremy Brooks should seek legal advice the next morning on the common law possibilities of bringing an action against a Crown servant, and the intricacies of the theatre licence situation at the Aldwych and Stratford-upon-Avon.

It was also felt that everything depended on George Farmer's reaction to the run-through.

Friday, September 30

Donmar, after lunch, the run-through began. The tension was unbelievable, and the electricity which came off from the songs, the Quaker meeting, the burnings, the journalist monologue, and above all MAKE AND BREAK, was riveting. The entire performance was an extraordinary theatrical event. The two sticks Peter had talked about were being ground together with an intensity that was often unbearable in the proximity of the rehearsal room.

Time was getting short, so in the second act, we simply played the Mark/Glenda dialogue, cutting songs and interpolations.

George Farmer was due at St. James's Palace to discuss with the Chamberlain immediately after the run-through. Lord Cobbold had consistently said, since his telephone call to Farmer, that he did not wish to see either Peter Brook or Peter Hall, but only deal with George Farmer as Chairman of the Governors. But when Farmer scurried for a taxi, both Peters went with him.

The Lord Chamberlain awaited them in full court regalia, complete with sword. After some delay, during which Peter Hall and Peter Brook waited in the street, the Chamberlain agreed to see all three visitors. He repeated his description of the performance, now modifying it slightly to 'bestial and left-wing.'

George Farmer made his position quite clear immediately by telling the Chamberlain that he had now seen the show, and was satisfied that it was a performance of integrity. He emphasized, however, that it was a show with a definite *point of view*, and that the Chamberlain should make no mistake about this. Speaking for himself, said Farmer, he was satisfied that the degree of personal endeavour which was going into the performance removed it from any easy propaganda posture.

The Chamberlain then asked George Farmer if he thought the show was anti-American. George Farmer said no; the show criticized Britain as much as the USA. The Chamberlain put it another way. Suppose, he said, suppose the American Ambassador came to the first night. Would he walk out?

No, said George Farmer, in a perfect theatre-of-the-absurd answer, not if he stayed till the end. (By which he meant that parts of the Act Two dialogue would have counterpointed the insolence of some of the Act One songs and actions.)

The Chamberlain then asked George Farmer if he was prepared to stand by the production as Chairman of the theatre's Governors. Absolutely, said George Farmer.

In that case, said the Chamberlain, I am prepared to issue a licence for the play. Great feelings of relief from Brook, Hall and Farmer.

But, said the Chamberlain, when I sent my list of objections to certain portions of the text, it is understood that there can be no negotiations over any of these.

Peter Brook exploded, virtually accusing the Chamberlain of trying to do a deal – 'if I let you put it on, you must abide by my cuts'. He insisted that the Chamberlain's objections to this text be treated just the same as those of any other play, i.e. subject to the submission of alternatives.

Sunday, October 2

Peter Brook to company before run-through on stage:

'The crisis with the Lord Chamberlain is an image of the whole war itself, the corridors of power, the power of rumour. Remember, if this crisis had taken place in Vietnam, some of us would be dead by now. I want you also to consider this as a small foretaste of the kind of response we are going to get when we open.

'The performance you gave on Friday was very good, but it already contained the seeds of its own destruction – many of you in the Quaker scene were so visibly moved you were shaking. This is something you could never keep up, not in that way. Keep your heads above water, keep your eyes on the goal ahead.'

The run-through was interesting for us above all technically: for the first time we saw Roger painted naked and rolled on paper, for the first time the dummy descended and we found out how uselessly heavy it was, decided to strip it to minimum structure.

We finished work in the theatre at 11 p.m, all went back to Peter's house to discuss Act Two. This was the first of a series of bitter arguments about the direction of the second act, arguments which were sharpened by the difficult position of Denis Cannan (arriving midway through the rehearsal period), and also by the ever-increasing tempo of the rehearsal process, which was now mounting towards the 'home-straight' – a time in which sober assessment was difficult, if only because there was so much to clarify in so little time.

However, deep divergencies split the team, and it is in order not to minimize the probability of these occurring with any other group of people working in this kind of collaboration that a summary must be given.

There were three such tormented discussions. They took place at Peter Brook's house, in a Lyons' Corner House, in the coffee bar of the Royal Garden Hotel and in a Wimpy Bar off Leicester Square. They all seem to have started at midnight at least, and to have ground to a halt in utter fatigue, even in tears, at any time from half-past two to half-past four in the morning.

Under these circumstances, the sharply-held attitudes of the early part of each discussion tended to degenerate into a desperate attempt to hold any thoughts together as time wore on. But basically, Adrian Mitchell, Albert Hunt and Sally Jacobs felt strongly that the girl character played by Glenda Jackson walked away with the play's 'moral' in Act Two; that the result was an apparently corrosive but in effect sentimental conclusion ('a girl in search of God,' said one of the team): and that the boy character, played by Mark Jones was not sufficiently eloquent to answer the massive onslaught of the girl's attacks.

Denis Cannan did not attempt to defend the characters, although in one particularly painful session, I felt he was crumbling before the attack in a paroxysm of self-accusation. Peter Brook, Geoffrey Reeves and myself tried as best we could to limit the argument within the practical bounds of what was possible in the time and circumstances, all of us nonetheless feeling that some demon of self-destruction had raised its head which needed to be faced more deeply than we had time for at that point. Extract from dialogue between Brook and an actor after the play had opened:

Brook: Every group contains the seeds of its own destruction.
Actor: Why does this have to be so?

> Brook: I can't answer that. You must find out how true or not it is for yourself.

Asked for practical solutions, Hunt, Mitchell and Cannan produced various speeches to follow Glenda's great outburst at the end: a speech for Vietnam, a speech for the English boy, a speech for the liberal journalist comforting Glenda imprisoned in her agony. We eventually played these speeches at one of the preview performances, but it was clear they weakened the dramatic line of the act, and Brook was adamant in returning to the original line, but using the presence and reactions and pressure of the entire company circling these two combatants to put the scene into some kind of frame, and not simply let Glenda 'walk away with it'.

Tuesday, October 4

Continuing the painstaking run-through on stage of the entire show, we reached the end of Act Two. Peter had asked the actors at the end of the run to come downstage, sit on the floor, and try to encapsulate their attitude to the war, and to taking part in this production, in as succinct a form as possible.

This would be the third time over the fifteen-week period of rehearsal that the actors had been asked to express their personal attitudes. The progression with each new statement – or attempt at a statement – had been gradually away from glibness, involving a greater and greater effort to assert.

Tuesday, October 11

Run-through of Act One. Because we were late starting, the actors were asked to keep their own rehearsal clothes instead of wearing costumes. Seeing them from out front, both Peter Brook and Sally Jacobs felt the reality of these fifteen-week-familiar clothes, and thus, forty-eight hours before the opening, we cut all the costumes from the show. First preview performance to RSC Club members.

Wednesday, October 12

The closed-circuit television system, which had never worked 100% and now showed signs of severe interference from the next-door Waldorf Hotel call-sign, was cut. Second Club preview performance.

Thursday, October 13

In the morning we cut fifteen minutes from Act One, which the actors took in their stride remarkably. The first-night performance got an electric silence from a hostile audience. The cannibal TV cameras were everywhere: Rediffusion on stage, filming the audience as the actors went down in paper bags (last remnant of a rehearsal game/exercise, which we cut after four performances because by then it had lost even shock value as a happening). In the foyer, the David Frost interview crew, seizing VIP audience members. Kenneth Tynan punctured the final actor's silence after the butterfly burning with 'Are you waiting for us or are we waiting for you?'

Friday, October 14

Company meeting in the Aldwych the day after the first night.

Peter Brook to the actors:

'The performance you gave last night was absolutely what I would have hoped for after all our work. Yesterday we changed Act One a great deal; and we changed it then because we hadn't been in a position to do so before. We're different from a Broadway musical in this respect: at a certain point in a musical, they "freeze" the work, because they don't want to reopen problems any more, they settle for the solutions they have found.

'But we found that the first two performances before a live audience – the previews – threw up new things, which we had to implement.

'Collectively, you took it in your stride. So that instead of the normal glazed brightness of first-night performances, you gave the audience something rock-solid, authentic. Remember what Grotowski said about the actor offering himself to the audience? That's what you deeply did last night; and you were rewarded by the quality of the audience's silence.

'Now I want to discuss the big question of the next step. From the first day of our rehearsal we have evolved a way of life. Now this must change. I shall no longer be seeing you every day. Now the life of our rehearsal has got to feed the playing of the show.

H

'The experiment we have been making since the start is, what is the relationship between theatre and everyday life? Grotowski offered one answer: he wanted to make it a complete and full-time way of life. And he does, in his small Polish provincial town, in that Communist/Catholic country, he can make it monastic. But here we are in London, with all the difference that implies. I myself am not prepared to give fifteen hours a day for the next ten years living with all of you. (Laughter.) I am not prepared to surrender all the outside world. So what are our possibilities?

'The last few years have thrown up possibilities for young actors to make their name very fast. This is as it should be, but it has a negative side: they can easily mark time, and after two or three years doing the same kind of work, what was originally hailed as exciting gets stuck in a rut where it either stays in the same place or goes downhill. Only a handful of actors have the god-driven freedom and drive to continue to open up and question. That's the self-renewing life you see in someone like Scofield.

'Now playing this show night after night on the stage poses the same question to everyone – and it is a question of inner burning. Each of you can cheat or not cheat. No one can tell whether you are going to be completely absent or present on stage. But if first one and then another of you start to shut off, the end result will be the total loss of the quality of the group's work. The seeds of destruction are already there.'

ACTOR: 'Why?'

BROOK: 'Because the whole thing is a process, and a process can always go two ways, go into reverse. Acting depends on bringing something all the time, otherwise it can turn in on itself and crumble. No amount of goodwill can keep it fresh – the only way is by bringing something constantly to it. This is the true question: whether you are interested enough to take the experiment further. In which case you will reopen daily the relationship between your work on stage and your daily life. Trying things out constantly.

'Have we compromised what we learned from Grotowski by playing in a large theatre and in the style we have found? I think not, if we keep it growing. His work is deep but narrow: our work here in London is more fragmented but possibly richer. What I am offering you is a technique. It may not interest you. But if it does it seems to me the only way of continuing. It seems a pity to settle for a casual relationship with what you are playing.

'How can you keep the life going? It is inevitable theatre-myth that the second night – tonight – is always a let-down from the first. But need it be so? Certainly, wishing it otherwise won't alter anything. Remember, when we had the critical arguments about the end of the play? Asking for something to redress the balance at the close, we implied disappointment at lack of a solution, at our failure to change the world. We imagined that we were falling short of something positive. But that something was there all the time. It is in the life, the degree of burning, you bring to the performance. People leaving at the end weren't crushed. All of you, sitting round Glenda, aren't crushed by the experience of going through all this. This is the point of the end: you sit there collectively taking the opposite attitude from either not caring or not worrying. This very quality puts Glenda's corrosiveness into perspective.

'Tonight we will make one really big experiment – we will leave everything in the show utterly unchanged.'

Laughter.

This is a glimpse of one of the most important (and I'm sorry to say, unusual) projects in the history of theatre for heaven knows how long.

This outline of ensemble work in this country indicates fantastic possibilities and opportunities. Judged by conventional standards and attitudes to the theatre, it was a failure. It didn't find its new language and it didn't ever make the impact its creators hoped. Lots of people reacted to the production – but not about Vietnam – more often about the failure of the piece to communicate. The fact that it is more interesting to read about than see and experience in the theatre only underlines the fact that the months of preparation were the most important aspect – they hinted at what possibilities are open to companies like the Royal Shakespeare Co. and the National. But alas, everything is back playing for safety again.

It is fortunate that in the middle of rehearsals for this project Grotowski should have paid his visit to the Company, so that in this we are reminded of the importance of his very quizzical approach to theatre.

The account also links thinking with happenings, censorship and community drama.

In addition, it is worth relating the method employed here with that outlined by Caldwell Cook in a very different context.

Note also:

1. the initial difficulties, and acknowledgement of some of the poverty of early explorations

2. the need to draw upon any and every experience which might throw light on the topic
3. the value of a Director (teacher)
4. the way in which varying personalities have to work together
5. the challenge of such investigations and performances to the day-to-day lives of those involved
6. the shock Grotowski's visit made and his insistence on a small audience
7. the comment that a way of life is a way to life
8. that each performance was a happening
9. the actors begin to dig inside themselves, finding a new kind of involvement and opening themselves more to outside stimuli.

18 Drama as Synthesis
John Hodgson and Ernest Richards

Ernest Richards and I began work on the book *Improvisation* in the summer of 1965. A few months before this, Stephen Joseph had paid me a visit, with a request that we discuss improvisation, because he found his work at Manchester was not proving as successful as he had hoped. This set me thinking that it would be a good thing to clarify my own thoughts on paper and I discussed the idea with Ernest Richards, with whom I was working on a course at Dillington House.

The book evolved from a utilization of practical experience: Ernest Richards drawing on his work with students and young people in the Liverpool Youth Theatre, of which he was Founder and Director; I drew from my experience in training actors at Bristol, where I had been Deputy Principal, and at Bretton working with intending teachers.

The book has three sections: the first is involved with background theory of acting; part two is concerned with drama built from ideas; part three discusses in practical terms the way in which improvisation can assist a more intelligent, thoughtful approach to a text.

Acting is an experiment in living . . . Learning how to live comes through experiencing. Improvisation is a means of exploring in which we create conditions where imaginative group and personal experience is possible. It is the spontaneous human response to an idea or ideas, or a set of conditions.

Man is a Unified Being

In most of our approaches to life, whether through science or through education in schools, and even through the training of the actor, we tend to look at man as a subject for analysis. In science, man becomes a study for one aspect: medical science, social science, or psychology, and education concerns itself with parts: physical education, religious education, arts education or training on the abstract mental level. Even the actor finds his tuition periods subdivided often exclusively into voice production, movement, dance, singing and so forth. So all through life there is very little attempt to look at man as a whole being, and inadequate concern to bring together these elements of training in development of the total personality. While some emphasis will always need to be placed upon differing aspects of development, we need to ensure that we spend adequate time in the unified living situation. From time to time we need to re-examine whatever aspects of existence we are working on and be sure that we have recognized their relationship to man in his environment. Kenneth Walker quotes the Indian tale:

> The elephant was in a dark house: some Hindus had brought it for exhibition.
> In order to see it, many people were going, every one, into that darkness.
> As seeing it with the eye was impossible, each one was feeling it in the dark with the palm of his hand.
> The hand of one fell on its trunk: he said, 'This creature is like a water-pipe.'
> The hand of another touched its ear: to him it appeared to be like a fan.
> Since another handled its leg, he said, 'I found the elephant shape to be like a pillar.'
> Another laid his hand on the back: he said, 'Truly this elephant was like a throne.'
> Similarly, when anyone heard a description of the elephant, he understood it only in respect of the part that he had touched.

On account of the diverse place of view their statements differed: one man entitled it 'dal' another 'alif'.

If there had been a candle in each one's hand, the difference would have gone out of their words.

If we really believe that the 'proper study of mankind is man', the best way of studying him is as he responds in relationships with people and things. There must be ample time devoted to allowing opportunity for the candles to be lit to enable us to see man as a whole.

Man as a Unique Being

While we are classifying man in the analytical process, stressing the common factors and trends in human behaviour, we must not lose sight of the unique quality of every individual. The body of human knowledge which enables us to classify and clarify various facets of human nature needs to have something to offset it, so that we recognize that in every man and woman there is a singular combination of the varying facets. This means that every single human being is a subject for research, and somehow we must accept opportunities in the growing process for everyone to be able to find out about himself and to discover the particular peculiarities of himself in relation to other people.

This may seem disturbing, for this concept of the unique nature of the individual means abandoning the idea of a safety measure of 'normality'. Society is nearly always unwilling to recognize anything or anyone that seems different, but this is an attitude which only adds to the conflict and complexity of man's existence, making individuals afraid of being different, and individuals afraid of the different. What we need to inculcate more is a sense of wonder at the uniqueness of the individual. We must learn to put this in place of the fear which results in the sneer leading to opposition and aggression.

Not only is every person different – every person has also unparalleled possibilities and potential. Everyone begins life with his particular heredity and personality make-up, modified by unique factors of environment which in turn bring their own variety of pressures, opportunities or lack of opportunities in the great range of experience that each individual undergoes. These factors are given further variety by individual differences in the rate of development which in turn contribute to the variety of human personality.

Generalized statements there may well be about the human situation, but we must always be on our guard lest we attempt to make human beings fit them, instead of using them to gain understanding of the individual. We all gain considerable comfort from realizing that we are not totally in a world unknown and unshared by others. We can gain help by talking about, and discovering, our similarities, but we should also feel that we can discuss and share our differences. There is a kind of paradox in which we need to appreciate the uniqueness of ourselves and of every other human being and that, though unique, we have had and are having experiences similar to others.

Poetry and the novel offer an opportunity for some understanding of the need to break down the fear that 'I am alone in my difference: everyone else is together in their similarity'. Both the private and the group level of experience are important, and in making discoveries about both these spheres of our life we have to accept the fact that only the individual can adequately discover himself for himself. This is a different kind of understanding from the accepted scientific knowledge where, once we have found how to split the atom, we can go on from generation to generation, if we wish, splitting it in the same way. On the human level, every single person in every generation has to have the opportunity of being able to find out about himself for himself.

The objective study of man in the social situation tends to leave part of man out of consideration. It has either to be a discussion of the situation after the event (for instance, the juvenile court or probation office), when rationalization is likely to take place, or an impartial observer viewing a situation from the touch-line (such as the social worker), from where it is only possible to grasp the externalized manifestations.

Drama is the only form in which we can fully use man in the exploration of himself in the living situation. Whether the living experience is recorded in a text or is set in motion by one or more ideas, its fullest discovery as personal experience must be realized through improvisation. Through drama, those experiencing the intensified situation can gain insight within controlled conditions

Science has tended in the past to distrust the subjective approach at all levels, believing it to be too prone to prejudice and self-deception. In improvisation, indulgence in a world of fantasy or self-deception is still possible and may well take place at some stages, but as it is taking place in a group situation, the final understanding arrived at will be part of exploration with others. This allows for the individual to work through the stage of fantasy or self-deception, and to reach his state of insight in concert with others. When the individual accepts the fact that the result of his personal research into his own working is to enable him to improve his own working, he quickly realizes the importance of identifying mis-representations. So, improvisation exists not just in the imagination, but is lived and moved physically alongside other human beings, in time and space. The feet of those improvising are constantly on the ground, sustained by other actors who help to ensure that all claims, hopes, fears and so on are referred to some clarified human response.

Throughout improvisation response will be from and with every part of the person, even though constantly attention will be focused on a particular aim.

19 How Far Ahead
John Hodgson

When the theatres in England were closed in 1642 the drama became severed from its roots. Prior to that point drama had in a broad sense been continually educational. It had been concerned with expression, experience, doubts and certainties in the lives of all classes of people. After 1660 the theatre developed for the most part as a pastime for the few, the aristocratic. The establishment of this literary, artificial and mannered form of sophisticated pleasure has led to theatre becoming associated with all that is shallow, artificial, showy and escapist. Right through to the Victorian period and still for many even at the present time, the theatre has remained a means of avoiding real life or a way of merely passing the time. Many actors who lived in the artificial world of the stage hardly dared to leave it: reality was too sharp a contrast. For some life behind the footlights was the land of promise. John Lahr in a review in 'The Village Voice' told that, when he heard his father humming musical comedy on his deathbed, he came to understand how deep the buoyant promise of that sound penetrated his personality and compelled him to perform. 'It was the first and last rhythm of his life: the jaunty beat which anticipated an excitement and happiness that real life could never touch. For him, and for many like him but less gifted, the stage was a place where they took revenge on the world for not living up to their expectations. Off-stage, they were ignorant, bewildered, stalled. They were victims: unprepared for a society which assured them that all they needed was pluck 'n luck. On stage, they stopped time. In a lifetime of waiting, they lived in the moment only for their audiences. They turned their private failures – the unchannelled energy, the unknown anger, the unspeakable longings – into public triumphs. They were never as free as when they were acting out their dreams. Some, like my father, survived to the end; others stashed their past into scrapbooks buried in bedroom closets. Either way, the yearning and violent competition, the appetite and the memory, took their toll. Innocence without wisdom is a desolation; and there was something missing, absent, even from the greatest performers. Yes, these old timers were haunted, but even when they were young they were escaping from ghosts in their past.'

The whole theatre ought to exorcise these spirits of the immediate past, re-examine its origins and begin to appraise the opportunities of the future. For the uses of drama are many and varied. They are also of much greater importance than most casual observers of theatre or classroom drama have ever dreamed of. If, as the subtitle implies, we regard *acting* as the central part of drama, the human being employing himself as the instrument in expressing and investigating his nature and condition, instead of merely escaping from it, we begin to appreciate something of the potential.

The theatre already growing in social significance could become a centre of many aspects of community life. The live theatre, as Barrault pointed out, enables direct communication between representatives of the world at large and prototypes, the quintessence of humanity at a particular moment in time – the unique experience. There is physical contact between the members of the audience and interrelationships between them and the actors. Present-day theatres are small enough for identity to be preserved and counteract the growing anonymity in the world at large. Theatre is collective without losing sight of the individual.

The material on which this interaction is centred might aim at universal relaxation and pure pleasure. Of course, it can appeal to the largely escapist side of our nature and enable us to somersault *for a while* out of our cares and complexities – the theatre turned fun palace. But the material might also be the means of focus of an issue vital to the local, national or international community. After such a performance, discussion and heated debate might follow – the theatre turned forum.

Always the theatre will retain that function of bringing to life great literature of past and present, giving insight to the human condition, expression to the intangibles and the incomprehensibles, materializing the fears, laughing at the foibles, scorning the failings, criticizing the shortcomings of men in this and earlier ages.

The company of actors working together, with adequate security and in touch with affairs could themselves be involved in experiment in ideas, in dramatic forms and ways of communication. Instead of being simply skilled interpreters and agile players only, they might also be creative performers, giving and developing ideas amongst themselves and with an audience. They could be receptive to new writers, directors and technicians as well as interested in developing their own artistic resources. So the theatre would be a centre of the new and the experimental.

The live entertainments in the theatre then, will vary in approach and impact; some may be designed to shock, some to soothe, some to stimulate thought; others will aim to titillate, tease or torment but none will strive to bore. There will be drama appealing to the intellect, drama appealing to the feeling and drama with an appeal to many levels at the same time. There will be drama presented in stark reality and drama drawing on all the techniques of illusion. Some will approach life bent on involvement – the presentation of imaginative truth; some will be designed to alleviate and present predicaments for objective reappraisal. The theatre can be the meeting of all the arts and an exploration of every technological innovation and development or it may demand concentration solely in the agility of the human mind, body and voice.

Every performance could be an exciting, an individual and a significant affair if we will only learn to use drama intelligently. Sometimes the atmosphere within the theatre might be quite formal, giving opportunity for taking part in a ritual and sense of occasion, a wining, dining, dressy and highly rehearsed festivity. At other times it might become more the workshop and the laboratory, a work in progress, a jeans-and-sweat-shirt, an overalls and what-do-you-think-of-this?-experience.

Drama used in schools opens up a wide range of opportunities. Still too often thought of as an extra, it could revitalize and give a great deal of the work greater interest and significance. In the first place the drama teacher has a chance to work alongside the young people in such a way as to contact and get to know them personally – drama demands a more total involvement and can draw upon heart and body as well as head.

To employ drama in school will involve the teacher in having a very positive educational philosophy since there is so much feedback and immediacy in the approach. As Caldwell Cook indicated, the drama room is a kind of laboratory of life where things can be tried out with control and safety. Here experience of some of the problems and difficulties can be externalized and sifted. Learning needs to be impressive and vivid if it is to be retained for long or it needs to be reinforced by practice and rehearsal – and drama is a useful means. In approaching history, geography, myth, religion or any area of the curriculum where there are human elements, the dramatic method can help both in investigating and researching the material and in unifying it towards an end product – whether that product is thought of as a showing, a presentation, or a production.

So many attitudes in education have ground down to a hardened, inflexible routine. Using drama will help to sharpen awareness, sympathy and understanding.

Drama is useful in setting up situations for language learning. After all it is in the group that most of us acquire our natural tongue and extend vocabulary – does it not also seem sensible that a second language could be approached in a similar (if perhaps more scientific) way?

In higher education too, it seems, we have not yet learnt the full value of drama. All kinds of lectures can be illustrated with live situations and applying the Moreno approach to all the social and human sciences would add a great deal to behavioural investigation. University drama departments have a very special opportunity not only to investigate world literature of the past but also to have a permanent laboratory inquiring into learning methods and human relationships.

Such an approach might well open up the potential in drama for all kinds of therapy and recreative (in a broad sense) activity. Social centres and evening institutes might do more than have groups putting on plays – drama could be seen as a continuation of much of the enjoyment in extending expressive and communicative skills begun earlier.

This interest might soon lead to a totally different approach to the mass media. We would become more critical of television and perhaps, especially in drama productions, there could be some cross-fertilization.

In the centre of every city, in the heart of every suburb there could be a theatre, counterpart to the library, the recreation hall, the council chamber. In every school, college, and university there could be at least one team serving all areas of learning, investigation and expression as well as assisting and stimulating the active involvement of growing people in making the most of their own education.

In every community centre there could be a group fostering the continued development of maturing adults and offering opportunities for participation in therapy and catharsis.

In a world of science, in an age of technology, in a time of ever increasing bureaucracy, drama looks at, draws upon and gives expression to the spontaneous, the living and the multifarious. In a world of categorization, in an age of analysis, in a time of collectivization, drama emphasises the individual, the unified and the personal. In fact drama used fully, re-establishes all that makes man unique, gregarious and human.

Select Bibliography

SECTION ONE

Theatre Today,		Arts Council
The Provision of Theatre for Young People in Great Britain,		Arts Council
Drama : Education Survey 2,		H.M.S.O.
Le Phenomène Theatral,	The Zaharoff Lecture 1961.,	Clarendon Press
The Theatre and Dramatic Theory,	ALLARDYCE NICOLL,	Harrap
The Unholy Trade,	RICHARD FINDLATER,	Gollancz
The Idea of a Theatre,	FRANCIS FERGUSSON,	Doubleday, N.Y.
Reflections on the Theatre,	J. L. BARRAULT,	Rocklilt
On the Art of the Theatre,	E. GORDON CRAIG,	Mercury

SECTION TWO

Early English Stages,	GLYNNE WICKHAM,	Routledge
Medieval Stage,	E. K. CHAMBERS,	O.U.P.
The Origin of the Theatre,	HUNNINGHER,	Hill and Wang
The Golden Bough,	J. G. FRAZER,	Macmillan
Beyond the Pleasure Principle,	J. FREUD,	Hogarth Press
Understanding Children's Play,	R. E. HARTLEY,	Routledge
Play in Childhood,	M. LOWENFELD,	Portway
Play, Dreams and Imitation in Childhood,	J. PIAGET,	Heinemann
Child Drama,	PETER SLADE,	Univ. London Press
Children's Games,	OPIE	Oxford
The Play of Man,	KARL GROOS,	Heinemann
The Education of Man,	F. FROEBEL,	Arnold
The Poetics,	ARISTOTLE,	Pelican

The Republic,	PLATO,	Pelican
The Laws,	PLATO,	Pelican
Apology,	PLATO,	Pelican
Story of a School,		H.M.S.O.

SECTION THREE

The Mastery of Movement,	R. LABAN,	MacDonald & Evans
Effort,	R. LABAN,	MacDonald & Evans
Modern Educational Dance,	R. LABAN,	MacDonald & Evans
Silence,	JOHN CAGE,	M.I.T. Press
Vital Speech,	HAROLD RIPPER,	Methuen
The Voice,	W. A. AITKIN,	Longmans
Voice and Speech,	G. THURBURN,	James Nisbet
An Actor Prepares,	K. STANISLAVSKI,	Geoffrey Bles
Building a Character,	K. STANISLAVSKI,	Methuen
Acting is Believing,	C. J. MCGAW,	Rinehart
The Method as Means,	CHARLES MAROWITZ,	Herbert Jenkins
Brecht on Theatre,	B. BRECHT (trans. John Willett),	Methuen.

SECTION FOUR

Dreams and Nightmares,	J. A. HADFIELD,	Pelican
Phantasy in Childhood,	DAVIDSON AND FAY	Routledge
Interpretation of Dreams,	S. FREUD,	Hogarth
Psychodrama I,	J. L. MORENO,	Beacon House, NY.
Psychodrama II,	J. L. MORENO,	Beacon House, NY.

SECTION FIVE

The Play Way,	H. CALDWELL COOK,	Portway
Drama and Education,	P. A. COGGIN,	Thames & Hudson
Development through Drama,	BRIAN WAY,	Longmans
Drama and Theatre in Education,	DODD AND HICKSON	Heinemann
Experience and Expression,	HODGSON AND RICHARDS,	Ginn
Declaration,	ED. TOM MASCHLER	MacGibbon & Kee

Drama in a World of Science, GLYNNE WICKHAM, Routledge

Introduction to Child Drama PETER SLADE, Univ. London Press

Story of a School, H.M.S.O.

SECTION SIX

Happenings, Dutton

US, R.S.C., Calder and Boyars

The Empty Space, PETER BROOK, MacGibbon & Kee

Encore Reader, ED. MAROWITZ, MILNE AND HALE Methuen

Experimental Theatre, JAMES ROOSE EVANS, Studio Vista

Rediscovering of Style, M. SAINT-DENIS, Heinemann

The Theatre and Its Double, A. ARTAUD Calder and Boyars

Theatre at Work, ED. MAROWITZ AND TRUSSLER Methuen

Improvisation, HODGSON AND RICHARDS, Methuen

Towards a Poor Theatre, J. GROTOWSKI, Methuen

MAGAZINES

The Drama Review
Theatre Quarterly
New Theatre Magazine
Creative Drama
Plays and Players
Tabs